THE BURNING BUSH

THE BURNING BUSH

On the Orthodox Veneration of the Mother of God

Sergius Bulgakov

Translated, edited,
and with an introduction by

Thomas Allan Smith

William B. Eerdmans Publishing Company
Grand Rapids, Michigan / Cambridge, U.K.

Published 2009 by
Wm. B. Eerdmans Publishing Co.
2140 Oak Industrial Drive N.E., Grand Rapids, Michigan 49505 /
P.O. Box 163, Cambridge CB3 9PU U.K.

Printed in the United States of America

14 13 12 11 10 09   7 6 5 4 3 2 1

Library of Congress Cataloging-in-Publication Data

Bulgakov, Sergei Nikolaevich, 1871-1944.
[Kupina neopalimaia. English]
The burning bush: on the Orthodox veneration of the Mother of God /
S.N. Bulgakov; translated, edited, and with an introduction by Thomas Allan Smith.
p.   cm.
Includes bibliographical references.
ISBN 978-0-8028-4574-0 (pbk.: alk. paper)
1. Immaculate Conception. 2. Orthodox Eastern Church — Doctrines.
I. Smith, T. Allan. II. Title.

BT620.B813 2009
232.91 — dc22

2008051812

www.eerdmans.com

Contents

v

Contents

A Note from the Translator

Bulgakov made use of the standard collections of patristic texts edited by J. P. Migne, *Patrologiae cursus completus. Series Latina,* 221 vols. (Paris, 1844-1890) (*PL* in notes) and *Patrologiae cursus completus . . . series graeca,* 161 vols. Paris, 1857-1912 (*PG* in notes), though occasionally he turned to Russian translations and paraphrases. In the notes, I have endeavored to provide the appropriate reference in Migne for the works used by Bulgakov, even though there are more modern editions available. Bulgakov was not always careful or consistent when citing sources. Where possible I have corrected mistaken references and provided missing ones. He also made extensive use of contemporary liturgical texts and of Russian and Slavonic versions of the Bible. The translation reflects Bulgakov's own versions of these texts, not necessarily English translations more familiar to readers. He gives the names of Old Testament books as they appear in Russian usage based on the Septuagint. With the exception of the numbering of the Psalms, which follows the Septuagint, I have adopted the names for the books of the Old Testament more familiar to English readers. Thus, Bulgakov's 1 and 2 Kings are 1 and 2 Samuel.

His use of modern theological works is no less muddied by imprecise bibliographic references. For the benefit of readers I list these works below. Works in German and French are cited in the original language. Russian titles are provided with an English translation, which is also used in the notes.

Bulgakov enjoys forming new words and using abstract nouns which are not readily translatable into English. A significant problem arises with the adjectival forms for Theotokos and Mother of God. While it would be possible to use the English "Marian," our vocabulary for the Mother of

God comes from the Latin Roman Catholic theological tradition and is laden with nuances and associations that would be misleading. Therefore, I have opted to use circumlocutions with the nominative form in order to render Bulgakov's adjectival phrase: thus, *bogorodichnyi prazdnik* is "feast of the Theotokos." An important abstract noun in Bulgakov's essay is *bogomaterinstvo* which he builds on the model of *bogochelovechestvo*. I have used "Divine Motherhood" and "Divine Humanity" respectively. Also, the Russian word *chelovek* has the same semantic value as the German *Mensch*. I have translated it either as humankind, human being, or human. A notable exception is "Son of Man," *Syn Chelovecheskii*, which is still used as a technical term in English. Uncharacteristically for Russian, Bulgakov capitalizes nouns such as mother, church, wisdom, burning bush, and I have kept his usage, since he seems to want to impart a theological value to the noun that would otherwise be lost. Finally, in transliterating Russian, I have used the standard academic system in use in North America, except for certain proper names which have become customary in English: Alexander, not Aleksandr, Soloviev, not Solov'ev or Solovyov, Florensky, not Florenskii. Also, orthography has not been modernized, except with the dropping of the hard sign at the end of words and the equating of *iats* with *e*.

Bulgakov's Sources

Blagodeianiia Bogomateri rodu khristianskomu chrez Ee sv. Ikony [*The Benefits of the Mother of God to the Christian Race through Her Holy Icons*]. 2nd ed. (St Petersburg, 1905).

Brianchaninov, Ignaty. *Izlozhenie ucheniia pravoslavnoi tserkvi o Bozhiei Materi. Sochineniia* [*An Exposition of the Doctrine of the Orthodox Church concerning the Mother of God. Works*], 3rd ed. (n.p., n.d.).

Denzinger, Heinrich, *Enchiridion symbolorum definitionum et declarationum de rebus fidei et morum* (Freiburg im Breisgau: Herder 1854[1], 1976[36]).

Dictionnaire de théologie catholique. 15 vols. Alfred Vacant, ed. (Paris: Letouzey et Ané, 1899-1950).

Dubosc de Pesquidoux. *L'Immaculée conception, histoire d'un dogme* (Tours, 1898).

Enchiridion Patristicum: locum ss patrum, doctorum, scriptorum ecclesiasticorum. M. J. Rouët de Journel, ed. (Freiburg im Breisgau: Herder, 1922).

Feofan the Recluse. *Pis'ma k raznym littsam o raznykh predmetakh very i zhizni* [*Letters to diverse persons about various subjects of faith and life*], 2nd ed. (Moscow, 1892)

Hefele, Karl Joseph von. *Conciliengeschichte.* 2nd rev. ed. (Freiburg im Breisgau: Herder, 1873-1890).

Hennecke, Edgar. *Neutestamentliche Apokryphen.* 2nd ed. (Tübingen: J. C. B. Mohr [Paul Siebeck], 1924).

Izbrannyia slova sviatykh ottsov v chest' i slavu presviatoi Bogoroditsy [Selected discourses of the holy fathers in honour and praise of the most holy Theotokos]. 4th ed. (Moscow, 1896).

Kirchen-Lexikon, oder, Encyklopädie der katholischen Theologie. 12 vols. Heinrich Joseph Wetzer and Benedikt Welte, eds. (Freiburg im Breisgau: Herder, 1847-1860).

Klee, Heinrich. *Katholische Dogmatik.* 3 vols. (1835, 1861).

Kleutgen, Joseph. *Die Philosophie der Vorzeit* (Münster, 1863).

Lebedev, Alexander. *Raznost' tserkvei vostochnoi i zapadnoi v uchenii o presv. Deve Marii. Polemiko-dogmaticheskoe izsledovanie [The Difference between the Eastern and Western Churches in the Doctrine of the Most Holy Virgin Mary. A Polemical-dogmatic Investigation]* (Warsaw, 1881).

Likhachev, Nikolai Petrovich. *Russkaia ikonografiia [Russian Iconography]* (n.d.).

Loofs, Friedrich. *Leitfaden zum Studium der Dogmengeschichte.* (M. Niemeyer, 1906).

Makary, Metropolitan. *Dogmaticheskoe bogoslovie [Dogmatic Theology].* (Moscow, n.d.).

Nikol'skii, A. *Sofiia premudrost' bozhiia. Novgorodskaia redaktsiia ikony i sluzhba sv. Sofii [Sophia the Wisdom of God. Novgorod redaction of icons and services of St Sophia]* (St Petersburg: St Petersburg Archaeological Institute, 1905).

Pravoslavnoe ispovedanie vostochnoi kafolicheskoi tserkvi [Orthodox Confession of the Eastern Catholic Church] (n.p., n.d.).

Pesch, Christian. *Praelectiones dogmaticae.* 4 vols. (Freiburg im Breisgau: Herder, 1909-1922).

Scheeben, Matthias Joseph. *Handbuch der katholischen Dogmatik.* 4 vols. (Freiburg im Breisgau: Herder, 1873-1887).

Schwane, Joseph. *Dogmengeschichte der patristischen Zeit (325-787 n. Chr.).* 3 vols. (Theissug, 1869).

Seeberg, Reinhold. *Lehrbuch der Dogmengeschichte.* 2 vols. (Deichert, 1895-1898).

Silvester, Archbishop. *Opyt pravoslavnago dogmaticheskago bogosloviia [An Attempt at Orthodox Dogmatic Theology].* 3 vols. (Kiev, n.d.).

Simar, Hubert Theophil. *Lehrbuch der Dogmatik.* 2 vols. (1879-1880.)

Skazaniia o zemnoi zhizni Bogomateri [Tales of the Earthly Life of the Mother of God]. 7th ed. (Moscow, 1897).

Staudenmaier, F. A. *Die Lehre von der Idee (Die Philosophie des Christentums oder Metaphysik der heiligen Schrift, 1-er Band)* (Giessen, 1840).

Stökl, Albert. *Die speculative Lehre vom Menschen und ihre Geschichte.* 2 vols. (Würzburg, 1858-1859).

Swete, Henry Barclay. *The Old Testament in Greek according to the Septuagint.* 3 vols. (Cambridge: Cambridge University Press, 1887-1894).

Terrien, Jean Baptiste. *La Mère de Dieu et la mère des hommes d'après les pères et la Théologie.* 4 vols. (Paris: P. Lethielleux, 1902).

Velichie presviatyia Bogoroditsy i Prisnodevy Marii [The Mighty Deeds of the Theotokos and Ever-Virgin Mary] (Moscow, 1845).

Toy, Crawford Howell. *A Critical and Exegetical Commentary on the Book of Proverbs* (New York: Scribner, 1899).

Introduction

A new wave of ecstasy with the world rolled in. Together with "personal happiness," my first encounter with "the West" and first delights before it: "sophistication," comfort, social democracy. . . . And suddenly an unexpected, miraculous encounter: Sistine Madonna in Dresden, you yourself touched my heart and it began to tremble from your call.

En route we hurry one foggy autumn morning to do what tourists do and visit the Zwinger with its famous gallery. My knowledge of art was perfectly insignificant and I hardly even knew what awaited me in the gallery. And there, into my soul peered the eyes of the Queen of Heaven approaching on clouds with the Pre-eternal Child. They had the measureless *power of purity and insightful sacrificial readiness,*[1] knowledge of suffering and readiness for voluntary suffering, and the same prophetic sacrificial readiness was visible in the unchildishly wise eyes of the Child. They know what awaits them, what they are destined for, and they come freely to surrender themselves, to accomplish the will of the One who sent them: She is "to receive a weapon in her heart," He goes to Golgotha. . . . I was beside myself, my head was spinning, tears at once joyful and bitter flowed from my eyes, the ice in my heart melted and a kind of knot in my life came undone. This was not an aesthetic emotion, no; it was *an encounter,* new knowledge, *a miracle.* . . . I was still a Marxist then and I involuntarily called this contemplation *a prayer,* and every morning, aiming to find myself in the Zwinger before anyone else, I ran there, "to pray" and to weep before the face of the Madonna; there will be few moments in life more blessed than those tears. . . .

Svet nevechernyi (Unfading Light), pp. 8-9

Sergei Nikolaevich Bulgakov (1871-1944) had this encounter in the spring of 1898 during an extended visit to Western Europe. He mentions it fleetingly in a letter to M. O. Gershenzon[2] and later gives this more eloquent recollection in his pivotal 1917 work, *Unfading Light,* where he also relates two other encounters with the Divine.[3] While the triad of revelatory meetings are of great importance for understanding the path of personal conversion taken by Bulgakov, not to mention their echoing of Vladimir Soloviev's (1853-1900) own three famous encounters with Sophia, for the purposes of this essay, it is the encounter with the Sistine Madonna that is most significant. It is ironic that a Western work of art depicting a very Catholic image of the Virgin and Child should occupy so important a place in the intellectual development of Bulgakov, particularly when considered in light of *The Burning Bush* with its sharp criticism of Roman Catholic doctrine and dogma concerning the Mother of God. At the same time, Bulgakov's experience before the Sistine Madonna is emblematic of his later essay on the veneration of the Mother of God, for he notes that the Catholic dogma of the Immaculate Conception, the criticism of which was the initial impetus for his essay, while erroneous in its formulation nevertheless conveys an essential truth about the Mother of God shared by the Orthodox, and thus, by implication, something fundamentally true of Christianity as a whole.

Bulgakov was born in the town of Livny in Orel province, the son of an impoverished priest in charge of a cemetery chapel. Since his family had provided parochial clergy for six generations, Bulgakov's entrance into the local seminary is not surprising. Like many other young Russian men of the nineteenth century, however, Bulgakov lost his faith at an early age. He left the seminary and pursued studies in the secular grammar school in Elets before proceeding to Moscow University where from 1890 to 1894 he specialized in political economy. He emerged as one of the leading Marxist thinkers in Russia. Upon graduation he took a teaching position at the Moscow Technical Institute and embarked on a publishing career. In 1898 he travelled to Western Europe, where he experienced a second spiritual crisis — to which the opening quotation refers — that would eventually lead him back to the Orthodox Church. From his return to Russia in 1900 until 1917 Bulgakov held a number of teaching posts in the field of political economy at universities in Kiev and Moscow. Very indicative of the direction his life would take was his involvement in the so-called Silver Age,[4] a movement of renewal in all aspects of Russian cultural and political life, and his participation in the "Circle of the Seekers of Christian Enlightenment" and the "Religious-Philosophical Society in memory of Vladimir Soloviev." His most important publications in the pre-revolutionary age were *From Marxism to Idealism* (1903), which captured the intellectual and spiritual transformation of many of his contemporaries, and *Philosophy of Economy*[5] (1912) and *Unfading Light* (1917) in which Bulgakov sets out the philosophical arguments for Sophiology. Bulgakov was politically active during this period, serving as an independent Christian Socialist in the Duma (Representative Assembly) of 1907. He would later be an active participant in the Russian Church Council of 1917-1918.

Whether or not *The Burning Bush* owes its genesis to those early mornings spent before the Sistine Madonna, there can be little doubt that the experience left a deep imprint on his soul. Beginning in earnest with *Unfading Light,* there is scarcely a major philosophical or theological treatise penned by Bulgakov that does not contain some extended reflections on the Mother of God, the Most Pure Theotokos, a not unexpected feature in the intellectual output of one so committed to rethinking that cornerstone of Christian theology, the incarnation of the Son of God. Furthermore, the wealth of liturgical materials — prayers, hymns, litanies, poetry — and icons dedicated to the Virgin Mother of God, not to mention devotional practices, make it seemingly inevitable that an Orthodox theologian would seek to incorporate reflections on the Mother of God into any serious theological discussion of the church's doctrine. In his memoirs Bulgakov with the benefit of hindsight draws attention to the impact that the Mother of God had on his early religious formation particularly with regard to the connection between the Mother of God and Divine Wisdom. He recalls the church in Livny:

> The church, obviously, represented a remnant of the old style: blue with white columns, the intimacy and charm of the old main part was moving, it was St Sergius' church, and built onto it was a main part with the altar of the Dormition — the dedication feast being 15 August. I never pondered why Sergius and the Dormition were joined here — clearly in harmony with the Trinity-St Sergius in the lavra. I did not know or understand that it was just as much a Sophianic temple as was the Dormition church in the lavra; I did not know then that

I received my name, was baptised and spiritually born in a *Sophianic* temple, that I was numbered among the choir of St Sergius, the servant of the Wisdom of God. I did not know that all my inspirations which in the future were fated to be developed into an entire theological system, basically were sown in my soul by Divine Providence in that affecting temple. Only now, in my old age, am I reaching that gift of God. . . . But on Dormition Day the festal icon was invariably decorated with autumn asters, velvet ribbons and mignonettes, and their fragrance has touched my heart ever since with the joy of the Dormition. This was not only an external association, but the fragrance from the grave of the Most Pure. And already the moonlit evenings are cooling off above the river from the platform around the temple. . . . Yes, here I received in my heart the revelation of Sophia, here in my soul was placed that pearl which I had sought in the course of my blind and confused life, I sought with mind and heart, more with the mind than with the heart, and when I found her I recognized her as the treasure given to me as a gift of God in my spiritual birth.[6]

Besides linking Sophia and the Mother of God, this passage shows that characteristic interest in the totality of religious experience which surfaces everywhere in Bulgakov's theological writings. Sophia, God's Glory, and God Himself are everywhere to be felt by the receptive human soul, and nowhere do they coalesce and assume such perfect concrete appearance as in the Most Pure Mother of God. L. N. Zander was one of the first and remains one of the few scholars to acknowledge the central place that Mariology[7] occupies in Bulgakov's writings, noting that "in Orthodoxy's veneration of the Mother of God, Fr. Sergius saw *realized Sophiology*, the ecclesial incarnation of that truth which was the alpha and the omega of his entire religious understanding and perception of the world."[8] Bulgakov's Sophiology remains his most controversial legacy to the theological community, and there is no question that one must come to grips with it in order to appreciate fully his Mariology; however, his writings on the Mother of God contain more than sophiological speculation. Anthropology, eschatology, original sin, human sanctity, sexuality and gender issues all receive their due as he explores the mystery of the woman chosen by God to give birth freely to His Son.

The Burning Bush (1927) is the first component in Bulgakov's so-called minor theological trilogy, whose other two members are *The Friend of the Bridegroom* (1927)[9] and *Jacob's Ladder* (1929).[10] Bulgakov considered *The*

Burning Bush and *The Friend of the Bridegroom* to go together as a two-part dogmatic study of the Deisis, an iconographic representation of Mary the Mother of God and John the Forerunner interceding before God for all humanity. With the third volume, which is devoted to the veneration of angels, Bulgakov completes his dogmatic statement on the joyous prayer and intercession of all creation standing before the presence of God.[11] The human dyad of Mary and John, on the one hand, and the angelic host, on the other hand, comprise all the possibilities of the creaturely condition — matter, spirit, embodied, temporal, rational — and serve as vehicles for the manifestation and realization of Sophia in the created order, at this stage in his thought principally conceived as glory.

Bulgakov wrote *The Burning Bush* initially to refute the Roman Catholic dogma of the Immaculate Conception, but in the course of writing the book he tempered this narrowly polemical approach in order to offer an exposition of Orthodox veneration of the Mother of God. The second part of the Deisis study, *The Friend of the Bridegroom,* has a similar intent, for in setting out how the Orthodox have traditionally venerated John the Forerunner, Bulgakov also critiques the Roman Catholic veneration of Joseph, Mary's spouse, who has usurped the Forerunner's place in Catholic piety as "greatest among those born of woman."

Since the Catholic dogma of the Immaculate Conception was promulgated in 1854, one has to ask why Bulgakov felt compelled to criticize it some seventy years later with such vehemence. From the Roman Catholic side, there does not appear to have been any contemporary Marian event, with the notable exception of the Marian appearances and locutions at Fatima in 1917, or any official, magisterial pronouncement on the Virgin Mary, to provoke Bulgakov's critique of the dogma and prompt him to give a positive statement of the Orthodox Church's attitude to Marian devotion. The publication on 12 November 1923 of *Ecclesiam dei,* an encyclical marking the three hundredth anniversary of the death of Josaphat Kuncevich, did elicit a sharp response from Bulgakov, who viewed it as little more than a proselytizing document,[12] but his reaction is indicative of a change of attitude rather than a direct stimulus for penning his words on the Mother of God. It is, rather, in an inner spiritual transformation that fundamentally reoriented Bulgakov's intellectual and religious world that a plausible explanation for the appearance of *The Burning Bush* is to be sought.

Zander accurately observes that Bulgakov, like so many of his generation, had been fascinated by the world of German idealism, German culture and political thought. Only after 1923, when he took up permanent exile in the West, does the dominance of German culture subside.[13] Indeed, when one looks even cursorily at the stages of personal development through which Bulgakov passed, Zander's observation is borne out. Having rejected his ancestral Orthodoxy, Bulgakov threw himself passionately into Marxist political thought as an ersatz belief system, and also devoured the thought of German philosophers such as J. G. Fichte (1762-1814), F. W. J. Schelling (1775-1854) and A. Schopenhauer (1788-1860). His adulation of Vladimir Soloviev (1853-1900) and exploration of esoteric forms of knowledge (particularly as espoused by Anna Schmidt [1851-1905], see below) brought him into contact with the Catholic intellectual world and the latinophile layer of the Russian intelligentsia. But even as he immersed himself in western, for him German, culture Bulgakov was moving back to his ancestral beliefs. As early as 1901 he was incorporating his religious beliefs in his writings, but this was not as yet a fully developed personal acceptance of Orthodoxy.[14] After years of doubt and internal struggle, he did "come home," and later he was ordained to the priesthood on Pentecost Sunday, 11 June 1918.

Many commentators note that Bulgakov was an emotional writer, whose inner life — whether wracked with doubts and fears or calm and peaceful — frequently found its way to the written page.[15] It would appear that *The Burning Bush* (and *The Friend of the Bridegroom*) was the fruit of one such interior struggle. Bulgakov, like his earlier much admired and imitated Vladimir Soloviev, fell under the spell of the Roman Catholic Church. Bernard Marchadier has characterized the years 1918-1923 as Bulgakov's Catholic Period.[16] Bulgakov expressed his catholicizing tendencies to his closest friend, Pavel A. Florensky (1882-1937), in a letter written from 17 August to 1 September 1922 in Yalta, from whom he clearly expected a withering response.[17] That same year he composed what is surely his most remarkable pro-Roman confession, his "dialogue" *U sten Khersonisa (By the walls of Chersonesus)*[18] clearly modelled on Soloviev's *Three Conversations*.[19] Bulgakov, seemingly despairing for the future of Russia after the Bolshevik Revolution, made a very impassioned case in favour of the papal form of church government and reunion with the Roman Catholic Church as the best means of preserving the Russian Orthodox Church. As he travelled into exile from his native Russia, thoughts of a personal acceptance of Roman Catholicism and conversion to that form of Christianity haunted him, but the further he moved from his native land, the more critical he became of the west and its Catholicism. The idealized image he had formed of Catholicism crumbled when confronted by the reality of the Church in Western Europe. His face to face contact with western Catholics (and western Christianity in general) had the effect of a spiritual cold shower. If in December 1922 on board the steamer *Jeanne* heading for Constantinople Bulgakov could write "I am going to the West not as if to a land 'of bourgeois culture' or a bygone land 'of holy miracles,' now 'rotting,' but as to a land that still preserves Christian culture, and chiefly, to the place of the most holy Roman throne and the universal catholic church,"[20] by February 1923 he could write

> The Catholic drama in my soul is so interminable, though there is not that gloom in it as in the very first days. . . . Militant Catholics settle the question simply 'by conversion,' reuniting the *separatos,* that is, annulling the question; in fact it would appear that it is impossible to see any other result because no one thinks about uniting the churches nor does anyone want to hear about it. And whom should one listen to? In Russia there is the 'living church,' Bolshevism, rot, Protestantism, here hierarchical sluggishness, displayed in Karlovtsi and everywhere, and among the Catholics the closed army of Jesuits ready for battle and acting as one man. But before the face of that army, that earthly power and worldly might I feel myself in Orthodoxy and as an Orthodox Christian more than ever before.[21]

His first shock was to observe Catholic missionaries at work in Constantinople; an encounter with a Fr. Gleb B., whose opinions on the church question Bulgakov shared but toward whom Bulgakov reacted with instinctive distrust,[22] further unsettled him. The most unfavourable impression of all was made by Jesuit Fr. Stanislas Tyszkiewicz, whom he met on 23 February (8 March) and again nine days later. This could well have been the decisive blow to Bulgakov's pro-Catholic leanings.[23]

Part of the difficulties that Bulgakov experienced in sorting out his religious and spiritual affiliation may be attributed to the negative impression made on him by the Orthodox in Constantinople. As his diaries show, Bulgakov heaped scorn on the Greek Orthodox Church as he encountered it in the Phanar in Constantinople, chiding the Greeks for their irreverent behaviour in church, accusing them of showing only ethnographic interest in an Orthodoxy that had become a nationalistic anti-catholic bastion instead of a living faith.[24] On 4 (17) April 1923 Bulgakov visited Eyüp and wrote "Today I took leave of Sophia and went to Eyüp, a corner of the Muslim world, with its mystique, piety, prayer, ancient trees, pigeons, faience, — ah, what a marvellous place, and how much more authentic piety is there than in that vulgar Phanar! How much higher the Muslims are than the Greeks!"[25] He grew increasingly frustrated with the disorder in his own Russian church at home and in its dispersion in the west, particularly agitated by jurisdictional wrangling. But instead of abandoning his church, Bulgakov began to develop a sense of responsibility for the Orthodox Church and his coreligionists. Daily reports of the violent suppression of the church in Russia unsettled his already troubled soul all the more. The indifference and weakness of the Greeks, the ignorance and rigidity of the nationalist Russian Orthodox, the militancy of Catholicism and the realization that his ideas about church unity were utopian and unrealistic compelled Bulgakov to cry out "It is impossible not to act, and it is impossible to act, and this *epokhé* at times gives a certain feeling of fatal irreparableness. Once more I repeat and acknowledge that I cannot live in breach with my native church and outside of it, and whether I have been reborn or still not grown up, the crisis of the church has happened inside me and made me powerless."[26] He would eventually find the strength to act, but only after several months of further turmoil as he travelled through Austria to Prague and finally to Paris.

Bulgakov arrived in Prague in May of 1923, a city teeming with Russian émigrés who were warmly received by the government. Bulgakov was given a position in the Faculty of Russian Law and became active in the Russian Christian movement.[27] But his interest in Catholicism was by now the subject of rumour and it elicited stinging rebukes from his fellow exiles. A public reading from his *By the Walls of Chersonesus* elicited general perplexity and George Vernadsky scolded Bulgakov for abandoning the fight against Latinity. His wife also played her part in tempering his Catholic love affair, but it would take some time for the suspicions of Bulgakov's orthodoxy to subside.[28]

The spiritual and intellectual distance that Bulgakov had travelled is tellingly revealed in the description of his second visit to the Sistine Madonna. He was eager to see the painting that had affected his life so profoundly and all but ran to the gallery where it still hangs in the Zwinger museum. But this time, his reaction was very different: "The first impression was that I *had not come to the right place,* and that She was not in front of me. But quickly I recognize and am convinced that it is *She* and yet, that it really is *not She,* or that I am *no longer he.* . . . What point is there in hiding or deceiving: I did not see the Mother of God. Here there is beauty, only wonderful human beauty, with its religious double meaning, but there is no graciousness. Can one pray before this image? That is blasphemy, an impossibility!"[29] From Bulgakov's journal of 16 (29) February

1924 Marchadier cites an even more forceful rejection of this painting and all that it represents: "truly, *ex oriente lux,* because what is here is not *lux* but a phosphorescent piece of rotten wood."[30] By the end of that same year, the break with the Catholic interlude seems to be complete. He writes "Yesterday I received my manuscripts and today *with horror* I look at myself in that mirror of death and see *what* I had come to there: catholicization out of despair, the dreadful sin of lack of faith and exhaustion!"[31] In Paris, the transformation would become evident in his first significant theological publications.

There is also some truth to the suggestion that Bulgakov's turn away from Catholicism was inspired by his undying fascination with Sophia, the Wisdom of God.[32] Since the heady days of his involvement in religious-philosophical circles and his two major philosophical presentations of Sophiology, *Philosophy of Economy* and *Unfading Light,* Bulgakov had written little about Divine Wisdom, seemingly preoccupied with the question of church union and Catholic theology and culture. But in Constantinople his visits to Hagia Sophia reawakened that slumbering fascination with heavenly Sophia. While his rediscovery of Sophia would pluck him from the arms of the papacy, his Sophiology would embroil him in the not too distant future in a bitter dispute within his own church that to the present day still casts a shadow over his theological achievements.

Discussions to establish an Orthodox Theological Institute in Paris took place while Bulgakov was still in Prague. In 1925 he was invited to Paris by Metropolitan Evlogii to become the head of the Institut St Serge and to teach dogmatic theology. His first publication in his new home was *Saints Peter and John: The Two Chief Apostles* (1926),[33] a short essay refuting Roman Catholic ecclesiology, especially as concerns papal authority. This was followed by *The Burning Bush* and *The Friend of the Bridegroom,* both of which offer strong critiques of current Catholic doctrine and piety. By attacking three features of contemporary Catholicism which could be seen as fostering an unmistakably Roman identity, namely, the papacy, the dogma of the Immaculate Conception, and the veneration of St Joseph, Bulgakov clearly distanced himself from Catholicism and offered instead a reasoned, passionate, and at times lyrical alternative in the doctrine, faith and life of the Orthodox Church.

Western readers will not immediately associate the title of the book, *The Burning Bush,* with the Mother of God, but will most likely think of the revelation of God to Moses on Mount Horeb (Exodus 3:1-15). Bulgakov's choice of titles, however, is more than appropriate to his purposes, and immediately signals to Russian Orthodox readers the topic and its elaboration. For the title refers to a popular Russian icon of the Theotokos, "the Mother of God the Burning Bush" for which a special feast day, 4 September, is fixed in the Russian calendar;[34] it refers as well to a frequently recurring epithet applied to the Mother of God in the hymnody and prayers of the canonical hours. Bulgakov refers to both of these facts of Russian piety and devotion as he elaborates his theme. By using an Orthodox liturgical epithet and icon as the emblematic title of his book Bulgakov would be professing both his orthodoxy and his adherence to the Russian Orthodox Church, which as we have seen, can be regarded as an underlying motive for the composition of the book in the first place. The icon of the Mother of God the Burning Bush stands at the opposite end of the spectrum of sacred art dedicated to the Virgin Mary and certainly sharply contrasts with the Sistine Madonna towards which Bulgakov had grown very cool by this time.

Coming some seven years[35] after his last major statement on Sophiology in *Unfading Light, The Burning Bush* is Bulgakov's first explicitly and consciously dogmatic treatment of the theme of Holy Wisdom.[36] Previously, Bulgakov had remained within the general parameters of sophiological speculation established by Vladimir Soloviev and Pavel Florensky, philosophically rooted in the Russian appropriation of certain themes from German Idealism (world soul, eternal feminine) and coloured by mystical experience both personal and gleaned from the esoteric writings of Jacob Böhme (1575-1624) and Anna Schmidt. He now sought to ground his reflections in the lived faith of the Orthodox Church and in a peculiarity of Russian Orthodoxy which early on identified Sophia not with Christ but with the Mother of God. Although the book picks up some of the threads from his earlier sophiological writings, the focus is on dogmatic themes associated with the Mother of God: her perfect sinlessness, original sin, human nature, Divine Glory. Tradition is the major source upon which Bulgakov builds his case: scripture, liturgy, patristic interpretation and icons. While his original purpose of criticizing the Roman Catholic dogma of the Immaculate Conception dominates the treatise, including a sustained literary debate with the great German dogmatician Matthias Joseph Scheeben (1835-1888), Bulgakov also chastises his own dogmatic tradition for its inconsistent treatment of the Mother of God, which at times slavishly followed Roman arguments or just as slavishly adopted Protestant objections to the Marian dogma as its own. Bulgakov offers a deeply felt meditation on the treasures of the Orthodox liturgy and iconography, showing in the process how natural it should be for Orthodox theologians to write about the Mother of God

from within Orthodoxy and how central a place she occupies in its dogmatic and devotional life.

It is by no means an easy task to describe the shimmering opal that is
Sophiology as developed by Bulgakov. A fundamental question underlies
all of Bulgakov's sophiological work: how can the gulf separating the created world from its Creator be meaningfully overcome? That he sought an
answer in Christology seems an obvious resolution, but Bulgakov takes a
novel approach for an Orthodox theologian. Classical Christian doctrine
holds that with the Incarnation there no longer exists an insuperable gulf
between God and the created order, for in Jesus Christ God has become
part of the creation while remaining fully divine. But Bulgakov believes
that more needs to be said. He wants to understand what it is in matter itself, and specifically in the human being, that permits, facilitates and in
an indirect sense brings about direct communication and communion
with God. For him, Sophia or Holy Wisdom is the answer. His efforts may
be compared with the physicists at the start of the twentieth century who
reconceived the structure of the atom and eventually elaborated the theory of quantum physics. According to Paul Valliere, Sophiology really concerns the engagement of Orthodoxy with the modern world, or rather, a
dramatization of the struggle of Orthodoxy to find its place in the modern world and contribute in a positive way to contemporary conversation
about the larger issues facing humanity.[37]

Bulgakov associates many concepts with Sophia: beauty, goodness,
glory, the feminine principle, chastity, holiness. In *The Wisdom of God, a
Brief Summary of Sophiology* (1937),[38] written a decade after the publication
of *The Burning Bush,* Bulgakov sought to set forth in as clear a manner as
possible his understanding of Sophiology. Sophia is the essence or ousia
of the Godhead.[39] While asserting with tradition that Sophia can be identified properly with each of the divine persons, Bulgakov holds that no
one divine person wholly subsumes Sophia, who is rather the self-
revelation of the Godhead belonging equally to the three persons and dis-
tinctly to each one of them.[40]

Important for grasping Bulgakov's thought about Sophia is his in-
sistence that nothing exists outside God; God is all. While the created
world is not God, because it is God's *other,* it too is in God. Sophia is a way
to comprehend the distinction between God and the created world as well
as their unity. Sophia connects God and the world, passively and actively,
and exists in two modes: divine or uncreated, and creaturely or created
wisdom.[41] The dyadic structure of Sophia can be understood as a func-

tion of the Christological dogma of two natures united in the one divine person of Christ and also reflects the distinction in God between the divine essence and the divine energies articulated in the fourteenth century by St Gregory Palamas.[42] Human beings are created in the image of the Triune God whose essence is Sophia; therefore, human beings are also sophianic in nature. Divine Sophia reaches out to the world actively and is received passively by creaturely Sophia who in effect welcomes her own self in this exchange. But because Sophia is both active and passive, human beings (who represent the created order) also actively or causally extend themselves towards God in accordance with their sophianic nature. This particular dimension of Bulgakov's Sophiology receives much attention in *The Burning Bush,* where the Mother of God appears as the perfect representative of the sophianic human being.

Bulgakov begins his essay with a consideration of the personal sinlessness of the Mother of God, something he finds grounded in the sparse gospel witness and the fuller liturgical tradition of the church. Ill at ease with the unresolved state of the question among the church fathers, Bulgakov argues that by virtue of her close association with the redemptive work of Christ, beginning in the incarnation and continuing to her patient suffering at the foot of the cross, the Mother of God appropriately shares in the sinlessness of Christ himself; however, he also quickly notes that her sinlessness is a result of Christ's redemptive action. He is sinless by nature, she is still subject to the power of original sin but is sinless thanks to her personal condition. Here Bulgakov seems to recast a fundamental notion found in the Mariological system of Scheeben, otherwise his sparring partner, who also held that the Mother of God was subject as all humans are to original sin because of her nature, but because of her personal relation to the Saviour was not subject to inherited guilt and so was sinless personally.[43]

He then moves on in chapter two to explore more fully how original sin can exert force in the Theotokos without her ever succumbing to its impulses and committing actual sin. He finds his answer in human anthropology, and here Sophia first appears. For the original human being, Adam, created in the image and likeness of God, bears creaturely Sophia within. The human being, thanks to its sophianicity, is not defective in nature but is created precisely for a relationship with God and equipped with all that is necessary to attain this relationship; however, as a creature, the human being is weak and unstable, it knows the possibility of life in and for God and of life in and for the world. Original sin consists in choosing life in and for the world. There follows a lengthy discussion on the nature of Adam (and Eve) as a generic being, not an individual, who passes original sin on to all his descendants. Two dimensions of original sin are transmitted by Adam to all human beings: the infirmity of nature, expressed most clearly in the process and fact of death, and sinfulness. While the first is a constant, shared without exception by all human beings, the second is a variable and may by the power of grace be entirely suppressed. This is true of the Virgin Mary in an exceptional way, but is also true of John the Forerunner and other holy persons whose feats are recorded in scripture.

Bulgakov in chapter three discusses the dogma of the Immaculate Conception in detail. In his view, the dogma rests on two premises which may be fairly criticized: how original sin operates in the human being, and how human souls come into existence. With respect to the first, a key weakness in the dogma is its resort to the exceptional privilege of grace given by God to free the Virgin Mary from original sin. Here he argues against the arbitrariness of God's action and the violence it does to human freedom. With respect to the second, Bulgakov weighs the merits of both creationism (each soul is directly created by God at the moment of conception) and traducianism or generationism (the parents generate the soul along with the body in the act of conception) and ultimately favours generationism, provided that the truth of creationism is included in it. Given the high value he puts on the sophianic character of human nature, such a conclusion is to be expected, for it alone allows the human being to act out of its essential nature synergistically with God.

The lengthy fourth chapter begins with a theological evaluation of the various liturgical festivals marking events in the life of the Mother of God, from her nativity to her Dormition and glorification in heaven at the right hand of her Son. At this point Bulgakov turns his attention to what we today would call gender issues and to an evaluation of sex. Both of these topics had occupied Bulgakov in the decade preceding the publication of *The Burning Bush*. As A. P. Kozyrev has recently shown, Bulgakov's handling of the themes of sexuality, male and female identity, and the masculine and feminine principle in the Godhead were intimately connected with his fascination with Anna Schmidt, a provincial mystic who presented herself as the incarnation of Sophia and the realization of Soloviev's sophianic mysticism, even inspiring the eroticization of Sophia in some of Soloviev's late poetry.[44] Bulgakov wrote three articles dealing with Soloviev and Schmidt before finally breaking free of her influence in 1921.[45] Be that as it may, Bulgakov continued to reflect on the meaning of sex and the masculine/feminine principle in his theological works from 1921 on. In particular, he would put forward the notion, now regarded as outmoded, that the feminine principle is passive and receptive — both in the relations of husband and wife and in the conceptualization of Sophia herself. Here too Bulgakov remains very close to the thinking of Scheeben concerning the feminine principle.[46] The chapter closes with a reflection on the theme of Glory in creation and its manifestation in the perfected creature, the Mother of God, who thus fulfils her role as the visible manifestation of Sophia.

The book concludes with three excursuses that focus on Scriptural and patristic evidence for his foregoing discussion of the Mother of God and Sophia. His first excursus, on the glory of God in the Old Testament, looks at prophecies, types and revelations of the Mother of God in conjunction with the revelation of God's glory, which for him is a revelation of Sophia. He concludes this excursus with a poetic effusion of his devotion to the Mother of God that sums up all that he has said in the essay: "She is Wisdom in creation, and in her is revealed the fullness of Divine triunity. She lives the life of the Holy Trinity and is the first of creaturely hypostases, the beloved Daughter of God and also Mother of the whole human race. She is the Glory of the world, the Burning Bush, creaturely nature, burning and not being burned up in the divine flame of the Holy and Life-giving Trinity." The second excursus looks at Old Testament passages that speak of Wisdom. Here Bulgakov wants to demonstrate how Wisdom/Sophia cannot be identified solely with the Second Hypostasis, as well as how she has a hypostatized quality without being herself a hypostasis. The third excursus examines the writings of Athanasius of Alexandria (ca. 298-ca. 373), Basil of Caesarea (330-379), and Gregory of Nazianzus (ca. 300-ca. 390) on the wisdom of God; but essentially he looks here at the meaning of mediation and mediator, first in the context of Arianism, and then as a way to understand the function of Sophia and by extension, that of the Mother of God and the saints.

The Burning Bush[47] is a rich, impressionistic text in which Bulgakov moves his sophiological thought forward, out of a religious-philosophical ghetto into what he no doubt hoped would be the main square of Orthodox theology. It also sheds light on the intellectual development of the most creative Russian Orthodox theologian of the twentieth century whose thought is finally receiving the attention it deserves.

THE BURNING BUSH

From the Author

The proposed sketch dedicated to the question of the Orthodox veneration of the Mother of God was conceived originally (a few years ago) only
as a critical analysis of the Catholic dogma of 1854 concerning the Immaculate Conception of the Mother of God. However, as work progressed it
became clear that a critique cannot remain only negative, but must be accompanied by at least some positive illumination of the question on the
basis of dogmatic teaching concerning the Mother of God which is held
by the Church and which is disclosed in various aspects in the church's
veneration of the Ever-Virgin Mary. The author recognizes the whole difficulty of such a theological interpretation and does not intend to give his
own personal conjectures greater meaning than that of a private theological opinion, in an area, moreover, that is little researched and difficult. Besides the explicit dogmatic determinations of the church, the Word of
God and patristic tradition, it is the Church's prayer life, prompted by the
Holy Spirit, her instructions and testimonies that present themselves as
the indisputable foundation for theologizing; in other words, dogmatic
facts are more primary than theological doctrines.

Most holy Lady Theotokos!
Strengthen my feeble and poor hand.

Paris
August 1926

The Burning Bush

The Orthodox Church honours the Mother of God as the most exalted of all creatures, "more honourable than the cherubim and more glorious beyond compare than the seraphim." It is not even possible to put into words that whole prayerful veneration of the Most Pure which every faithful soul together with the holy Church bestows on her. "No mind comprehends how to praise fittingly" that purity and holiness which surpasses every mind. It seems that it is already impossible to add anything to this veneration, impossible to favour or exalt the Most Pure Virgin more than the holy Church has already exalted her. And yet, in accordance with the general spirit of Orthodoxy, for which life is more adequate than formulas, the Church, as a matter of fact, does not possess a comprehensive *dogmatic definition* concerning the Mother of God except the decision of the third ecumenical council concerning *the Theotokos*.

The veneration of the Mother of God, which rests, of course, on defined ecclesiodogmatic doctrine about her, is confirmed by church *practice*, primarily through the liturgy which is actuated by the Holy Spirit and which expresses the prayed life of dogma. On the contrary, school doctrine about this subject in Orthodoxy is inconsistent and unclear, it is absent to a significant extent or, what is far worse, it falls into a polemical dependence on Catholic dogmatization, digressing from its straightforward and positive task. In the present essay the principal task is to disclose one aspect of this doctrine, namely, the *sinlessness* of the Mother of God.

CHAPTER 1

The Absence of Personal Sin in the Mother of God

Does the Most Pure, the All-Immaculate One have any kind of *personal* sin? Is it possible even for a moment to conceive this dreadful abuse? And yet, as strange as it may sound, to just such an admission do those Orthodox theologians tend who are tempted by excessive zeal to shatter to its foundations the unsuccessful Catholic dogma of the Immaculate Conception of the Mother of God. Even stranger still, in patristic literature the church's point of view was far from being settled straight away and not only Origen but also St Basil the Great, St John Chrysostom and several others deviated from it.[1] In the end, however, the interpretation of Saints Ephrem the Syrian, Epiphanius, Gregory Nazianzus, Ambrose of Milan, blessed Augustine, and others triumphed which expressed more precisely the church's veneration of the Mother of God.

First of all with respect to the absolute personal sinlessness of the Mother of God it is necessary to establish on the basis of the facts of the gospel tradition as well as according to the evidence of immediate feeling that there exists no possibility of ascribing to the Mother of God the committing of a personal sin in whatsoever moment of her life. In fact, if we turn over in our thoughts all the stages of her life, which one of them "will the hand of the vile brush against"? Would Mary, graced already in her mother's womb and born of the holy and righteous ancestors of the Godman, have committed a sin in her childhood, a time that is considered a blessed state for all people? (Cf. the "Service for the burial of a child" in which the idea of the incorruption of this age by sin is repeated a number of times: "before the taste of earthly weakness took him, Christ our Saviour, this spotless child . . . uncorrupted . . . most pure . . . blessed, like a pure bird into heavenly purity . . . in the future age you prepared for him a space, Abraham's bosom, and in keeping with angelic purity, sacred places" and so on.) True, one can object that the idea of the blessed and sinless state of children refers only to "those reborn in water and spirit," that is, to the baptised; but baptism became possible only after Pentecost. However, the absence of a personally committed sin, besides original sin, constitutes the general characteristic of childhood, and it distinguishes this from the later stage, which invariably proves to be open to sin despite baptism. Outside baptism this negative childhood sinlessness, non-participation in sin by virtue of the absence of conscious and responsible actions, does still not, it is true, give salvation.[2] But with respect to personal sin is it really possible that the Virgin Mary, graced from the womb by the Holy Spirit, proves to be different from all people in an unfavourable sense?

Is it possible to ascribe personal sin to the Theotokos in her childhood years, in those blessed three years which she spent under the pious roof of her parents? It is enough merely to pose the question aloud in order to feel without delay its impiousness. Furthermore, will the wicked mind dare ascribe personal sin to the Ever-Virgin in those years of her childhood and youth when she was preserved in the temple, feeding on the bread of angels and in communion with them, devoted to prayer and the contemplation of God? Or will it do this with respect to those months during which the Most Pure, having left the temple, remained in the protection of righteous Joseph and prepared herself for receiving the annunciation? Surely this would have happened later, if the Pure One proved to be in sin, would it not? Let there be no place given to such an evil idea. After the annunciation, when the Holy Spirit descended upon the Graced One, "cleansed[3] her, and her womb became a heaven" when she carried in her womb the Divine Infant — will profane thought dare ascribe to her the possibility of any sort of sin whatever? Or is it possible to think this relative to the time when the Mother of God was raising the Divine Infant, uninterruptedly illuminated by the light of His Divinity? This strange idea is occasioned by the prophetic words of Simeon the Just concerning "the weapon" which must "pierce the soul" of Mary (Lk 2:35) and interprets this image in a disparaging sense, as doubt or lack of faith. Later this idea is stuck on to the tale about the boy Jesus preaching in the temple. The mother's words "your father and I were greatly worried about you" and what he said in reply "but they did not understand the words spoken by him" (Lk 2:48, 50) are interpreted as a sign of lack of faith. A similar exegesis is applied to that occasion when mother and brothers are looking for an opportunity to speak with the preaching Jesus (Mt 12:46,

50; Mk 3:31-35). Both cases — in the temple and while he is preaching — present themselves as a temptation on the human path of Mary which she passes through in her earthly life on the path of her Divine Motherhood. She continually had to sacrifice the natural feelings of human mother-hood for the service of her Son which required a complete self-renunciation. These sacrifices were not offered easily or gratis; a weapon continually passed through the Mother's heart — even earlier than Golgotha, for her whole life until then was indeed a path to Golgotha, its pre-initiation. With the usual informational reserve amounting to parsimoniousness in all that concerns the Mother of God, the Gospels nonetheless imprinted both these cases of temptation's trial, silently half-opening for us the sufferings of a maternal heart, its struggles and temp-tations on the way to Golgotha, its human exhaustion (for humanly even her divine Son was tempted and exhausted). And still in these texts which speak about the temptations of the Mother of God there is not the least indication of an assault of sin. She remained sinless all along this path which terminates in her unwavering station at the cross. The Mother's station on Golgotha at the cross of her Son reveals the purity and the sin-less sacrificial quality of her entire life which prepared her for Golgotha. Where, then, and what grounds can there be for ascribing sin to her dur-ing the Saviour's earthly life when she offered her own tribute of maternal suffering in the work of redemption? But perhaps sin found itself a place after the resurrection, after Pentecost? The mere posing of this question only exposes its complete inappropriateness. In a word, there are no grounds in the Gospels for ascribing to the Most Pure any sort of assault of sin at all, and if this is sometimes done, then it is on account of certain dogmatic inventions of a misunderstood character (as for example is the case with Origen who ascribed to the Virgin at the cross not only the greatest grief and sufferings but also doubts on the sham grounds that without the presence of personal sin the Lord could not be her saviour and redeemer).

In its countless divine services dedicated to the Mother of God, the Holy Orthodox Church firmly and clearly teaches the absolute sinlessness of Mary in her birth, her holy childhood and adolescence, in the Annunci-ation, in the birth of her Son and throughout her entire life. We shall pause at only the most important dogmatic witnesses borrowed from the services of Theotokos feasts.[4] As is evident from these witnesses, the Most Holy Virgin is called in her very birth "Holy of Holies," "living heaven," "temple of all kings and thrones," "sole immaculate one," "the true divine temple pure from infancy on," "hostile to the course of sin," etc. The question arises: is the idea of any sort of assault of sin, which even some fathers of the church, and with them other orthodox theologians, allow, compatible with this veneration? Obviously not. The Mother of God was sinless, not a single attack of sin approached her most pure soul, the bearer of perfect virginity. But in that case is she not made equal "to the one sinless" Lord Jesus? No, and therein is the whole point. Sinlessness belongs in a unique and exclusive sense to the Son of God conceived without seed from a virgin who had never known a man, in that He was a stranger not only to every *personal sin but also to original sin*. The latter had absolutely no power over the new Adam. He appeared only "in the likeness of the flesh of sin" (Rom 8:3) but not in sinful flesh, and by a free act of ascesis He *made himself small* (Phil 2:7). For the sake of our salvation He accepted and endured the infirmity of human nature, the weakness and lassitude of the body and death on the cross. As before the fall Adam was not susceptible to natural death for it was not in his nature ("God did not create death," Wis 1:13-14, 2:23-24), so too the new Adam was not subject to the natural law of death but freely submitted only to a violent death which revealed the whole counter-natural character of this death for Him, "for death could not hold him" (Acts 2:24). By virtue of His unconditional sinlessness His death gained a redemptive meaning for all people, for strictly speaking He had no sins and there could not be any in Him. In this manner, the likeness of the flesh of sin, assumed in keeping with His self-abasement, according to the plan of human salvation, only revealed the full sinlessness and incorruptibility of human nature in the Godman. It is quite the opposite in the case of the Most Pure and All Immaculate One: in her, *original sin* preserved *its entire power* with all its fatal consequences — weakness and mortality of the body (for death is only the final revelation of this weakness). The Theotokos died a natural death in fulfilment of the natural law, which she bore in her human nature. Death was defeated only by the salvific power of Christ's resurrection and was ultimately annulled by it. The Lord Jesus is in this sense *the Saviour* for the entire human race, and in it of His Mother as well, which is why the Most Pure even sang in her song "my soul magnifies the Lord and my spirit rejoices in God *my Saviour*." The immaculateness and sinlessness of the Ever-Virgin refer not to her nature but to her condition, to her *personal* relationship to sin and her personal overcoming of it. This requires a purposeful explanation: can personal sinlessness be united with the presence of original sin, or is there here a contradiction?

Appendix 1

Nativity of the Theotokos

At the "Lord I have cried" — Today God who rests upon rational thrones has prepared for himself *a holy throne on earth;* he who in wisdom has made the heavens firm has created in his love for humankind *a living heaven. . . .* Anne gives birth to a maiden, *from all generations foreordained* to be the dwelling of the king and maker of all, Christ our God.

At the Lity — *she who was predestined* to be the queen of all, God's habitation. At the aposticha — Through the angel's foretelling *the all holy fruit* of Joachim and Anne the righteous ones, the virgin, today comes forth, the heaven and throne of God, a *tabernacle of purity* — for behold today is born *she who was foreseen before the womb* to be the mother of our God, the vessel of virginity.

The canon of Andrew, ode 1: *The Holy of Holies* is placed as an infant in the holy sanctuary to be reared in the hands of angels; ode 3: Virgin, *brought up in the holy of holies,* Most Pure Theotokos, you have appeared higher than creation; ode 6: Your chaste parents, pure one, offered you *who are the holy of holies* in the temple of the Lord to be raised honourably and to be made ready to become His mother . . . we sing *your holy nativity* (cf. the kontakion), we honour your spotless conception, O one called by God to be both bride and virgin; ode 7: *O womb* (of Anne) which made room for God's dwelling place! O womb that has carried her who is more expansive than the heavens; holy throne, intended life of sanctification; ode 9: You have inherited through a promise *O Mother of God, a worthy nativity for your purity* . . . we venerate your swaddling clothes, O Theotokos.

At the lauds sticheron "on the parents of the Theotokos" — O wondrous miracle, the fountain of life is born from a barren woman and grace begins radiantly to bear its fruit. Rejoice, Joachim, that you were the parent of the Theotokos: *there is no* other *parent of those born of earth* like *you, O pleasing to God* . . . living pillar of chastity and brilliant tabernacle sparkling with grace, Anne has appeared glorious and truly given birth to the palisade of virginity, the divine blossoming.

Service for the apostle John the Theologian on 26 September

The canon for the Theotokos, ode 1: As a beautiful one, *as a most good one, as a spotless one among earthborn ones,* God has chosen you.

Entrance in the Temple

At small vespers to the "Lord I have cried" — *The Holy of holies is fittingly brought to dwell in the sanctuary* . . . let the gates of the God-pleasing temple be opened: *for the temple of the king of all and his throne* being received today with glory within, Joachim exalts having consecrated her to the Lord.

At the aposticha — Heavenly gates receive the virgin into the Holy of Holies, *the unsullied tent* of God almighty. Host of virgins, bearing torches, receive *the pure virgin* into the holy of holies like the bride of God the king of all. To the "Lord I have cried" — Today *the living temple* of the holy glory of Christ our God, *the sole pure one blessed among women* is accompanied into the temple of the law. . . . Into the holy of holies *the holy and spotless one* is led by the Holy Spirit. . . . After your nativity, O Lady Theotokos, you came to the temple of the Lord to be raised in the holy of holies *as one who is consecrated.* Then Gabriel was sent to you, *the all spotless one,* bringing you food. All the heavenly beings marvelled when they saw *the Holy Spirit take up his dwelling in you.* Therefore most pure and unsullied one, you who are praised in heaven and on earth, Mother of God, save our race. . . .

At the Lity, the stichera: behold . . . *the one who has been sanctified to God as his dwelling* today is brought into the temple like *an unblemished offering.* . . . Today the temple where God has his place, the Theotokos, is brought to the Lord's temple . . . come all you faithful, let us praise *the one unblemished woman* proclaimed by the prophets and brought into the temple, *the mother who was foretold before the ages* and in the final days appeared as the Theotokos.

At the aposticha — Heaven and earth rejoice as they behold *the rational heaven* approaching the divine house to be raised honourably *the sole and unblemished virgin* . . . divine Anne revealed grace and leads with joy into God's temple *the pure ever-virgin one given by grace.*

Sessional hymn — *before your conception, pure one, you were consecrated to his God, and after you were born on earth you were offered as a gift;* now to him fulfil your parents' promise. In the divine temple *as one who is truly a divine temple, O pure one from your infancy,* you have been offered with holy candles, you appeared as the tabernacle of unapproachable and divine light.

Sessional hymn after the polyeleos — Let David the Psalmist rejoice and Joachim and Anne be glad, for *a holy fruit* has come forth from them, Mary the lamp bearing the divine light.

The Canon, ode 5: *Strange is your nativity, strange the manner of your growing, strange too all the glorious things about you, O bride of God,* everything is unutterable for humanity. Ode 8: Anne once brought you into the house of God *most pure temple.* . . . Ode 9: Your miracle, pure Theotokos, soars above the power of words: for in you the body understands more than words, *being hostile to the course of sin.*

At the lauds — let the gate of the God-pleasing temple be opened, *for the temple of the king of all and of thrones* today is received with glory within, Joachim exalts having consecrated her to the Lord.

The Sunday of the Holy Ancestors

At the "Lord I have cried" — O faithful, today as we commemorate our ancestors we pray to Christ our Deliverer who has exalted them among all nations . . . and who has shown *from them the power of life to us,* the one who knew no man and child of God, Mary *the pure one.*

Troparion — by faith you justified our ancestors, *having betrothed the church beforehand from the shadow of the nations;* the saints praise you in glory, *because from their seed is a blessed fruit, she who bore you without seed.*

Annunciation: aposticha — *God has loved you from the ages and has chosen you for his dwelling place.*

From the service for 9 December, the conception of St Anne when she conceived the most holy Theotokos

Stichera to the "Lord I have cried" — He who from an undampened rock makes water flow gives as fruit to your womb, O Anne, the ever-virgin Lady, and from her will spring forth the water of salvation. . . . The prophetic words are now fulfilled, for the mountain of the holy ones is firmly established in the womb, the divine ladder is planted, the mighty throne of kings is made ready, the place of God's entrance is ornamented, the burning bush begins to bud forth, the myrrh-maker of the saints already flows, the barrenness of the river of wise Anne whom we bless with faith.

Sessional hymn: A new heaven is formed in Anne's womb, by the command of God the all-fashioner, the unfading sun shines out from it, illuminating the whole world with the rays of Divinity, with a superabundance of loving kindness, the one lover of humankind.

The Canon, ode 1: Holding in her womb the book which, the prophet foretold, is printed by the Holy Spirit, Anne cries out to all: the one whom all the scriptures reveal is exalted, for I have brought her forth today. — The divine and saving temple finds a place in the womb and is formed in the maternal entrails, the ladder is planted which raises the whole human race to the highest places. Let her conception be celebrated with faith. Ode 8: The earth in which the maker of the earth has settled, the holy sceptre, the new life, the jar of manna in the maternal entrails, begins to bud forth her who bears him. Ode 9: As you are conceiving, life-receiving fountain Anne wise in God, receive joy now, for having welcomed the holy temple within your womb you magnify the one who is resplendent with the creator's light of truth.

Stichera for lauds: He who before the ages unutterably from God revealed the origin of the divine and dread mysteries of faith proclaimed to mortals, the conception of the pure Child of God, proclaims through her the cessation of the deeds of darkness and the passions. Come joyfully today every rank and human generation, let us celebrate brightly with the angelic hosts the most glorious conception of the Theotokos: patriarchs celebrate the mother of the king of all; prophets, the one who was proclaimed to all; forebears the one who from you is Mother of God; elders the ancestors of God, ancestors of God the child of God, virgins the ever-virgin, for assurance the root of faith, consecrated ones the all holy temple of God, the choirs of all the saints the cause of your assembly, the hosts of angels the one who bore the master of all and the saviour of our souls.

CHAPTER 2

The Power of Original Sin
for the Mother of God

In order to respond to the question posed we need to focus our attention on that corner stone of dogmatic theology on which Christian anthropology and, in particular, the doctrine of redemption, rests. The human being is created by God according to His image and likeness. This means that God imprinted on the spirit of the human being His tri-hypostatic image and along with this placed him in the creaturely world as if in His own place, and made him a creaturely god. In creation the power of the tri-hypostatic divine revelation was made evident, and the primordial human being was created pure and unblemished. Therefore he was a personal bearer of Divine Wisdom, of creaturely Sophia, as it were: *the divine image,* with which the human condition was not at variance, is the *divine likeness* in him.

In Catholic theology beginning with medieval scholasticism and continuing down to the present day a distinction was established between *donum superadditum, justitia originalis,* and *status naturae purae.* According to the sense of this doctrine, it is necessary to put forward even before the fall that distinction in the human as a creaturely being that was disclosed only after the fall, namely, between that which belongs to the human as a creature, and that which is given to him only in virtue of an extraordinary gift of grace but which itself *does not* belong to him. According to Catholic doctrine, neither immortality nor freedom from lust *(concupiscentia carnis)* is proper to "the pure nature" of the human: the natural human being was created by God free from neither death nor lust. Only the extraordinary gift of grace *(donum superadditum)* frees him from the one and the other, together with the gift of original righteousness *(justitia originalis).* Both principles — the natural and the graced — in relation to the primordial human are imagined in Catholic anthropology as distinct and even opposite, and the only foundation for the fact that the first human was endowed with these gifts is the free will of God, if it can be so expressed, the arbitrariness of divine love and goodwill towards people. *An ontological link,* an internal necessity, does not exist here.

Of course, this doctrine encounters the direct testimony of the Word of God that God did not create death and, on the contrary, that everything created was made "very good," while *concupiscentia,* introducing a lustful inclination into the human essence, is not good even before the judgement of limited human reason, so that this doctrine is shown to be insulting to the Creator and creation. It in fact removes the power of the divine image in the human, since it reduces him, even in the *original* outline, to mortal life in lust. Even if this condition is concealed and stripped of power in the primordial human being by the *donum superadditum,* still in relation to human nature it happens *super,* forcibly, counter-naturally, and thus even *super naturam,* like some *Deus ex machina.* The possibility of such a distinction or *dualism* in the interpretation of human nature, by virtue of which some of its properties are humanly natural while others are super-meritorious and superhuman, is linked to the general absence in Catholic theology of a clear anthropology which would rest on firm foundations and not yield to the influence of legalism in the theory of redemption. Such a basis for anthropology can only be the doctrine of Wisdom as the pre-eternal foundation of creation, pre-eternal humanity, by virtue of which the earthly human is created according to the image of Christ the heavenly human (*ho anthrōpos ex ouranou* — 1 Cor 15.47). It is enough to take in earnest only this fundamental correlation in order to clear away like a cobweb the constructions of scholasticism concerning what is owed to the human and what is not owed, is *super.* With the human being the image of God shone in creation, the tri-hypostatic divine Sophia was revealed, by virtue of which the creaturely human hypostases were made. In *the creatureliness* of the human lies the cause of the precariousness *of his condition,* his incompleteness, the possibility for him to fall into sin. The ontological basis of the *fullness* of human nature consists in his sophianicity. His creatureliness is not at all revealed in the defectiveness of his creaturely nature *according to essence,* as Catholic theology teaches, ascribing to him both mortality and concupiscence precisely by virtue of this creatureliness, but only *in the image of possession* of this his fullness. The incorrupt and virginal human has in himself both the power of life — *posse non mori* — and the power of chastity — *posse non peccare* — not by means of an extraordinary gift — *donum superadditum,* but as an internal norm, the exact *essence* of his nature. Both death and sin, although *possible* in the human owing to his creatureliness (as sin up to a certain time was possible even for the world of bodiless powers: this is proven by the fall of the Morning Star and his angels and the battle of Michael and his hosts with him in heaven, who definitively resisted in this battle and conquered), were for the human precisely *not normal and contrary to nature.* Meanwhile according to Catholic doctrine this results in exactly the reverse, so that it becomes incomprehensible and ontologically inappropriate by what manner in general the fall into sin became possible, since it was not his own freedom that preserved the human from sin but a supernatural divine power. In what way was this power rendered powerless before the temptation of the serpent, or how could the human of himself — by his own or satanic powers — overturn that grace? From the Catholic perspective the original fall into sin is presented as impossible, unclear and incomprehensible; here is ascribed to the human not the naiveté of ignorance proper to his stage of growth, and not the weakness of an as yet untempted will, but precisely a satanic uprising against grace, a blasphemy against the Holy Spirit, which is not forgiven either in this age or in the future. But such was not Adam's fall into sin.

Already this very distinction of natural and graced, in the sense of given and superadded as applied to the primordial human nature, is false; it constitutes the radical defect, *prōton pseudos,* of Catholic anthropology. It is necessary to take the idea of the *divine image* in the human in all of its ontological significance, with which such defectiveness cannot be reconciled. Here as applied to the primordial human the distinction of two aspects of grace is unsuitable: in creation *(creativa)* and in providence *(providentialis),* which became customary in scholastic theology, for here either all is natural or all is graced. The world before the fall, although as yet it had not become that world in which God is all in all, is nonetheless *the pre-inception* of that same world. Likewise the human was completely open to the action of Divinity, to pre-inceptive divinization, but only in virtue of his immaculateness and sinlessness: God came in the cool of the day to converse with the human being, as with a friend, and this "conversation" was not *donum superadditum* in relation to his incorrupt nature; on the contrary, this divine communion was given and set in it. For this sake and precisely as such was the human created to be a mediator between God and the world, by communing in divine life. In a word, the Catholic opposition of natural and graced in the human is cancelled by his radical ontological determination: the human bore the image of God and, although he is a natural creaturely being, as the image of Divinity he still is open and accessible to the influences of Divinity. He was filled with grace and divinized from measure to measure, becoming through this a god in nature, a god-world or a god-human, and not some sort of ontological centaur, an animal, merely concealed in its animality by the *donum superadditum*. To put it bluntly, Catholic theology undermines in the same way without noticing it the very bases of Christology, linked with anthropology.

It is entirely possible to accept and ontologically to understand the incarnation of the Logos in a human which by nature is conformable with the Logos himself. But completely impossible and unacceptable is the incarnation of God in a lower creature, mortal and concupiscent, in some sort of half-animal, not only by reason of its given sinful *condition* but also by reason of its *nature*. Thus, the primordial human was neither mortal nor concupiscent according to his nature, for in *his very nature* was included a life of grace in God and with God, for he was created in the world for God. But, as a creaturely being, he had in himself the creaturely weakness and instability of nature; in it lay the possibility of life not only in God and for God but also in the world and for the world. And in original sin the human extinguished the life of grace within and tore asunder his direct graced communion, "conversation" with God; he committed homicide against himself, ceased to be a human, a friend of God, and instead became a natural being, and plunged into *cosmism*. This fall, this homicide was at the same time suicide: as the soul is the life of the body, so God is eternal life for the human, the life of the soul. Having turned away from God, the human lost the power and fountain of life within and, weakened, he could no longer contain and bind his body. Death entered the world. At the same time, being the ontological centre of the world, its soul, he lost the very faculty "of having dominion" in the world. The world fell into an orphaned state; it was left without a master. The fall was a cosmic catastrophe, "a curse" for the earth; it happened not just in the human but also in the whole world (and through this it condemned the human to labour in the sweat of his brow). The world fell ill with the human, and until the present day the whole creation groans and is tormented on account of "the one who accused her" from whom she hopes for her deliverance (Rom 8.19-22). Although the world in the human being remained sophianic in its first principles, essentially *a divine world*, it ceased to be a world-*cosmos*, but became a world lying in evil and suffering. Having corrupted his body, the human being harmed the whole world; having become the law of his life, evil in the world began to bear fruit and multiply just as it did in the human. After the fall a new world epoch begins, a particular state of the world in impairedness and groaning, and we sons of Adam no longer know this "very good" in which the world was created. If the fallen human being, according to the word of the apostle, has "another law which is in our members, a sinful law" (Rom 7.11, 20), then this disorder extends into the whole world.

So, wherein are the power and essence of original or hereditary sin? Like all sins it has two aspects: a subjective and an objective aspect, guilt *(reatus)* and its consequences — impairment and corruption; in it there are its own freedom and its own necessity. In Adam himself, evidently, both aspects of original sin are joined: here there were his free self-determination and the personal sin of disobedience, unbelief and hatred for God, in virtue of which he got the false idea that spiritual might and immortality could be obtained by the powers of this world, by eating the forbidden fruit. Adam fell into *cosmism* or practical atheism and was punished precisely with this cosmism: he became a natural, cosmic being. The objective consequences of his sin were of necessity linked with this cosmism — sickness, toil, anxiety and death. In as much as Adam's fall into sin is regarded as a personal human sin with personal responsibility, this is sufficiently understandable. However, all the difficulties arise before theological thought when the sin of Adam happens to be understood as an ancestral "original" or general human sin determining by itself the fates of the whole of humanity. Theological thought, from blessed Augustine down to our own days, wears itself out clarifying this transfer of Adam's sin to his heirs. In agreement with the teaching of the apostle Paul, "as by one man sin entered the world, and by sin death, so too has death passed into all humans, in as much as all have sinned" (Rom 5.12), "by the transgression of one person death has reigned by means of the one" (Rom 5.17), "by the transgression of one person judgment has come to all human beings" (Rom 5.18) — the sin of Adam has a universal meaning for the whole of humanity, and was for it the source of impairedness *(hamartēma)*.[1] How is one to understand this representation of the one for everyone in perdition which the apostle parallels with the representation of the one in salvation: "by righteousness is justification for all humans to life" (Rom 5.18)? The usual answer to this question, since the time of blessed Augustine, is that Adam committed his sin not only for himself but on behalf of his descendants to whom it is passed on through birth; carnal conception is the channel through which sin flows into all humanity. At the time of birth the human being receives as it were the inherited disease of sin which perverts his soul. In this sense original sin *peccatum originale* is an innate sin *peccatum naturae* (*hamartēma* in the apostle Paul as opposed to *paraptōsis* or *parabasis,* personal sin). All people constitute a single race with respect to physical origin; thus one person can perform services or give satisfaction for many, one person can be their representative, similarly to how Sodom and Gomorrah could have been spared for the sake of five righteous men.

In Adam's sin the *corruption* of the whole of human nature occurred; this is the *natural* side of original sin or its consequences (in Catholic theology this is called *peccatum habituale,* a sinful condition). This idea constitutes the general conviction of the fathers of the church and is expressed in different forms by them.[2] But there is another side of original sin: every sin has its source in the bad use of human freedom, and it is in this sense *personal* sin. The original sin committed by Adam is *the personal* sin of everyone, actively committed by them — *peccatum actuale.* Both aspects of original sin must find their explanation.

Let us first of all stay with *the natural* consequences of original sin. We have already shown that it has its spread not only in human life and the human body but also in the whole of nature in as much as the human is the focus of the world. It was not given to the human being to create the world, but in virtue of his superior situation in this world it proved possible for him to ruin it. From the moment in creation when it was said to the primordial human "have possession of the earth and hold dominion over every creature" (Gen 1.28), the human became as it were the responsible guardian of the universe such that his personal self-determination was also the fate of the whole world. In this sense the human, not being in any sense creator of the world, was the responsible participant in its fates and condition. The whole world would be other if it were not for the sin of Adam. Having *cosmic* significance, Adam's sin had *a general human* significance as well, so that the sin of one became the lot of all. This signifies not that Adam was the *representative* of the human race in a juridical sense, as one of many and on behalf of many, but that in him this entire race existed; *the whole* of humanity was present as a single, all-encompassing nature and essence. This must be understood ontologically.

Humanity can be thought of in two ways: as an *aggregate* of identical or similar individuals, repeating one another in a certain sense and at the same time different from one another and mutually impenetrable: A B C . . . etc.; their single *humanness* being an abstraction, universal, deducible in parentheses, but really existing only in individuals. This is the *nominalist* understanding which, being interested in the logical operations of thought, refuses to see their metaphysical basis and comes to nothing more than description as comprehension. We can think of humanity, or more precisely, humanness, *realistically* as a certain spiritual essence or force, one in its being, representing in itself the organism of the world (microcosm), but as a plural, multi-hypostatic essence in its realizations. Because one sees only this plurality, nominalism is seduced by it. Individuals are for the realistic perspective only splashes, hypostatic appearances of *a single* humanness. Whence follows a certain ontological solidarity of the whole human race which is grounded in its metaphysical unity: not that "all are guilty on behalf of all" as Dostoevsky said, but all are *one,* and each, acting for himself and on behalf of himself, acts in the whole of humanity and for its sake. This is a strange and even awe-inspiring thought, because it reveals to every human being his bottomless depth and eternal fate. Each individual human being turns out to be not only determining but also determined by his nature, namely, he is a peasant indentured to sin, a captive to the flesh, and a slave of sin. His nature is for him already determined, in his personal existence.

There was, however, a time when it was not thus determined, but was still *determinable,* and depending on this determination it could become either one thing or another. This was in Adam's *paradisiacal* state, before the fall, when the ontological commandment not to eat the fruits of the tree of knowledge of good and evil, and the double possibility for self-determination towards God or towards the world appeared before Adam. After the choice was made, this possibility of *choice,* of alternatives, disappeared not only for Adam but also for all his descendants. In this sense the choice stands beyond the limits of history and even of this very world in its current state; although it is indeed an *event,* it is not in a series of events that begin after it as its consequences. It is the *beginning* of our time, of our age (eon). Being on the one hand *only an individual,* Adam comes forward as *the all-human,* with his own definition defining his nature where it concerns not its essence but its condition. In just such a special status of the individual all-human Adam lies his personal particularity, which is not repeated in any of his descendants, who had before them the already accomplished fact of Adam's self-determination and bore it in themselves as their own proper nature. The decisive significance of Adam's act is intelligible because of the *unity* of humanity and humanness; however, in that relation it is not entirely clear why and in what capacity precisely Adam was that individual, that hypostatic bearer of humanness, who proved to be the ruler of destinies for the whole human race. Here one ought first of all to bear in mind that the critical moment of choice, of trial and self-determination lay unavoidably on the human's path owing to his *creatureliness,* and perhaps, to the *double* possibility objectively deposited in him: if he turned towards God, he could become a god by grace for the sake of the whole world or, if he turned away towards the world, he could become its slave and give power to the elements of non-existence and death. This self-determination entered God's plan for the creation of the human being, who in this self-determination realized as it were his own self-creation. But this self-determination or self-creation *humankind in general* could accomplish only *as a hypostasis,* in an individual form, as an individual, for without a hypostasis, humanness is not realized, it is an abstraction.

What kind of hypostasis was it that was charged with accomplishing this determining act at the critical moment? Whatever it was, it is clear that owing to the very properties of its position connected with this moment, this primordial hypostasis, as *the first,* is *unique in its class.* Namely, it starts the counting of further hypostases; without itself being counted it grounds the counting by itself, beginning it from itself. Such in general is the characteristic of the *first* — it is not only an ordered magnitude, one out of many, after which immediately follows and to which adheres the second, but it is also unique, the one that, strictly speaking, stands outside every series, as the one that begins it. Adam's hypostasis is just such a first and unique hypostasis *according to its position:* Adam is not only the first human, he is also unique in his class, the primordial human, the forefather. And this very position is *ontologically* founded in the nature of the human, as a free-spiritual being, created by God in the freedom of his self-determination (and by this the creation of the human differs from all other living beings, to which this self-determination was not given other than with the human and in the human). One such hypostasis in the human race must be the primogenitor, Adam, who by the same token alone in himself begins beforehand and holds in himself all people and everything. Given this, his primordial state, his being unburdened by sin, his clarity of sight and proximity to God are the fundamental immanent characteristics of such an Adam. And by means of his primordial position, his proximity to God who converses with him in paradise, is determined all his immeasurable pre-eminence in comparison with which all of his *personal qualities,* in the sense of individual endowments, genius or talents, as we now distinguish them in people, are completely annihilated, and seem insubstantial, as if they did not exist. In other words, as sinless and primordial, Adam *does not have* individual personhood in the sense in which we now understand it, for in our understanding every such individuality, as determinateness, is also limitedness *(omnis definitio est negatio)* — and now the concept of the individual is precisely the antithesis of the universal, the all-human. In this sense Adam *was not an individual,* although he was a hypostasis, for a sinless human is at the same time also *a human in general,* is the all-human, free from the bad *limiting* influence of individuality.

Individuality in our current sense is a fruit of the fall, something that ought not to be. It is distinct from hypostasis, which is a centre of love, an intelligent ray of Sophia; her property, and the property of chastity, wisdom, wholeness, is that all these her rays are of equal worth and of equal strength, all points are equally central. From here we arrive at the paradoxical conclusion that Adam's own individuality has no specific significance, for it was his *position* as primordial that was decisive here, and in relation to this primordial purity and chastity none of the descendants of Adam, placed in his position, *would be distinguished from him at all,* each one would be Adam. In this sense Adam was the authentic all-human, the real representative of the whole human race. All people are not only of equal value but are also equal, equally of genius in their primordialness and chastity, for they participate in Sophia herself, the Wisdom of God; distinctions in individual endowment and strength come later, only in the fall, in its limiting and hence differentiating power. Consequently, in as much as Adam committed his own sin as the primordial human, he committed it as *a human in general, as the all-human,* and hence the question loses meaning; it becomes senseless to ask what would have been if the primordial had not been Adam but, for example, Seth. Each primordial would have equally turned out to be Adam, and we cannot suppose two *different* Adams. Thus, we arrive at the conclusion that *Adam's own individuality* did not exist before the fall, even though there was a hypostasis, a personal centre, as the possibility of love.

Adam's individuality, as *one of many,* who possess his own fate and place, arises only with the fall into sin and its consequences ("you shall be as gods knowing good and evil"). Then too Adam and Eve recognize themselves as separate, uncoordinated, unrepeating and mutually impenetrable centres, in the multi-centrism or ex-centrism of existence. And humanity, instead of being one multi-hypostatic entity, one nature in a multitude of hypostases, disintegrated into a multitude of individuals, separate representatives of humanity, who can even ask themselves if humanity exists as one.

By the metaphysical unity of humanity is grounded also its empirical unity, which in the succession of generations is expressed as *heredity,* or the living link of ancestors with descendants who through this live a certain common life of the race. The human, being an individual, is left as a generic being in which the race lives. Interlacing among themselves one generation after the next forms the genealogical tree of the human race. Original or hereditary sin, as original, is a manifestation of the common power of heredity, of the unity of human nature. Adam's sin in this sense is a general determination, not so much sin as a determined state of human nature, and in it of the whole world. As the world is not created anew for each human being but there is one common world for all humanity, so too human nature, realizing itself in different hypostases, remains one and does not reconstitute itself.

The question still remains: could Adam have avoided original sin? Is it not a fatal predestination relative to the human? Or, perhaps, if *another* representative of the human race stood in Adam's place, could he have avoided it? The second question has already been answered above: in relation to and in the position of Adam *there is no difference* between separate representatives of the human race. It would still be possible to refer here to divine providence, to which the powers and destinies of every human are open and known, and by which the most appropriate individual is selected for the decisive trial; however, this consideration is of little use here and for this reason it is simply superfluous.

To the first question about the fatality of the fall one cannot but point out that primordial humankind's freedom realistically understood includes in itself, as blessed Augustine himself acknowledged, *liberum arbitrium indifferentiae*, as a real possibility to choose freely, i.e., unmotivated, *out of itself*. At the same time, in the still untempted Adam, this harboured within itself the unavoidable possibility of falling, as had already been indicated in the highest though still creaturely spirits. The fact of the divine command, directed towards the freedom of the human and containing in itself the ontological disclosure of the foundations of the human, testifies indisputably to *the possibility* for the human to resist sin although, at the same time, the possibility of Adam's fall was known to God. For this reason, before the creation of the world God planned its salvation through the sacrifice of his Only-begotten Son. Divine foreknowledge is not doubled. God divines the freedom of creaturely beings in their self-determination. But by virtue of this Divine foreknowledge sin does not stop being the work of a spiritual-moral being, that is, an action of its freedom. And with respect to the human, sin was not necessary, or more precisely, it could equally have been both defeated and accepted *with freedom*, the freedom of a creaturely being. There was here no necessity, in the sense of being fatally doomed. But for that reason sin, as indeed every action of freedom, *is inexplicable causally*. It is a free, i.e. creative, self-determination of creation in the human. As a consequence of this, sin is imputed to the one who has committed it as something that ought not to be.

Apropos of original sin, as a sin *of nature* having force for *the whole* human race without *any* exception (the Sole Sinless One, the Lord Jesus, does not represent such an exception for He is *the new Adam, the new, true* human), one can still ask oneself: why does the fall of the Morning Star and his angels *not* spread to the whole angelic nature and, on the contrary, why was it sharply localized?[3] The nature of angels is unknown to us, but from this fact we necessarily must draw the conclusion that although they compose harmonious hierarchies, the angelic *assembly,* angelic spirits do not form *an angelic race* in the sense of the unity of origin through re-production, i.e., through repetition according to essence of equally val-ued, equally substantial, naturally identical hypostases of the one multi-personal Adam. We have no direct indication in the Word of God and tra-dition of the church about whether this signifies that each of the angels is created by a separate creative act, which eliminates reproduction as a repe-tition of the similar to itself, or whether in the angelic world particular re-production does have its place. Essential and decisive here is that a gov-erning focus in the world is given only to the human, a summons to govern and command creation is entrusted only to the human; only he is the lawful king of this world (the power of "the prince of this world" is a stolen one, and sometime he will be expelled in order to yield his place anew to humankind, headed by the new Adam, Jesus Christ, to whom "is given all authority in heaven and on earth").

Ontologically the human being is the world, and his self-determination, just as his fall into sin, has force for the whole world. An-gels, although they are servants of God, "second lights" standing before the Throne of God, nevertheless are not the world; thus even among themselves they compose an *assembly* but not a race — separate rays, in the aggregate revealing the glory of God but ontologically apart. (For this rea-son it can be said that the Aristotelian definition of the unity of substance as *koinon en pollois* can be applied to the angelic world whereas on the other hand the Platonic *hen en pollois* is applicable to the human world.) Thus the category of original or natural sin which spreads out into an en-tire nature is inapplicable to the angelic world: its head, the Morning Star, determined by his fall only his own personal fate, for there is no single na-ture of angels as there is in human beings. Each angel has its own nature, and is in itself its own personal self-enclosed world. The salvation or eter-nal perdition of angels happens therefore by their own particular immediate path of personal turning to the Godhead. At the same time the destinies of the angelic world are obliquely linked with the human world, which angels are predestined to serve, for the human being, and not the angel, is the microcosm, the lord of the universe. So too Lucifer, in order to find cosmism, to become a cosmic being, the prince of this world, out of a lonely, homeless and rootless pilgrim, an eternal beggar, finds by stealth and deception a fulcrum in the human and through the human in the world (out of which he is expelled by the exorcizing prayers before holy baptism).

One ought to note particularly the consequence of natural sin indicated above: human personality is born in it not only as a hypostasis created by God in His image, *but also as an individuality,* which keeps aloof and separates itself from others. Through this the natural, ontological equality of people as multiple centres not only of a similar but also of a common single life becomes obscured and perverted. The wholeness of the human race collapses and comes unravelled together with the loss of chastity, and in place of multi-unity multi-difference appears, bad plurality, in place of concentricism there is eccentricism. This plural number contains the satanic lie, namely the *like gods,* which knows not only good but also evil, i.e., its own limitedness, and which is always carrying with itself its own shadow. *Individuality* is the reflected light of the Morning Star on a human being whom he desired to pervert according to the image of his metaphysical egotism — a multi-hypostaseity *without love.* It is in this sense the consequence of original sin: fallen humankind knows hypostasis only in the form of individuality, and the whole of humanity decomposes into individualities which logic considers possible to unite only in the abstract, by mentally inferring in brackets universal signs.

The loss of one's soul for the sake of Christ, that is, liberation from the captivity of individuality, is the condition of Christian salvation. But in the fallen world individuality is the sole form for the life of the soul, just as a sinful body is for the life of the flesh, and only life in Christ *liberates the hypostasis from individuality,* leading it into the multi-unity in love that is necessary for it, into the Church. Thus, we repeat once again, quite out of place is the question of whether the individuality of Adam has no decisive meaning for original sin: before the fall into sin there was no individuality, separating him from others, and Adam really was the *representative* of the entire human multi-hypostatic race. In him and his person every human hypostasis lived and acted harmoniously. So it was *before* the fall into sin, but after the fall it became otherwise: every hypostasis began to live after its own reckoning, as an individuality, and together all proved to be enslaved to the debt of sin, and became children of wrath — *tekna orgēs* (Eph 2.3).

The first objective consequence of Adam's fall into sin is the falling away of humankind from God, and in it, of the whole world, the disruption of the internal norm of humanity's being, and consequently, *a deep abnormality or depression of its state,* with the liberation of the lowest, creaturely element in humanity, passionate lust — *concupiscentia.* In this sense sin is inherited sickness hanging like fate, like calamity, over the whole human race. If the essence of original sin were exhausted in this alone, then it would not be so much sin as misfortune, as any inherited disease appears to our eyes. Sin becomes sin only as personal guilt, linked with personal freedom. In this sense the sin of Adam is the personal sin of every person. To say it another way, did each one of us commit original sin, and if so, when and how? In principle we have to answer this question affirmatively, for first of all Sacred Scripture and tradition give completely clear evidence of this. Redemption from sin, the shedding of blood by the Lord Jesus Christ for the remission of sins is immediately linked with the original sin of the *one* through whom death entered. True, here we are talking about *sins* in the plural number, but these sins are the consequence *of one* sin, which occasioned *sinfulness* and generated sins. And this very sinfulness is linked with the personal guilt of each person, with their participation in the sin of Adam.

The practice of the ancient church concerning the baptism of infants has prevailed in the Church. It was clarified in the Pelagian controversies and also corresponded to the shape of blessed Augustine's thought in his fight with Pelagius. Baptism is given for *the remission of sins,* and on this basis — say the Baptists following the Pelagians — baptism is possible only for adults and not for children for whom it is not even needed owing to the absence of personal sins in them. But with the decrees of the council of Carthage[4] the Church confirmed the necessity of baptism for children too, as ones who carry in themselves the burden of Adam's sin. By this very fact the council established the difference between the condition of baptised and unbaptised children after burial, even though this did not receive further disclosure and more precise definition. And this fact — the baptism of infants for the remission of sins — though oblique is indeed the fundamental dogmatic argument in favour of the necessary "remission of sins" through baptism even for "blessed" and "unblemished" children, that is, liberation from original sin. (Cf. the prayers of exorcism before baptism.)

To this it is necessary to add a further consideration. The Lord conquered death and healed the entire human race from original sin. To Him belongs all authority in heaven and on earth, and He will resurrect the whole human race (for the Last Judgment) and renew nature, once the new heaven and new earth have appeared. The world is saved by Christ, for the power of His Resurrection acts in the world. The new Adam has already taken the place of the old one, and if the latter is still decaying and with his decaying body covers the flesh of resurrection, then here the empyrean does not correspond any more to the authentic reality, as in the sacred mysteries the empirical reality of bread and wine do not correspond to the real presence of the Body and Blood. If original sin were only inherited disease, then healing would have finally ensued, not only as a possibility for each one but even as a reality. But the Lord established *baptism* for the remission of sins and it is the only path to salvation, according to His unassailable word. True, here we encounter the mystery that baptism is not accessible *to everyone,* through no fault of their own: it proved to be inaccessible for the whole of Old Testament humanity, for paganism and for the entire non-Christian world. Their destinies and their salvation is a mystery of God for which there are indications in the preaching in Hades about several other paths of salvation beyond the grave unknown to us; but for Christians to whom the mysteries and the keys of the mystery have been entrusted here on earth there is only one means of salvation — through baptism. Thus the baptism of children, necessary even after the already accomplished healing from the disease of original sin through Christ's incarnation and resurrection, indicates the presence of sin in them, in a subjective sense (*reatus*) just as blessed Augustine correctly testified.

But if it is so, if all people are sinful, even though they have lived only one hour on earth, if new-born children are sinful, then wherein is this sin, where and when is it committed? Behold the fatal question for theology over which the theory of original sin uselessly exercises itself. On this difficulty is also based the theory of the reincarnation of souls (or of their pre-existence), which wishes to explain the unknown through the unknown, postulating previous existences in order to understand the present one. But with this the question only grows more complicated and confused, for the reincarnations of what has gone before demand a similar explanation.

How very unsatisfying is that poverty-stricken theory of the arbitrary imposition *(imputatio)* on descendants of the sin of their ancestors or the no less arbitrary Catholic theory according to which God deprives humans of supernatural grace already before birth, as a result of which humans are born in an unworthy state in sin. And so, does not only the sin of condition — *peccatum habituale,* but also actual sin belong to each one of us, sons of Adam? Or, as it is usually thought, is the latter the condition of Adam alone, while remaining foreign to his descendants, who in this manner are his unwilling victims? One senses something amiss in such a notion.

First of all in the depths of our spirit we feel a certain fundamental fault of our whole being, *not sins* but precisely *sin,* a fundamental anomaly or impropriety: that struggle of the will with good and evil, "another law" ruling in our members and pulling us not towards what I want but what I do not want, about which the apostle Paul testifies (Rom 7.18-24). This muffled but deep consciousness of some sort of primordial self-determination, as something that ought not to be, is the evidence of our *personal participation* in the original sin of Adam: not only Adam but each of us personally, with him and in him, but for ourselves, committed his sin and commit it, and this sin is in some sense *our* sin, that is, it is an act of our freedom and not only of our unwilling. But on the other hand, this very sin of Adam is not just *one* out of many sins, the first in succession, belonging personally to Adam. No, it is a completely particular sin, not one of many, but the sole one which is the metaphysical source of moral sins. It is the sin of human freedom against humanity's own nature, an untrue and improper metaphysical self-determination. It stands, strictly speaking, beyond the limits of individual historical destiny, on its very bounds, on the threshold of life. Adam's sin, as was explained already above, was not his *individual* sin, for then there was as yet no individuality in the current sinful luciferian sense, but it was a sin proper to the *status* of the primogenitor who enters into life and is there self-determining. As a result of this *non*-individual character of sin it is impossible to consider it the individual sin of Adam by which only he sinned, but another human in fact did not sin or would be able not to sin. No, in original sin Adam sinned not as Adam or not only as Adam but as *every* human. And every one, all of us, each one of us were co-present in him, co-participated in that metaphysical sin, burdened with which we are born already as *individualities* possessing our own particular fates and our own particular sins. In other words, Adam as the one who committed the original sin as a *real* and not only an ideal or juridical representative of humankind, as *everyone,* is not more sinful or more just than all people: in original sin all are equal, and as much as this is sin, all are equally sinful. That which happened with Adam happened — metaphysically — for all and with all of his descendants still unborn though consubstantial with him, and this occurrence is realized in birth, and is made real anew for each person.

The Church condemned (at an ecumenical council) the Origenist doctrine about the pre-existence of souls, which was in Origen linked with the Neo-Platonic conception of the origin of the world as a consequence of falling away from the Deity, and the body as a consequence of falling out of the Divine world. The *pre*-existence of human souls *without* bodies or *outside of and up to* the body contradicts the firm church doctrine that the human being *by its nature,* on account of the Divine plan for it, is an incarnate spirit, consisting of body and spirit. There is and was no other time preceding the time of its existence: the human first arises in the divine creative act. But this negation *of pre-existence in time,* it stands to reason, in no way eliminates the existence of all that is *outside* time, in eternity, in God, as a creative foundation for all that happens in time. On the other hand, this does not eliminate the possibility that something happens *at the bounds* of time in human life, no longer in eternity but still not in time.

The Lord creates the human soul after His own image and likeness: this signifies that He creates it not as He does all other creatures of the world, by the power of His almightiness, without asking them about it. He creates these souls by His own creative power but in their freedom, by virtue of which is given to them to participate as it were in creation, concurring in their own existence. In the mysterious and inexplicable act of Divine creative love the Lord resigns Himself to acknowledge the self-determination of the creature in His act of creation. Therefore in every living soul exists its *will towards life.* (This is why metaphysical suicide is insanity and a direct *contradictio in adjecto,* but every empirical suicide is only the spasm and convulsion of the will towards life.) But in that extra-temporal moment, on the bounds of time, in the creation of the soul one's share in the original sin of Adam is already realized personally by everyone for himself.

When the soul is created (no matter how closely understood is this creation, about which below) it is joined with a body *not against its will, but willingly.* That is, by its will *towards life,* it takes up its abode *in this world* already having fallen away from God sick with sin; and in its free incarnation, in this will towards life its solidarity with Adam and its *personal* participation in original sin are realized. The latter is not repeated but is realized anew in each new hypostasis of a single human being.[5] In the same sense it is correct that we *are born in sin:* in lawlessness have I been conceived (this is from the perspective of the body, the world), and in sins did my mother give birth to me (this is from the perspective of the soul which received this sinful world). This fall into sin occurs in birth, on the bounds of this world, but the fall of Adam also occurred, though in time, on the bounds of the present sinful world, in another still pre-sinful state of the world. True, Adam was created in an unblemished state. He showed his will to sinless life at the time of creation, but this self-determination still remained incomplete, and after it, a second followed — in the fall into sin. Both of these acts or moments of Adam's self-determination already merge into *one* for his descendants, by virtue of the unity of the human race and the world. This duality of moments for Adam belongs once again to his *position* as the first-formed, and not to his individuality.

But perhaps some will inquire: why then does the soul not know and not remember its own accomplished self-determination, its agreement to incarnation in a sinful body, an act of the will towards life? Is this not a fantasy and a dream? This question would be pertinent if the discussion were about a separate act of life, or its occurrence in time which could either be remembered or not remembered in a series of other events. (The idea of such temporal pre-existence was condemned by the Church in Origenism.) But in the given case the discussion is not about an event but about a beginning and consequently not about a temporal but about a pre-temporal act. It cannot be remembered as an event of the temporal life, but the soul does preserve a recollection of it, an anamnesis, and wears its seal. In this sense the soul *always* remembers it and unceasingly recalls it in consciousness of the impropriety and impairment of its being, of its personal responsibility for this and of its sinfulness. The correctness of this recognition is attested by the Church which extends *the guilt* of original sin *to all* and in baptism absolves precisely that pre-temporal guilt, original sin, which is committed in the very act of birth.[6] By the will towards life and towards incarnation in a body defiled by sin and in a world polluted by sin the soul participates in the common human original sin, in the collective identity of all humanity.

In this case the soul is self-determining, as humankind in general, as ancestral humanity, and in this self-determination all are one, all are equal. But at the same time this self-determination is fully individual, for along with sin and in a certain sense even thanks to sin, individuality is born: *principium individuationis* is original sin. By becoming cohesive in sin, which essentially is the chaotic and corrupted state of integral existence, its decentralized condition and the resultant multi-centricity and eccentricity that corresponds to it, humanity itself loses the wholeness of its consciousness, and is scattered into individuals. Humanness as the single spiritual essence of *all* people, as their nature in the one Adam, becomes the latent basis which is realized only in individuals and their generations. The freedom inherent in the human spirit assumes in personality an individual character fitted with qualities and, along with the unity and solidarity of all humanity in its nature, it receives the power, inequality and distinction of individuals in their *freedom* and the distinction of their destinies entailed in this. One must assume that people receive not only different destinies at birth but that they are born already *different* and that each human wears a more or less precisely articulated *quality*, a certain "mentally accessible character" which, as Schopenhauer correctly observed, lies at the basis of the empirical. In other words, if with original sin individuality in its individualism is born, then original sin is realized in everyone individually, souls arrive in the world not the same. This is what daily experience tells us: usually we observe only external inequalities and differences in the destinies of people, but we do not see through to the much more essential interior differences. Since the birth of human beings with souls of a determinate quality is the work of God, it is an axiom of faith that the external destinies and circumstances of birth are likewise the work of God; in other words, a pre-established harmony exists, an internal correspondence between the soul and its visible destiny.

For divine foreknowledge the freedom of creaturely beings and their possible self-determination are not closed. Divine Providence, which governs the world and leads it to its determinate goal, knows *all* the components of this world and all their mutual relations. God knows the secrets of the human heart and He knows everything. In this sense the apostle said, "whom He foreknew, these He also foreordained . . . and whom He foreordained, these He called, and whom He called these He also justified, and whom He justified, these He also glorified" (Rom 8.29-30). In particular, it is said about Isaac and Jacob, "when they were still not born and had done nothing evil or good, Rebecca was told: the greater will be in servitude to the lesser" (Gen 25.23). As it was written "Jacob I have preferred and Isaac I have despised" (Mal 1.2-3). "What shall we say? That God is unjust? Never!" (Rom 9.11-14). God sends souls individually fitted with qualities into bodies individually fitted with qualities, i.e., here are included all the circumstances of birth and earthly destiny. This preordained harmony is completely incomprehensible for creaturely reason but it is a postulate of faith in the Creator, in the depths, divinity and knowledge of Divine reason. The only thing clear to us in this is that although humanity is individualized in its destinies and in the realization of its humanness, this individualism does not destroy the general ontological bond which is manifested in the heredity of original sin as well as in particular series of particular heredities which lead above and below and in different directions. Individuals do not exist entirely apart but as families, each human leaf is attached to a branch which is secured on a common trunk. Different possibilities, which are realized in the common background of heredity, appear in clans and generations, which consist of corresponding individuals.

One must consider that this special heredity has its basis in the freedom of the pre-worldly self-determination of the soul, and that here neither chance nor arbitrariness exists, although it does not admit for itself *a comprehended,* that is, a rational explanation (an attempt at which is the notorious reincarnation). On the basis of special heredity not only individual movement upwards or downwards but also movement intensified by it is possible, an accumulation of individual differences arises and the self-creativity of individuality moves beyond its bounds and becomes ancestral. Spiritual energies are held back hereditarily and accumulate, and diverse clans represent as it were condensers of these energies. From the outside it can even seem that they determine entirely by themselves the individualities that come under their influence. On the contrary, owing to the principle of pre-established harmony, they are themselves determined by those who bring energies with definite qualities into the world in their free self-determination, but who find for their realization an appropriate means or body for their own incarnation. Thus in the Bible two possibilities or two paths in the one family of Adam are contemplated from the very beginning: Cain and Abel and then Seth, the Cainites and the descendants of Seth; later the clan of Abraham, Isaac and Jacob is selected, the people of God, and in its composition the tribe of Levi, the branch of the priesthood, and the tribe of Judah, the royal branch. Finally, in these tribes and in their particular heredity the chosen clan is singled out, or "the genealogy of Jesus Christ our Saviour"[7] which the evangelists Matthew and Luke deliberately set forth in a different way. The summit of human ascent in the stock of ancient Adam, which was impaired by original sin, is reached in the Mother of God.

The effect of sin comes to light first of all as *the infirmity* of nature, expressed in *the mortality* of the human being: its spirit takes insufficient possession of the body at birth, such that already from the time of birth itself the energies of destruction begin to develop and accumulate along with the energies of life; mortality is already a fundamental interior quality of life, its incompleteness which appears at the end of life as the deadly outcome. The sickliness of the body is only a particular expression of its mortality. With this is bound also its dependence on the natural elements, on hunger, cold, on the weakness of the body, its weariness, on the weakness and limitedness of the mind and cognition, on the weakness of the will and its vacillations, on the affectivity of the whole passionate essence of the human being. All these properties, burdening and limiting human life, can be expressed more sharply or more weakly, but in every human being they form the source of *infirmity.*

Although it is *the consequence* of original metaphysical sin, this infirmity, which can be paralyzed only in the order of grace, is still not personal sin. This is demonstrated more graphically than anywhere else when our Lord, alone sinless, took on Himself "the likeness of the flesh of sin, the infirmity of nature." It is sin as a disease, *hamartēma,* but it differs from *sins* as human acts, transgressions — *paraptōma* — as the works of evil in the world. The latter, although having a basis in the infirmity and limitedness of nature, tolerates the broadest differences and vacillations. Hereby the power of sin in a human can increase to the point of becoming satanic (Antichrist) or enfleshed (antediluvian humanity), but it also weakens to such a degree that it is capable of being exalted to the highest sanctity, the summit of which is attained in the Virgin Mary. The All-Pure Virgin originated from the holy forebears of the Godman who had absorbed into themselves the whole of Old Testament holiness and blessedness. By her natural origination from Adam, having in herself all the power of original sin as an infirmity, she remains free of every *personal sin,* of every participation in the work of evil, with the help, of course, of divine grace.

The infirmity of her nature is expressed all the more graphically in that she was subject to the natural law of death, which she accepted in her honourable Dormition. To be sure, Divine omnipotence would be entirely permitted to free her from this general human outcome, as the just men Enoch and Elijah were freed from it without possessing her exclusive and unique holiness. But in her death the infirmity of human nature was providentially revealed, and overcome in her glorious resurrection. Catholic theology, which after the 1854 dogma of the Immaculate Conception is forced to prove the freedom of the Mother of God from original sin, finds itself obliged to deny the connection between death and original sin despite direct religious obviousness.

According to the opinion of Catholic theologians (see the likes of Scheeben), the human being by nature, in virtue of his bond with the body, is subject to death, as well as to diseases and passionate lasciviousness, *concupiscentia.* Only an extraordinary gift of grace, taken away from him after the fall, saved him from all of this. (It follows from this that the

Mother of God, as one who is freed from original sin, must be freed as well from human infirmity and from death; generally speaking, she lives in a paradisiacal state in the midst of an unparadisiacal world.) This assumption bears witness to the deep and radical defect of Catholic anthropology, which sees in the bond of the human with the body not the particular *privilege* of the human being, placing him above the angels, but the cause of his fateful and unavoidable creaturely mortality. Despite the teaching of the Word of God that God did not create death, here the exact opposite is affirmed, that God created the human being mortal. The human being, this image of God, this creaturely god, bears death in his nature, is created mortal and is only preserved from death by grace, which can even be taken away — such is the thesis lying at the basis of all Catholic anthropology. On the contrary, in accordance with Orthodox doctrine, death entered the world through sin, in which the human literally perpetrated suicide against himself, having turned away from God and lost through this the life of the soul; he realized in his soul the force of death which was deposited in it only as a possibility. This relates to all the other manifestations of the infirmity of human nature.

This infirmity of nature causes, of course, the active power of sin, engenders *sinfulness* in which is realized the power of the devil, "the prince of this world," over humankind. But this power of sinfulness can be weakened and approximated to the state of potentiality. The law living in the members of a human being and opposed to the good through "the body of death" can be rendered powerless to a greater or lesser degree, which is why the active power of sin can be changed. Here, of course, exists the radical difference between the Old and New Testaments, or more precisely stated, between the condition of those who have received baptism and those who do not know it (such is the whole of Old Testament humanity). In the waters of baptism *the guilt* of original sin is washed away and the grace of new life is bestowed, but *the infirmity* of human nature is not rendered powerless, and it preserves its power of the law of sin which opposes good in the body and will of a human being, such that even a baptised human has the capacity to sin and needs as it were repeated baptisms in the sacrament of penance. In *this* respect the status of an Old Testament human in relation to sin does not differ so much from that of a New Testament one, whose sin is *forgiven* and to whom the graced mysteries of the church are given for the sake of rebirth, although the sinful infirmity of nature preserves its power, the consequence of sin.

But grace was not scarce even in the Old Testament, for it likewise knows great righteous people, holy prophets, who spoke, acted and wrote by the Holy Spirit. To be sure, the action of the Holy Spirit in the world was other than it is after Pentecost. It was preparatory, preliminary, like the action of the Word in the world before His incarnation. None the less Old Testament humanity was not in the least deprived of the grace of the Holy Spirit, and in particular, the Old Testament Church, with its God-established priesthood and divine worship, was not deprived of it either. All of this had only a prototypical character, it spoke about the future; however, prototypes are not allegories but symbols, religious significances and realities. The feats of Old Testament faith, about which the letter to the Hebrews (chapter 11) speaks, bear witness to the presence of grace, for such faith is a gift of grace. The host of forebears and fathers of the Saviour, of prophets and righteous ones, clearly testifies to this abundance *of preliminary* grace: *the fulfilment* of these promises concerned the New Testament, the Resurrection and Pentecost, but it was foretold in the Old Testament Church. In other words, would Enoch and Noah, Moses and David, Elijah and Elisha, Isaiah and Jeremiah, and the other prophets, not have had the Holy Spirit? Consider what was proclaimed by the angel about John the Forerunner, about whom it was said that he was the greatest of those born of woman and yet less than the least of those in the Kingdom of God: "he shall be filled with the Holy Spirit already in the womb of his mother" (Lk 1.15). The holy prophet Jeremiah bears witness to the same thing about himself (Jer 1.5). So why is it possible, generally speaking, to deny the effect of sanctifying divine grace in unredeemed and still unregenerate humanity, as a pledge of future blessings? Similar to this, the blessings of the present age are likewise a pledge or a prototype of the blessings of the future age about which it has not entered the human heart what God has prepared for those who love Him.

This brings us back to the question about grace and blessedness. What kind of mutual relation is there between grace and freedom, divine and human? According to Orthodox understanding, grace does not force or impose itself, but is sought out by the human being and bestowed on the one seeking it. God in His love for creation abolished the abyss lying between Him and creation and made humankind for divinization. In its primordial condition, before sin, humankind had that power of divinization as the direct consequence of the harmonious structure of its spirit, the power of chastity. Adam was, so to say, naturally blessed, apprehending by his uncorrupted spirit the grace of a life in God and with God streaming into him. He was not separated from God, and thus there was not even a place *for opposition* of the natural and the graced in their indivisibility, in the power of the divinization of humankind which began with his creation. His real likeness to God makes understandable and natural his blessedness, as the fulfilment of the creative plan for him. This blessedness is not something arising from the outside, which could even not exist, but is rather interiorly, immanently grounded in humankind by a creative act, as by creaturely Sophia.

Here we again collide with Catholic doctrine which annihilates the Sophianicity of humankind, which tears asunder and opposes in it righteousness and blessedness so that one is thought of in complete isolation from the other, and blessedness itself seems to be the *donum superadditum*, an act of merciful arbitrariness. This *donum* can be separated or removed *without* harming nature itself, in fact as something *added* or *superadded*: this is precisely how the removal of grace in original sin is considered, as a punishment, but not as a consequence of the human's deviation from its norm, that is, from Sophianicity with its chastity. True, the scholastics maintain that as a result of sin the human proved to be *spoliatus gratuitis, vulneratus in naturalibus,* but this *vulneratio* is only an indirect consequence of a less fortunate condition of human nature, which remained in itself unchanged and uncorrupted.[8] Catholic doctrine, on the one hand, infinitely alienates the human being from God and practically denies his Sophianicity or the Divine image, since he is bound with natural lust and mortality (for there can be no image of God in animals). But on the other hand it makes the divine condescension in bestowing grace ontologically ungrounded and completely arbitrary: the human is not opened here to grace by the power of the image of God present in him, but is only *an object* for grace, remaining himself and preserving his nature both before and after its removal. The divine-human act which is the divinization of the human in his bestowing grace (the human is not only its object but also its subject, a gracious-natural, supercreaturely-creaturely being) is here regarded only as an act of God *upon* the human and not *in* the human, from the outside and not from inside. The mechanical and superficial character of this entire understanding leaps to the eyes together with its inappropriate legalism: God gave the human a commandment as the juridical basis for an agreement; the human broke the commandment and was deprived of the corresponding blessings, and was thus left only with himself. That's the whole story. Therein results the full and complete rupture between God as the source of blessedness, and the human being as His successor.

Fallen humankind was left without grace, and at the same time it remains possible to return this grace by a one-sided act of Divinity, by divine arbitrariness, for the whole change occurred from the side of God, who took away the superadded gift, and *not* from the side of the human, who was left unchanged (for *Vulneratio* is ontologically immaterial). By this, of course, the very foundations *of the process* of the divine economy of our salvation are destroyed. The sanctification of humankind for the reception of God, for the divine incarnation, is thus not the ascent of the human race itself towards divine incarnation, but the act of God *upon* a human being, namely upon the Virgin Mary, to whom the forfeited *donum superadditum* is returned.

The whole Orthodox understanding proceeds from entirely different anthropological premises and in particular from a different teaching on original sin. In uncorrupted sophianic humankind everything was moved by Divine grace; this was not *donum superadditum,* but the breathing and life of the human being by which it still possessed the image of God as the divine basis of its nature. Now, this image was given not only as its sophianic basis, but also as a task toward the realization of the *likeness:* to say it in another way, the appropriation of the Divine image was itself entrusted to the freedom of humankind. The condition of blessedness before the fall was normal and in this sense *natural* for humankind (just as the "natural" condition of humankind in sin is against nature and does not correspond to its authentic nature). But already in the very creation of the human spirit God, by summoning it into existence out of non-existence and imprinting it with His power, makes room for the freedom of its self-determination. Thus the created human being, in the foundations of his existence, is imprinted with the image of God and is therefore a God-receiving, natural *vessel* of grace (but in the idea of vessel is contained also the idea of accumulation, not as *donum superadditum* but as *donum*). In his freedom he either realizes the image in the likeness or he does not. In this is expressed human self-creation, which at one time was expressed in general and fundamental existential self-determination, but afterwards is accomplished in particular in a series of things produced.

Original sin deprived the human being of the gifts of grace belonging to him *in keeping with his creaturely rank* (and not *super* him) thanks to which *the nature* of humankind is broken in him: he grew sick, as a result he lost power over himself and became mortal. But this infirmity, no longer surmountable by the powers of the human being himself, and overcome really only through the *donum superadditum* in the person of the new Adam, did not abolish in him the image of God as the interior bases and norms of his nature. Neither did it abolish his freedom, no matter how much it was diminished by sin, or his self-creativity, although this was already in a weakened state.[9] Humankind changed after sin in its whole *con-*

dition, but it did not lose anything essential, nothing was *removed* from it as an externally imposed punishment, except what it could no longer receive: the fullness of blessedness and communion with God, as well as immortality, which is incompatible with a sinful life, as something needless and improper for it.

In this way is obtained the exact reverse of Catholic doctrine. *Privatio* is not in the beginning with *vulneratio* as its result, but the other way around: *vulneratio* has as its result *privatio*. Fallen Adam is not at all deprived of the gifts of grace, for immediately after the fall God gives His promise about the seed of the woman. Adam, moved by a prophetic spirit, gives the woman a name: Eve, or life. His sons, evidently, following the instruction of their father, are already familiar with the offering of sacrifice. In the time of Seth the Divine Name is pronounced; Righteous Enoch by walking before God is freed from death. Melchizedek, unknown to the world, is worthy of receiving a gift from the father of the nations, with whom God had already entered into direct communion and concluded a covenant, etc., etc. In a word, even after the fall the ontology of God's relations towards humankind did not change; humankind in its freedom shook and weakened the human dimension of that ontology. But whenever human freedom restored this breach, in the measure of this restoration God gave His sanctifying and strengthening grace to humankind. The ladder between heaven and earth was not broken off, and the angels sent to humankind descended and ascended on it.

In contrast to the condition of the human before the fall, grace is here, really, *donum superadditum,* a special Divine influence on fallen creaturely nature. That *justitia originalis,* which in the opinion of Catholic theologians and according to the definition of the Council of Trent (Session V, I)[10] was an extraordinary gift of grace, the result of *donum superadditum,* is precisely *the natural* condition of a sinless human being opened to the influence of God: in this openness his nature is like God according to grace ("you are gods"). The condition of being closed to grace, which the human caused by the power of his sin, the reduction of his graced divinity to simple potency, signifies an abnormal condition for humankind. And grace can reach him only by a supernatural path, the *donum superadditum,* which is traded to fallen nature. The divinely established cult and priesthood in the temple are so to say the regular means of giving grace, like a channel through which grace flows uninterruptedly into the world to humans. The extraordinary, personal and direct blessedness of the ancestors, patriarchs, prophets, kings, saints and finally of John the Baptist and the Virgin Mary is the irregular means. To be sure, even here grace does not compel, in the sense that it selects vessels that are worthy of it: the ascetic feat of *human* holiness, hands lifted up and opened towards heaven, does not remain without its reward, and by this, really, *donum superadditum,* fallen nature *is restored to such a degree* that is completely inaccessible to human powers. In this sense saving grace operates in the Old Testament, before the advent of the Saviour. This extraordinary grace, in keeping with the will of God inaccessible for human comprehension, is limited by the boundaries of the Old Testament Church, of the chosen people of God, who are the saving nursery for all humanity. All the rest of humanity lives by the gifts of grace which are received at the moment of creation, *gratia creativa,* and although they are weakened in their effect, in no way are they removed from the world as its supernatural sophianic basis. (The verse "O Christ, light of truth, illuminating and sanctifying *every human* who comes into the world" is read in the first hour.) And here the difference between individual people and nations remains. "God is no favourer of persons, but in every nation the one who fears Him and approaches in truth is pleasing to Him" (Acts 10.34-35); in other words, a place remains for effort and freedom. But this topic does not now lie on our path of consideration.

Let us sum up what has been said. In fallen humankind original sin reveals *its power* as *an infirmity of nature,* bound with the impairment of the whole world in humankind and with the suffering of the whole groaning creation, a sickness and mortality, and as *sinfulness,* the power of sin which fetters and paralyses human freedom, as captivity and service "to the prince of this world." The first, infirmity, as the general lot of the whole world and humankind cannot be overcome by individual human power and is in this sense *a constant.* It is defeated only by the power of Christ's hominization, divine incarnation and His glorious resurrection. Even the very exceptions to this common law, the liberation from the infirmity of mortal nature, like the cases of the assumption into heaven of Enoch and the prophet Elijah while still alive, only confirm this. For it is not overcome here but only abrogated by the deliberate action of Divine omnipotence, and besides, as must be thought, only for a time, not finally. According to the faith of the church they will both appear in the world before the second coming in order to taste death in keeping with the common lot (Rev 11.3-12).

The second power of sinfulness is a *variable.* It can be less or more, at one time thickening until the pre-flood depravity and abomination of Sodom, at another time becoming lucid until reaching the righteousness of Moses the friend of God and the purity of John the Forerunner. Here, the extraordinary grace of God fills up what has become depleted and heals what is infirm, raises the human being to a condition higher than nature, really, by bringing him near to *justitia originalis* (except for the guilt of original sin, of the fall in birth itself and at the time of birth, in the sense explained above). The question arises: *to what limit*, by the assisting grace of God, can this weakening of the power of personal sinfulness in humankind be brought, and can *that limit* be indicated in general? It can be indicated only *from below:* we will not defeat or eliminate original sin, as *an infirmity of nature*, by any *human* holiness. And this *preserves its full force even with respect to the Virgin Mary*, in so far as she is in fullness and in truth a human being, but only in virtue of this could she serve the true and unalloyed hominization of Christ.

In as much as sin through the paralysis of human freedom engenders *personal* sinfulness, this latter can be weakened to a minimum and even brought down to the condition of full potentiality: *posse non peccare* (though before redemption and before baptism the condition of *non posse peccare* cannot be reached). To be sure, such a maximum achievement is unthinkable for fallen humanity without the help of Divine grace which, however, only assists freedom and does not compel it. In other words, when original sin as infirmity is kept in force, *personal freedom from sins* or personal sinlessness can be realized by the grace of God. In harmony with the firm and clear consciousness of the Church, John the Forerunner already approaches such personal sinlessness. The most holy Virgin Mary, the all-pure and all-immaculate, possesses *such* sinlessness. Only by virtue of this sinlessness was she able to say with her entire will, with her whole undivided essence, *behold the handmaid of the Lord*, to speak so that the answer to this full self-giving to God was the descent of the Holy Spirit and the seedless conception of the Lord Jesus Christ. The smallest sin in the past or the present would have broken the integrity of this self-giving and the power of this expression. This word, decisive for the whole human race and the entire world, was the expression not of a given moment only, but came out of the depths of Mary's unblemished being. It was the work and the sum of her life. The inadmissibility of personal sin in the Virgin Mary thus becomes axiomatically trustworthy provided we understand *what kind of* answer was demanded here of Mary. This was not the particular agreement of her will to a particular action, relating only to a given moment of life; no, this was the self-determination of her entire being.

The Virgin Mary is often called the new Eve. Like every comparison this one has force only within definite bounds, by maintaining the *tertium comparationis.* But this is exactly *the personal sinlessness* of Eve (before the fall) and of the Virgin Mary; in all remaining relations the old and the new Eve differ from one another. In particular the primordial Eve did not know the burden of original sin which the Virgin Mary carries within. Hence the personal sinlessness of Eve remained as yet untested, unjustified, gratuitous, whereas the Virgin Mary's freedom from personal sin was not only her personal accomplishment but also the accomplishment of the whole Old Testament Church of all the forebears and ancestors of God; it is the summit of the ascent of the whole human race, the *lily* of paradise that blossomed on the human tree. In this manner Eve *naturally* has the advantage *of position,* in the sense of freedom from original sin; *her personal* righteousness recedes decisively in the presence of the personal immaculateness of the Ever-Virgin who in herself defeated sinfulness.

There remains, however, a puzzling question: is it possible to admit such personal sinlessness, understood not in the sense of overcoming the sinfulness of nature but only of its manifestations, of personal sins, that is to say, not a substantial but a functional sinlessness, in the presence of the corruption of human nature by original sin? Does not the Apostle Paul testify here (Rom 7.15-25) against this opinion when he speaks about the sin living in us and prompting us to do evil even in spite of our will? This evidence, however, cannot be used against the personal sinlessness of the Virgin Mary if only for the simple reason that for the given case it tries to prove too much and thus does not prove anything. In fact could these words really be applied to the Most Holy Virgin: "I do not do what I want, but what I hate I do . . . the good that I want I do not do, and the evil that I do not want, I do" (Rom 7.15, 19)? If anyone dares to touch God's Ark with these words, let him provide a full account of his audacity and show where, when and in what the Most Pure committed the evil that she herself hated. It suffices merely to pose this question in order to be horrified by it.

No matter how great, holy and wonderful the apostle Paul was, what he said here about himself in justified self-reproach, and in his own person about the whole sinful human race, cannot be applied to the Most Immaculate One. Here, besides personal holiness, connected with the inherited accumulating holiness of the forebears and ancestors of God, full force must be given to her unique and exceptional blessedness. Even if the idea of Catholic dogma about the freedom of the Mother of God from original sin by virtue of a special act of Divine grace is incorrect, it will be perfectly correct to accept here the action of divine grace in a completely exceptional degree, for humankind unique and unsurpassable. For if the prophet Jeremiah, and then the Forerunner John, were sanctified by the Holy Spirit while they were still in their mother's womb, would this have remained without consequences throughout their lives, and would not the battle with the power of sin have been alleviated through this? But with respect to the Graced One, who was blessed by grace already in her very conception and in her birth, would not the preserving, preparative and sanctifying grace of the Holy Spirit have worked the whole time in order to render "that other law operative in the members" powerless and to crown her effort, her struggle, with complete victory?

It is self-evident that this personal sinlessness is not realizable by human powers alone without the grace of God. Yet, even grace does not accomplish it mechanically but by the participation, with the efforts and ascetic struggle of a human being who in sin has preserved the sophianicity of his being, the nobility of his origin, and his lofty predestination. In this, *and only in this* sense can and must it be said that the Most Pure by a special grace of God was preserved from every sin, whether committed in deed or by intention. By the grace of God which filled in her own personal effort, no sinful assault whatsoever, no sinful desire, ever touched her most immaculate soul. She was accessible to temptations only as *trials* in keeping with the infirmity of her human nature, but not as transgressions entering inside and poisoning her heart with their venom and staining it. Her relation to temptations is completely like that of her Divine Son in Whom "we have not such a high priest who cannot suffer with us in our infirmities, but who like us was tempted in every way except sin" (Heb 4.15), who "Himself endured having been tempted, and can help those who are tempted" (Heb 2.18). Thus the Lord, after the forty-day fast in the desert, "became hungry afterwards" (Mt 4.1) because of this infirmity of human nature which He assumed out of love for the human race. But the attempt of the devil, when he made use of this infirmity to turn it into sinfulness, to lodge in it the assault of sin, at first if only in the guise of sinful intentions, was put to shame and he was told "get behind me, Satan: for it is written 'Worship the Lord your God and obey him alone'" (Mt 4.10). Here are distinguished and contrasted completely clearly the *infirmity* of impaired, weakened human nature which was assumed by the Lord, precisely in order to return to it its power, and *the sinfulness* which has its foundation in weakness and was nonetheless forever overcome by Him and repudiated. In the Virgin Mary we have precisely this separation of infirmity from sinfulness, with the difference that in the Godman this overcoming is achieved not only by the graced sanctification of human nature but by the power of the incarnate God, whereas in the human Mary it was totally a consequence of the all-powerful cleansing of human nature by grace, by the human ascent towards Divine Motherhood.[11]

43

To this comparison one can add some further considerations. Original sin as infirmity is the general lot of all; however, this lot can be accepted in different ways. And if it is true that souls at the time of their origin are determined in freedom, then it is fully necessary to recognize that the entrance into this world, the reception of original sin is accomplished in diverse ways and in a different sense. The Lord, remaining free from original sin, assumed along with "the likeness of the flesh of sin" its consequences — infirmity, and He assumed it out of love towards humanity in order to overcome it from within, once He had expiated sin. Of course the relation of the Godman Himself to the flesh of sin and its infirmity remains completely unique, as *a sacrifice* of love, whole and unconditional. But some *sacrificial readiness* must be admitted even respective of the Virgin Mary at the time of her being born into this world with the assumption no longer only "of the likeness" but also of the very flesh of sin. She was prepared *even before* her birth by the heroic struggle of the Old Testament Church for the type of holiness that can hardly be united with a greedy, self-loving submersion in the flesh of the world, but more readily compels us to suppose a sacrificial assumption of common sin as the common fate of people for the sake of their salvation.

The Mother of God, although non-independently, femininely and so to say in a suffering way, passively, accompanies her Son along the whole path towards Golgotha, beginning from the manger in Bethlehem and the flight into Egypt, and she receives the torments of the cross. In her person Eve, the mother of the human race, suffers and is crucified. In church hymns she is called *Lamb* together with the Lamb. But if this seems beyond doubt relative to the earthly life of the Saviour and the Mother of God, why can this same correlation within certain limits not be extended to her very nativity itself? Why not accept that given the holiness of her spirit, even her all-pure birth, her participation in the burden of original sin[12] by virtue of her acceptance not only of the likeness but also of the very flesh of sin, also has a *sacrificial* character, to a certain degree? Out of love for suffering humanity self-renouncing physicians inoculate themselves with the most frightful diseases and settle in the midst of lepers. But precisely this same power of sacrificial readiness, of saving love is accumulated in the whole series of ancestors of the Mother of God, and it gives a completely exceptional meaning and uniqueness to her own nativity. In any case one must not forget that *this birth* was foreknown and proclaimed by God Himself in paradise ("the seed of the Woman will trample the head of the serpent") and it was announced by the Holy Spirit to the prophets David, Solomon, Isaiah and others.[13] And so, the Mother of God by the power of her personal freedom and the grace of the Holy Spirit is completely free of every personal sin during and after her birth. Therefore, original sin has power in her only as an infirmity of human nature, but it is deprived of its seductiveness and is powerless to summon sinfulness even as an imagined assault of sin or an involuntary movement of lust. Such is the understanding of this question in Orthodox doctrine, in as much as one can establish it on the basis of the whole prayer life of the Church. (See the addenda of the author.)

CHAPTER 3

The Catholic Dogma of the
Immaculate Conception of the Mother of God

In Orthodoxy, belief in the personal sinlessness of the Mother of God is like fragrant incense, a cloud of prayer condensing out of the incense of her pious veneration in the Church. If one asks the question what precisely signifies and how one must express in theological language the force and purport of such veneration, then precisely these or similar dogmatic formulas automatically suggest themselves. Yet, such formulas, unavoidable for doing theology, have until now in Orthodoxy only the status of private theological opinions, *theologoumena;* they have never been the subject of broad church discussion. In the present case, as in many others, the Church, while maintaining a true veneration of the Mother of God, and consequently an orthodox doctrine contained in it, did not proceed to expound this doctrine in dogma. This becomes a necessity either owing to the reverential penetration of the mind towards the mysteries of the knowledge of God, in keeping with the needs of Christian contemplation and speculation, or because of the practical needs of the struggle against false teachings and heresies.

If we do not consider the ancient heresy of Nestorius, already defeated and condemned by the Church, who taught that Mary was not the Theotokos but the Christotokos, new heresies about the Mother of God have appeared only in more recent times, primarily in Protestantism which has completely rejected veneration of the Mother of God. This heretical doctrine is the cause as well as the consequence of the distortion, impoverishment and withering of Christian piety in Protestantism. In fact what a profound and many-sided change would arise in our whole religious life if we were to remove from it all those thoughts, feelings, experiences and dispositions that are linked with our reverence for the Mother of God, with our living, experiential knowledge of the Mother of God's presence in the world. Christianity with Christ alone but without the Mother of God is essentially a form of religion other than Orthodoxy, and Protestantism is separated from the Church not by its particular false teachings and arbitrary divisions into sects, but above all and more substantially of all by its lack of spiritual sensitivity for the Mother of God. How such spiritual insensitivity arose and became possible in the Christian world is a puzzle and a mystery of Protestantism, more correctly of all western Christianity.

Catholicism reveres the Mother of God generally speaking no less than does Orthodoxy, but that reverence has been subjected to the general spiritual yoke weighing down upon the whole Catholic world. The necessity to manifest and feel the absolute authority of the pope in everything, particularly in matters of faith, to dogmatize from above, to issue dogmatic laws where life does not in the least require them, proclaimed itself here as well. Indeed the new Catholic dogma of 1854, issued by Pope Pius IX and *de facto* anticipating the dogma of the Vatican Council concerning papal infallibility in matters of faith, was just such a law, called forth by nothing other than the desire to exercise dogmatic authority. True, a poll of the bishops was formally conducted by mail and telegram, and of course, their agreement was obtained, but in general the shadow of future events cast backwards, namely, of the Vatican Council and the Vatican dogma, already lies on this dogma.

The dogma of 1854 was not provoked by any vital necessity (unless one considers the voices of church parties or the visions of individual pious souls which still do not represent dogmatic authority). For Catholicism a time existed when the need for a dogma concerning the veneration of the Mother of God was really present, namely, when the Reformation repudiated it. But not having done this at the proper time, it no longer had this need, now that the church rivers have entered their banks and the Protestant denial of the Mother of God has been exposed in its full antiecclesiality. In any case, the new dogma has no significance for the struggle with Protestantism. The Dogma of 1854 was in this sense an arbitrary doctrinaire attitude of separate parties and voices and reflected all their influence with its one-sidedness.

In general the Catholic dogma is *an incorrect expression of a correct idea about the personal sinlessness of the Mother of God,* and it does this by completely unsuitable means. Indeed, it introduces problematic and even false doctrines as fundamental elements of dogma and formulates completely falsely the very idea, quite denying the power of original sin in the Mother of God.[1] In itself it is a dogmatic misunderstanding and even simply a mistake. But it forces Orthodoxy to clarify the true dogma concerning the veneration of the Mother of God as the sinless, all-pure, all-spotless Ever Virgin, which is vigorously maintained in Orthodoxy. Unfortunately, Orthodox polemicists in their excessive sincerity began to deny not only the false dogmatic formula but the very truth itself, and they began to speak of the non-sinlessness of the Mother of God.

The Catholic dogma of 1854 proclaims that the Most Holy Virgin *"in primo instante suae conceptionis fuisse singulari omnipotentis Dei gratia et privilegio intuitu meritorum Christi Jesu Salvatoris humani generis ab omni culpae labe praeservatam immunem,"* that is, "from the first moment of her conception, she was preserved free from every stain of sin by a special grace of almighty God and in virtue of a special privilege, in consideration of the merits of Jesus Christ the Saviour of our race." The subject of the *immaculata conceptio* is the Mother of God from the first moment of her conception or in accordance with the interpretation of Pope Alexander VII (Const. *Sollicitudo omnium ecclesiarum* 1661),[2] in the instant of the creation and in-pouring of Mary's soul into her body. In this there is no word about the immaculate state of the generative activity of the parents in the moment of conjugal union, *conceptio activa* or more precisely *generativa,* but likewise the conception itself of the child *(conceptio passiva)* is not the object of the privilege. For, if one means that *concupiscentia passiva* which is the immediate product and content of the generative principles *conceptio seminis, conceptio carnis, conceptio inchoatae personae,* and which in time or at least according to nature precedes the inpouring *(Eingiessung)* of the rational soul, then it still does not contain in itself Mary's personality. In any case *privilegium* corresponds only to that passive conception, which by more recent theologians is called *conceptio passiva adaequata et consummata,* and by early defenders is named *conceptio germinis* (in opposition to *conceptio seminis*) and *conceptio spiritualis sive personalis,* and sometimes *vitalis sive animalis* (in opposition to *conceptio carnis*) and coincides with *nativitas personae in utero.* Immaculateness is ascribed to the product of generation not as a result of the means of origin but despite them, by a special divine action, through which Mary's soul was created and poured into the body.[3] With respect to human conception, *conceptio humana,* this is designated as *conceptio divina,* that is, *a Deo.* The Immaculate Conception designates that freedom from original sin which is given at the time of baptism, and is perhaps the baptism of Mary before her birth and consequently, before the nativity of Christ.

The dogma being examined in its theological formulation is bound up with two premises: (1) the Catholic doctrine concerning the operation of original sin in humankind in conjunction with the doctrine concerning its original state; (2) the doctrine concerning the origin of human souls by means of a new creative act, creationism. Only in light of both of these doctrines is it possible to understand the fundamental idea of the dogma and to evaluate it on its merits.

Really, here we are concerned with the gift of *justitia originalis,* which had been removed from humankind during the fall but was restored to Mary in the guise of a special exception of grace at the creation of her soul. Her body resulted by the usual path, but this is not an obstacle for "the immaculate conception" because by itself the body is not injured by sin. The whole power of sin consists precisely in the removal of the gift of original righteousness, whence its mere restoration *suffices* for the Immaculate Conception. Here that peculiar and of course quite disputed doctrine determines by itself the content of the dogma of the Immaculate Conception, in this way introducing scholastic doctrine into the very heart of dogmatics and thereby giving an example of scholastic doctrinalism. With the elimination of these school teachings from the dogma, nothing remains except the general pious and fully correct idea about the sinlessness of the Virgin Mary. Nevertheless it is impossible not to detect a certain gaping contradiction in the dogma even on the basis of these premises. Mary's body, conceived in natural conditions, remained not purified and not blessed with grace for a certain time, even if in an embryonic state. About the body it is said that it is "a filthy and depraved vessel and like a lead weight it weighs down and binds the body."[4] But let us analyse in more detail both premises.

The Anselmian–Duns Scotus doctrine about the original nature of humankind and about original sin, connected with the theory of satisfaction and representing so-called Semi-Pelagianism, triumphed in the doctrine of the Catholic church not only thanks to the promulgation of the 1854 dogma but also thanks to the condemnation of the doctrine of Baius (sixteenth century), by the decree of the council of Trent (Session V, 1, 2, 5). What was Adam like before the fall and what did he lose in it? The answer which is given by Catholic doctrine, beyond every mitigation and reservation, is this: human nature in itself *did not* change, only the supernatural aid, graciously regulating human nature, was removed, as Bellarmine says concerning the integrity of the first human: *integritas illa, qua primus homo conditus fuit sine qua post eius lapsum homines omnes nascuntur, non fuit naturalis eius conditio, sed supernaturalis evectio . . . fuisse donum supernaturale.* (Robert Bellarmine, *De gratia primi hominis,* 2 ibid. 5).[5]

A modern theologian plainly says that the character of animal life with all its imperfections is inherent in the human being in keeping with the weakness of the body, *infirmitas carnis* — not owing to the fall but according to his very creation. In other words, the human being is an animal and like all animals is subject not only to the possibility but even to the necessity of the diminution and cessation of life, unless the food, created for him by God, preserved him from this forever;[6] which is why the presence of the tree of life in the midst of paradise was required.[7] In other words, the human inclination to sin and the weakness of his nature flow out of his being joined with a body that obscures the divine image in the human being.[8] In this is displayed the peculiar combination of practical Semi-Pelagianism and Manichaeism which penetrated Catholicism through Augustinianism, a characteristic unawareness of the body as the fullness of the Divine image in the human being.

Human nature according to this opinion is defective owing to its being joined with a body; the primordial, immanent harmony and natural grace that is based in the sophianicity of the human is not inherent to it. Therefore it can be supported only by an influence from outside, transcendentally, by supernatural grace, by an act of divine arbitrariness, if one can thus express it, by a *deus ex machina,* not in conformity but in nonconformity with and in spite of human nature. This very nature in its contradictoriness is likewise an act of divine arbitrariness which has called into existence a being that is wittingly defective, self-bifurcating, in this sense lower not only than angels but also than animals. Of course it is completely incomprehensible that such a being is placed at the head of the whole of creation and given the lordship over the whole animal and vegetable world; that it is "made little less than the angels" and is "the joy" of Divine Wisdom. Here too the divine incarnation, which becomes completely incomprehensible in the face of the internal and unalienable defectiveness of the human being, is a similar act of Divine arbitrariness, having no foundation in human nature itself. Therefore what takes place in the incarnation is not the disclosure of true nature, the fulfilment of human nature with the tracing of the fullness of God's image in the human, but once again violence against human nature by an operation from the outside. The incarnation thus becomes an internally contradictory act, and the very foundations of Christology (and Soteriology) are undermined by Catholic anthropology. Naturally, the incarnation itself becomes a kind of fortuitousness, summoned . . . by the fall of Adam, by the merit and fruit of this fall. *"O felix culpa, quae talem ac tantum meruit habere Redemptorem. O certe necessarium Adae peccatum"* as the Catholic Church sings.

51

"Inherited sin can be drawn in here only to the extent that the clothing of grace, which has covered him insufficiently and hindered their manifestation, is stripped away thanks to it," and in any case it "can be drawn in only as *meritorischer Grund,* whereas *physischer Grund* for all that must be sought in the joining of the soul *mit dem korruptiblen Leibe.*" The body is now constructed in essence no differently and joined with the soul no other way than it was in the first human being (ibid.). The joining of the soul with the body constitutes the fundamental deficiency — *Mangel* — on the basis of which sinfulness *peccatum habituale* arises, out of which comes *peccatum actuale.* "It is impossible to be astonished that the human being with the exceptional complexity of his nature out of the high and the lowly, making him the centre and connecting link of creation, one according to his nature, is in less of a condition to satisfy his own particular status and vocation than the purely spiritual beings above him and the animals below him. Therefore it would be quite arbitrary and criminal to desire in the interests of honouring the Creator that the human being in virtue of the construction of his nature would be such that of himself he could satisfy the full realization of his idea" (234).

On the contrary, his complexity and incompleteness allows the Creator to show to him a particular assistance of grace and to exalt him more than the angels. [These paragraphs appear to be a note, but the Russian original does not print them as such. Translator]

In their understanding of grace in relation to the human being, Catholics mainly emphasize its supernatural, super-creaturely character, the moment of divine condescension as divinizing power, but they do not give full value to graced creaturehood, to the Divine image in the human being, an image that is real and living precisely because it receives and, one can say, draws towards itself heavenly grace — by its natural graced state, by the very image of its nature. Hence the mechanical quality and the coarseness of outlook of Catholic theology with respect to *status naturae purae, elevatae, lapsae.* According to the doctrine of Divine assistance, *adjutorium divinum,* Adam possessed an equilibrium in his nature and an original righteousness, *iustitia originalis;* he bridled the disorderly lasciviousness inherent in him, like the rider of a horse. But if the human being's power was not in its particular god-bearing nature with its inherent inalienable freedom, but in *donum superadditum,* which in the well-known sense *coerces,* changes human nature and gives it powers that do not belong to it, then it becomes incomprehensible *how* the human being could sin, how it could repudiate this *coercion* of grace. Or has grace itself proved to be powerless? Lacking a convincing answer to this question, Catholic theology is forced in essence to understand original sin as *carentia or nuditas justitiae debitae,* that is, as a mechanical and arbitrary *removal of donum superadditum*. If it is still possible at a stretch to interpret it as punishment for Adam, with respect to his descendants it is an act of pure arbitrariness, something that *is confirmed* by the dogma of the Immaculate Conception: what has been arbitrarily removed can just as easily be arbitrarily restored.

Catholic doctrine introduces dualism into anthropology, the result of which is a mechanical understanding of how the divine and the human are joined in a human being: in this is its Manichaeism. Its Semi-Pelagianism is expressed in its failure to distinguish between the condition of natural and fallen humankind, except in a collective respect; the *vulneratio* of nature about which the scholastics speak, consists in the weakening of human powers, but not in the change of the very image of humanness in the human being. According to Orthodox understanding, sin committed by a human being in his freedom influences him *immanently* in his nature, by the force of its perverseness depriving nature of the knowledge of God and the direct reception of His gifts. The punishment for sin likewise is not something externally imposed but only something confirmed by the Divine will, by the self-determination of human nature, by the consequence of sin. It acquires an ontological meaning, just as the Divine commandment was ontological for humankind, although it had a deontological form: it was invested in a command. Its observance was the ontological condition of the humanness of humankind, its violation an ontological catastrophe, introducing in humankind a new law and a new life, famously contrary to nature, not responding to the ontological norms and tasks of humankind.

Among Catholics it is quite the contrary: *status iusitiae originalis* is contrary to nature for the human being even in the sense of his supernaturality, and, vice-versa, *status naturae lapsae* corresponds more to *status naturae purae*. The condition of humankind before and after the fall is here determined externally, as a law, transcendental to its nature, as an act of God's almighty will, *not in the human but upon* the human, or on the human, at first as kindness, then as judgment and forensic sentence, as punishment: in this way what is essential here is that *the condition* of human in its relation to grace changes, but humankind itself does not change. The Catholic Church expressed this idea in its condemnation of the teaching of Baius in the bull of Pope Pius V in 1567. Baius taught that the original condition was *status naturae debitus* (as opposed to *indebitus*) and that all the advantages of the primogenitors in paradise were linked with this primordial human nature.[9] All the sufferings of humankind, even death, are punishments for sins, and this has force even with respect to the Virgin Mary. This doctrine was condemned in the form of a series of anathematized theses (*Enchiridion Denzigeri,* 1001ff),[10] and in the process it was established that humankind could have been created by God in the same condition in which it now finds itself and independently of guilt, and consequently that the grace of the original condition is supernatural, *that is, superhuman;* humankind is more *an object* of the influence of grace than its subject.

A second time, a similar teaching was condemned in the nineteenth century in the persons of Hermes and Günther,[11] who likewise affirmed that the original state did not have a graced but a natural character: divine blessedness and wisdom would not have permitted the creation of a human being without original righteousness, under which is understood the subordination of sensuality to reason. The flashes of doctrine about the primordial sophianicity of humankind were condemned at the provincial council of Cologne (canon 15).[12]

And so, the present-day received doctrine of the Catholic Church concerning original sin and the initial condition regards sin as *privatio,* a pushing aside of grace which by the will of God can be restored to humankind; in this same manner humankind is re-established *fully and entirely* in its original state. Therefore the Mother of God is fully and entirely assimilated to Eve before the fall. Here the peculiar *deus ex machina,* recourse to divine arbitrariness, is applied to such a degree that the whole human side of the preparation for God's incarnation becomes insubstantial and unimportant. Essentially the meaning of *the genealogy* of Christ the Saviour is cancelled. In fact, given such an understanding this act of restoration of *iustitiae originalis* could have come at any moment of history, and not in the fullness of time, and generally speaking, history as the *common task*[13] of humanity, as the sole and coherent act which has the incarnation as its centre, does not even exist in such an understanding. The whole mechanical quality of the Catholic outlook is displayed in this anti-historicism, which cancels the power and sense of the Old Testament preparation of humanity for the incarnation of God, and essentially repudiates freedom for humanity. The result is that the Virgin Mary is inherently holy, but not because of her personal hereditary righteousness, accumulated through the centuries in Old Testament humanity. It was not she who drew to herself the extraordinary, exceptional gifts of the Holy Spirit, but the one-sided act of divine election, which even before birth or in birth itself placed her in a privileged *(privilegium),* exceptional situation in which she was able not to sin, though no longer by her own power. In this way human freedom and dignity are abased, which are so inviolably preserved in Orthodox doctrine.[14]

To this one must add that the idea about the *anticipation* "of the merits" of Christ with a view to the redemption of Mary from original sin likewise suffers from a crude legalism in the understanding of salvation. Of course, if salvation is to be understood as *a ransom* "by merits," as payment of a debt owing, then perhaps it is still possible to imagine such a credit transaction by which the debt is taken into consideration before its actual payment. True, this is an injustice, a partiality towards one person that could have been shown towards everyone, thereby averting the consequences of Adam's original sin for the whole world. Here only recourse to the omnipotence of God remains, which is free to forgive and have mercy, that is, the direct path to Calvinism with its doctrine of arbitrary predestination. But already the very possibility of such a preliminary amnesty demolishes the whole ontology of original sin, according to which it is as much guilt *(peccatum actuale)* as a state *(peccatum habituale)*. This ontology resolutely opposes Catholic thought about redemption on credit, before the redemption accomplished for all. The latter is not a juridical act of imputing merits but first and foremost a real change of all human nature through the incarnation; it is the graced creation of the human being anew, which is realized for each one in holy baptism. For this reason the anticipation of redemption about which the Catholic dogma of 1854 speaks, even if it can still be thought of as an amnesty, that is, as a juridical act, can in no way at all be understood as the most profound regeneration of human nature. Such a thing cannot be anticipated earlier than its actual accomplishment. In this sense baptism is also not anticipated, and the idea that the Most Holy Virgin would have been baptised before the institution of baptism, that is, before the coming of its very possibility, is inwardly contradicted — in ontology there is no place for *privilegium* — the very idea of which exposes the anti-ontological legalism of Catholic theology. Examined from this side, the dogma is an ontological misunderstanding, an experiment conducted with means inapplicable, i.e., unsuited, to the present instance.

But it has yet another dogmatic premise. This consists in the doctrine that souls at the birth of individuals are created by God every time by a special creative act, and in this act they are already deprived of extraordinary sanctifying grace, *justitiae originalis,* in advance. Owing to this they are born as children of wrath, weighed down by original sin (although, it would seem, that if it is so, then there is no personal guilt in this deprivation, and it is incomprehensible why the ones who are deprived of this gift over and above what is owed must still bear personal responsibility because of this deprivation). In accord with this general idea of creation, it is supposed that a human being is begotten by God as a *tabula rasa* with respect to sin, free from every sinful assault but needing a special gift in order to be protected against it which he does not receive. Here, the body proves to be the sole source of sin, and bodily generation is already the beginning of sin. But such a role for the body contradicts to a certain degree the Catholic view concerning the absence of change in Adam's nature after sin. On the other hand, this unavoidably compels us to suppose that the body must have infected the soul of Mary with original sin too, although it is free from original sin by virtue of her *privilegium*. But then her immaculate conception turns out *not to be realized*. All of this merely shows the particular absurdities and ambiguities of a dogma that was introduced in a hasty procedure of papal administrative-dogmatic pronouncement and bears on it the traces of that haste. Its one-sided orientation to the doctrine of the immediate creation of souls by God is of importance, whence that doctrine, sufficiently debatable and in any case not fully clarified, is also dogmatized (to be sure without any internal necessity and without sufficient motives).

The unwieldy question about the manner of the soul's provenance, dragged in here, has its own complex and lengthy history determined primarily by the conflict of two views: according to the one, souls are immediately created by God — creationism (to this is united the Origenist doctrine of pre-existence, still condemned by the Church, according to which souls existed before their taking flesh; this latter event is the result of their growing heavy or their falling away from God). According to the other view souls are generated by the parents — generationism or traducianism, the result of the power inserted by God at the creation of humankind: "be fruitful and multiply." In ecclesiastical literature there was no lack of opinions favouring both the creation and the generation of the soul, although the majority opted for the first opinion.[15] In the Western church creationism triumphed decidedly, and in Orthodoxy too some theologians (Metropolitan Makary, Archbishop Silvester) regard it as the norm for Orthodox doctrine, which by the way does not prohibit others (e.g. Archbishop Filaret of Chernigov) from supporting an entirely opposite opinion.[16] The Word of God gives no decisive answer, so that by their own admission the texts produced by defenders of both opinions essentially do not support them.

Gen 1.28, 2.23 is cited in favour of traducianism, while against it are cited Is 57.16, Is 32.15, Wis 8.19, Eccl 12.7. Even less decisive are arguments from reason, clearly exposing the impossibility for rationalizing thought to reach the secret of its own generation, or the origin of the soul. The chief argument advanced against the possibility of generation of souls by the parents is, after Thomas Aquinas, the simplicity, indivisibility and uncomposite nature of the soul which the idea about the generation of the souls of children by the souls of parents contradicts. On the other hand, the generationists point out that the idea of a new creation of souls destroys the unity of the human race, renders the transmission of hereditary sin incomprehensible, and in general does away with any form of heredity. Besides this, the parents prove to be here the givers only of flesh for their children and in essence are no longer parents. Others point out that the idea of uninterrupted creation destroys God's Sabbath rest at the conclusion of His creating the world, seemingly subordinating the creative will of God to human desires and acts of conception. No small difficulties arise for creationism in the doctrine of the divine incarnation, which in this instance proves to be the assumption merely of a body. One comes to the conclusion that even the Theotokos cannot be called by that name, for she gave only flesh to her Son.

Finally, this question sometimes is complicated by a question about the dichotomous or trichotomous structure of human nature: does a human being consist only of *two* parts, flesh and spirit, as many texts directly state, or of three: spirit, soul and body (in support of which can be cited 1 Thess 5.23 and Heb 4.12)? Prejudice against trichotomy is partially explained here because Apollinarius adhered to it, and relied on this very doctrine in his heretical Christology.[17] The trichotomous structure of the human being naturally considers that only the spirit originates immediately from God, whereas the soul and body come from the parents. Using a dichotomous structure, it is more suitable to think that the soul is created by God while only the body is created by the parents. By the way, this question is not posed in this connection in the history of dogma, although it suggests itself naturally and, as it seems to us, unavoidably.

And so, is it incumbent upon us as well to speak out without fail in favour of one or the other of the school doctrines, to make a choice in favour of creationism or generationism (traducianism)? Or is a third outcome possible here, one that frees us completely from having to choose between either point of view, and as a result leaves us with the possibility of seeing here a series of misunderstandings? That is precisely how the affair presents itself to us: the whole question has acquired an unnecessary, anthropomorphic formulation as a result of the application of the category of time to the life of the Godhead. The choice between generationism and creationism in this sense would signify one thing: *when and how* does God create the souls of individuals? But this *when,* when applied to the operation of God, is already a misunderstanding, because the category of time is inapplicable to God. Everything that God creates, He creates sempiternally and in eternity, and only for the creature, for humankind, is this revealed in time, as concrete filled time. It is false to think that time has its limiting power even for God, hence to admit, for example, that there was a time before the creation of the world when God was not yet the creator. This is the same question that blessed Augustine brushed aside irritably: what was God doing before creating the world? There can be only one answer to this question: in God there exists *no when whatsoever,* and every *when* in Him is pre-eternal, supratemporal, for which reason there does not exist *a never* either. Everything unfolding in time occurs from eternity in God.

Thus on the one hand it is said that God created the world in the course of six days and afterwards rested from His works, having created the world in its fullness. But at the same time, according to the testimony of the Word himself, "My Father is working until now and I am working." This in no way signifies the continuation of the acts of creation in time, as theologians usually imagine, but His sempiternity: every temporal creation (and all creation is temporal, for it is in time) is sempiternally in God. This in no way signifies the Origenist doctrine of the pre-existence of souls which was condemned by the Church, for the Origenist doctrine distinguishes namely *two* times and it locates yet another pre-earthly time prior to our earthly time, that is, it quite simplistically lengthens and somewhat complicates earthly time. Besides, our idea refers to that which has power *before* time, or, more correctly, *over* time, as its foundation. God has with Him pre-eternally the world in its prototypes and the world is a sophianic eternity that has been reflected in the course of time. In this way every being proceeds from God in eternity and develops in time, once it has been summoned by the creative act *let there be.* For God nothing arises, but all is pre-eternally there. In this way the truths of creationism and generationism in their most general sense are completely combinable, that is, as a doctrine about unceasing emergence, through an apparently always continuing, though once and for all accomplished creative act — creationism, and about the autonomous, immanent formation or development of a fashioned creaturely world that received in itself the fullness of creative powers of existence — generationism. In dogmatics the two aspects are differentiated, as Divine Creation and Divine Economy which is an unceasingly continuing act of creation, that has appeared once and for all in all its originality and diversity: "You send forth your Spirit and they are created, you remove your spirit from them and they disappear and return to their dust" (Ps 103). Besides this, although everything arises in time, and consequently is limited by its bounds, *at the same time* it pre-arises earlier than its own showing up. Everything is sowed in everything[18] and is supported in its being by a uniquely-supratemporal creative act. Generally speaking this is applied to the common foundations of being. Now let us examine this same question in relation to the creation of humankind.

Humankind occupies a special place in the universe. On the one hand it is created together with the whole world out of the fullness of the divine *all,* and in this sense it is one with the world. On the other hand, God breathed into it Himself the breath of life and honoured it with His own image. The latter is of course not simply a likeness, "a property," but an essence, *ens realissimum* in the human being who is a created god, in the image of the real God. Which concepts, philosophical and theological, are needed to express this insufflation of a living soul by God Himself in Adam can and must constitute a particular theological problem. There is no doubt that originating in such a way Adam's spirit does not cease to be a created, creaturely spirit. It is a second creation, just as are the angels, "the second lights" which streamed from the single, first Everlasting Light. Adam does not obtain through this origin any share in the pre-eternal life of the most holy Trinity. But, as the image of God and in some sense the repetition of the Godhead itself in the world, an image that arises *not* only out of creation through the word *"let there be,"* but also out of a mysterious inner apportionment from the core of the Godhead, through "the in-breathing" of the soul, Adam is the pre-worldly being, from all eternity, in the world. In other words, in some sense Adam is created and not created, rather, he is issued by God; he is a creaturely and non-creaturely being, temporal and eternal, the world and the not-world, the supra-world, God in the universe, a citizen of this world and through this its master. In this way, in his very *composition* (in no matter what terms we may express it: dichotomous or trichotomous, for this does not belong to the essence of the question) the human being *is dual,* ontologically complex, bicomposite. As a citizen of the world he is created in the world and with the world, and in this sense he does not have a special face, does not require a special creation.

But he also arises from God by a special act not of world-creation but "of in-breathing," of issuing. This duality or bicompositeness of the human being (dichotomy) is the metaphysical basis for his essence, which is unchangeably reproduced in every human being: he receives his hypostasis, his countenance, his I, from God as His image, as a mirror of

Divinity in which It reflected Its countenance. All these images in a certain sense flow together in *the one* image of Adam, the old Adam, and afterwards in the image *of the New Adam,* for the Godhead which determines this image by itself is one. But at the same time they are really plural for each one has in itself the reflection of the whole Godhead, possesses His image and through this is *ens realissimum,* like many reflections of the one sun in pluriunity. Such are the foundations of human nature, reproduced in each human being.

It is out of place, immodest and even naïve to inquire whether it was enough for God to have breathed a living soul into Adam's body *once only* and thus to have reflected His image in him, or if this is repeated over and over again. The one and the other are already contained in the single creative act[19] of the creation of humankind. In it every human personality exists for God forever and does not arise by chance or self-capriciously, as a result of the play of earthly forces. In this way the truth of creationism is that in the composition of humankind, in its very nature, there is a supraworldly principle which cannot arise by earthly forces, even if by the power of heredity, but presupposes the direct participation of Divinity. As Adam or together with Adam and in Adam, each human being is specially created by God, is a repetition of His Image, as a godlike spirit issuing from God, as a hypostasis bearing in its very self the seal and mark of its sempiternity and its divine origin. However, this refers not to chronology but to ontology: we are speaking here not about God "pouring in" some sort of spiritual essence at a certain, fixed moment of time in the development of an embryo into this latter. Thus do Latin theologians think (and in part some Eastern patriarchs led astray by them).[20] On the contrary, in each birth the form *is realized,* God's pre-eternal behest and intention for every human being is fulfilled. In God and for God there exists His one image, one human being in the person of primordial Adam, but in this image are given all images of this Image, all his individual *hows,* which are realized in time as individualities. And thus, the question about the time of the "pouring in," about its means — expressly, occurring one time only, or by a common single creative act — is simply out of place. It is a type of misunderstanding, for here it is possible to ask only *what, and not how.*

Creationism simply expresses in crude and naïve form the truth about the supramundane provenance of the human hypostasis. The truth of generationism lies in the fact that, as in Adam God breathed in the breath of life only after his body had been created out "of earth," that is, of the world, so too in the descendants of Adam the image of God, the spirit, the hypostasis, is realized only in the human being who is begotten out of worldly nature, from the tree of Adam. In other words, the body, and not only the body but also its quickening animal soul, are created by natural conception and birth, which is as incomprehensible an operation of the omnipotent God as the generation of the soul. For in fact what does the living body of the human being, thirsting and waiting for the seal of its divine spirit, represent? Is it simply a pile of bones and flesh? Is it really less and lower than animals which have a living soul in their "blood," according to Moses? Does this special animal soul have in itself not only power over the body but also its own, though lowly, spiritual energies, its own mind, its own body, its own character? But on the human body with its animal soul is likewise imprinted its innate hereditary character; a human being is not born *tabula rasa*. His hypostasis, his divine spirit, the image of God lodges in a definite dwelling and as we have attempted to explain above, the soul *consents* to this indwelling, co-wills it, assumes it, as it were works by its own act and becomes on account of this responsible. Here genealogy, heredity enters in force. If it is expressed dichotomously, one must say that the living quickened body of a human being is born from the seed of the parents and in this body the soul is implanted. If it is expressed trichotomously (which essentially is one and the same thing; thus in the Word of God we encounter both dichotomous and trichotomous expressions, see Heb 4.12; 1 Thess 5.23), then one must say that from the parents is born not only the body but also the animal soul, the empirical character, and in this joining of body and soul the spirit takes root.[21]

Generation by the parents *only* of the body, first of all, would humble the human being, even before animals: the human being's place at the end of the six days supposes its full mastery over everything created on the preceding days. The sixth day is the ontogenesis of the human being. It is first of all the perfect all-animal, possessing in itself everything that animals have, in particular a living animal soul. Secondly, the separation of the body from the soul and the origin of the one and the other particularly, one through birth and the other through creation, is in any case no less incomprehensible than the birth of the soul from the soul of the parents. Strictly speaking, the one and the other are equally impossible to understand in their *how* and it is a mystery of Divine creativity, a miracle. The metaphysical necessity of a separate origin really exists, not in relation to the body and animal soul, but in relation to the body in conjunction with a soul or simply in relation to a living body on the one hand and to the spirit, hypostasis, Divine image, on the other hand. For the first things make up the cosmic, animal principle in the human, the second, the divine. And of course they cannot be confused in the sense that the one can proceed from the other.

But at the same time a well-known bond, conjugateness, correspondence, exists between them — there exists the individuality of the body and soul, the individuality of the spirit appropriate to them. If creationism wants to abolish or weaken this conjugateness, to destroy these bonds, then it bumps against one obstacle here that is completely insuperable for it and which confused blessed Augustine, namely against original sin and heredity in general. In as much as creationism includes in itself this principle it becomes colourless. It loses its chief power — the opposition of soul and body as mutually independent principles. Radical creationism's affirmation concerning the full independence of the soul being created from the body being generated would entail the full negation of heredity and genealogy, the unity and bond of the whole human race, original sin and the whole Old Testament economy, including the Saviour's genealogy. For the meaning of the last named things reduces to the preparation of a body for the Saviour at most, remote from any spiritual power. Creationism in this sense is a crude and naïve occasionalism and atomism in its understanding of human destinies; each human being arises separately, has its own proper destiny, is separated from those who are similar to it through its own provenance, owing to a new creative act. In its consistent construction this doctrine tears asunder all Christology and Soteriology as a doctrine about *a single* Adam, old and New. In as much as creationism is prepared to include in itself *a pre-established* relationship between a spirit created by God and a body generated by parents, it in effect surrenders its positions and represents only a variety of traducianism.

The doctrine of the Immaculate Conception of the Mother of God in the 1854 dogma is struck by this same occasionalism. To introduce this disputed, dark and unelaborated doctrine into the very heart of a dogma, to execute such a rash and unwise act was necessitated because by this means it appeared all the easier to promote the sinlessness of Mary as a *privilegium,* given on credit, in an extraordinary order, and thus to resolve all the dogmatic difficulties connected with the question of the veneration of the Mother of God. Mary is removed from the general order at the creation of her soul. In that moment the *donum superadditum* that had been removed from everyone else is restored to her. But in as much as this is the act of a one-sided divine arbitrariness, this *privilegium,* it seemed, would be possible for all the descendants of Adam. In essence this undermines the whole implacable power of original sin that joins everyone not

only in divine reprobation but also in salvation. In this way this rash dogma shakes the very foundations of Christian dogmatics. More than this, it deprives the Most Pure Virgin of her own merit in sinlessness, for it endows her with immunity with respect to sin beforehand *gratis,* as a *privilegium.* Thus, although it pursues a good goal — the glorification of the Virgin, the dogma does it by completely unworthy means and is an example of dogmatic arbitrariness and haste.

According to the idea of the Catholic dogma, "the immaculate conception" of the Mother of God signifies simply *another creation* of her, in distinction from all other people: she is endowed with a special gift with which other people are not endowed, nothing more. And this corresponds, really, to an advantage received in the sense of *privilegium.* Here we have an example of the mechanical coarsening of theological concepts, eliminating human freedom in favour of an arbitrary predestinationism and an unwarranted application of the principle *ex opere operato.* Withdrawn from original sin, Mary would turn out to be withdrawn from all humankind, separated from the tree of the old Adam. By the way, it is precisely through her that a new branch ought to have been grafted onto that tree.

The extraordinary outpouring of the gifts of the Holy Spirit, unique in its type, at the moment of the Most Holy Virgin's conception, in her conception and in her birth, was a divine supplying for human infirmity. It was, first of all, because of the obvious righteousness and holiness of "the ancestors of God" Joachim and Anne, and of the whole God-pleasing series of their forebears; the holiness of birth corresponds to the holiness of the parents. Secondly, it was because of the holiness of the Most Pure Virgin herself, shown even before her earthly birth in her pre-temporal and pre-worldly self-determination. And however much it is possible to speak about "the immaculate conception" and nativity of the Most Pure and Unblemished One, even here grace does not automatically or mechanically select for itself an object that remains passive in this election; rather it responds to the counter-movement of human nature itself. The Mother of God acquires freedom from personal sinfulness, preserving in her nature the whole power of natural sin and its infirmity. It is incorrect to speak about her baptism *before her nativity and that of her Son.* The Mother of God was baptised along with all the apostles on the day of Pentecost. And besides this, in keeping with the law of sin, she tasted death. She did not possess that freedom from death which for our primogenitors was connected with the absence of original sin.

In a word, from all sides the newly invented dogma presents itself as a superfluity and a fabrication.

CHAPTER 4

The Glorification of the Mother of God

According to the sense of the Catholic dogma of the Immaculate Conception, the decisive event in the life of the Mother of God occurred before her birth, in her conception, when she was freed from original sin. Everything further was only the realization of this act of *deus ex machina* in her — the restoration to her of the *donum superadditum*. Orthodox veneration of the Most Pure, on the contrary, does not know such a single threshold, for her whole life is a series of steps in an uninterrupted ascent from earth into heaven. In relation to original sin there are only two possibilities: to have it or to be set free from it. On the path of personal holiness, on the contrary, there is a continuous growth in sanctification: the exact sophianic image of the creature, which is the ontological basis for its holiness, as well as the power of existence, is realized in creation all the more vividly until such time as it emerges with full power. Then the creature is already the revelation of triune Wisdom, in which the Word of God, begotten by the Father, is embraced by the Holy Spirit. Such namely is the path of the Mother of God.

In the life of the Mother of God one can point to a series of events which the Church marks with particular celebrations or prayers and which represent thresholds in her spiritual increase and glorification. Such events are: the Nativity of the Mother of God, the Entrance into the Temple, the Annunciation (and connected with this the Visitation of Elizabeth), the Nativity of Christ, further, a series of events of His earthly life from the flight into Egypt to her station at the cross, the Resurrection and Ascension of Christ, Pentecost and the Dormition of the Mother of God.

In celebrating the Nativity of the Mother of God, the Church points to her special pre-elect holiness already in her generation, owing to which her subsequent development towards Divine Motherhood proved possible. The Church celebrates likewise the Nativity of John the Forerunner, as an especially blessed event along with that of the Mother of God, bearing witness thereby that the holy birth being celebrated is not yet an "immaculate conception" with liberation from original sin's power, but is only the beginning of a holy life increasing all the time in sanctification. Childhood purity and holiness, bound up with ignorance of sin and special divine election, must be tempered and perfected and increase in strength — the absence of sin must be replaced by its being victoriously overcome.

The entrance into the temple of the living Temple of God, the templification[1] of the Virgin Mary, corresponds to the next step in the sanctification of the Mother of God. The temple was the only place on earth hallowed in peace where God lived (cf. the prayer of Solomon at the consecration of the temple — 1 Kg 8.14f; 2 Chr 6.3f.). This was the place of paradise in the earth of the curse, which here was removed from the world and creation, for the temple was holy. In this holy place, where angels would descend, the Most Holy Virgin was brought into communion with them, led into the Holy of Holies by the High Priest, in accordance with prophetic inspiration. Since that time the power of the Old Testament Temple already begins to be abolished as the sole place of encounter of humankind with God. Mary becomes the Temple of the temple, and receives on herself the power of the temple's consecration. The significance of the temple is already exhausted, and it is left to be but a place of prayerful encounter until that moment when the curtain will be torn asunder and the Old Testament temple sanctuary abolished.

The Annunciation is already the completion of Divine Motherhood. The descent of the Holy Spirit and His indwelling in the Mother of God, who by virtue of this indwelling received the capacity for a seedless conception, is generally speaking the highest blessing that can ever be thought for creation. The indwelling of the Holy Spirit already signifies the divinization of human nature in the person of the Mother of God. At the same time it was not yet salvation, but only the preparation for salvation. Life in the Holy Spirit was revealed for humankind only through Christ and in Christ, who prayed His Father to send down the Holy Spirit after His ascension. Before this the Holy Spirit is revealed as a surmounting power which acts on humankind in a certain sense from the outside, transcendently, but not from the inside, not immanently; the latter became possible only when Christ took on flesh and became immanent to

66

humanity. Thus the singular and unrepeatable indwelling of the Holy Spirit in the Virgin Mary, not shared by any other creaturely being, does not exclude Pentecost for her. It does not close the possibility of receiving the grace of the Holy Spirit already as the principles of the proper life of a human being, as its interior divinization. The Virgin Mary became the Temple in which the Holy Spirit dwelt for the purpose of Christ's incarnation, but as a human being, for the sake of her own nature begotten in original sin, *as indeed every human being,* she needed baptism and the reception of the Holy Spirit and she received the fiery tongue of the Holy Spirit *along with and equally with* all the apostles, with the whole Church. The grace of the Annunciation proved to be compatible with the grace of Pentecost. As a human burdened by original sin, Mary needed redemption through the blood of her Son and the appropriation of this redemption through the gift of the Holy Spirit; to speak in the language of church sacraments, she needed baptism (with the Holy Spirit and with fire) and chrismation (sealing with the Spirit). This in and of itself sufficiently refutes the Catholic dogma. Otherwise there would be no reason for her to be present at Pentecost (it merits notice that *the sole* recollection about Mary in the Acts of the Apostles concerns precisely this account, and in icons of the descent of the Holy Spirit the Mother of God is always depicted in the centre of the apostles receiving her special fiery tongue).

This compatibility of the Annunciation and Pentecost is very meaningful; it bears witness that even the fullest reception of the Holy Spirit for the sake of Divine Motherhood did not remove the necessity of baptism and redemption, which is why the Mother of God names her Son without a moment's hesitation *her Saviour:* "My spirit rejoices in God my Saviour." The Holy Spirit who descended at the Annunciation gave the power for seedless conception. He made her the earth of God from which sprouted the Body of Christ, the new Adam. The action of the Holy Spirit at the Annunciation is therefore an unmediated influence on the body of the Mother of God (analogously to how the Spirit of God hovered over the waters at the beginning of the universe), although of course with the participation of the spirit; Pentecost, on the contrary, was a new spiritual birth, in keeping with the word of the Lord in his conversation with Nicodemus.

Beginning with the Annunciation the Virgin Mary becomes the Mother of God, as Elizabeth, the mother of the Forerunner, calls her in a prophetic illumination, and in whose person the entire Old Testament church welcomes her: "and how does it happen to me that the Mother of my Lord comes to me!" Becoming Mother of God does not signify a merely temporary state, which continues during pregnancy and ends with the birth of Christ. It is a property that lasts forever, for we always bless the Mother of God as the true Theotokos, not in a fleeting past alone but also in the present, as this is expressed in the iconographic depictions of the Mother of God with the Child in her arms. The bond of a mother with her child is generally speaking a sort of *common life*, although it is recognized only dimly. The bond of this common life is expressed in the unity of flesh, which despite becoming separate, is at the same time common. In no way is the bond interrupted or terminated by birth; rather, it extends throughout life. This inner, invisible power of motherhood, manifested in human birth, is, so to say, a natural icon or prototype of Divine Motherhood. Through the visitation of the Holy Spirit the flesh of the Most Holy Virgin acquired the supernatural capacity of conceiving without a man, becoming by this means the principle of humanity in the New Adam. The action of the Holy Spirit here exceeds the powers of human nature; it exceeds the natural powers of the Most Holy Virgin herself and in a certain sense forestalls her own particular path. Personally for her, Pentecost, which regenerates the spirit, ought to have preceded the Annunciation, which immediately exerts influence upon her body (this postulate about the baptism of the Mother of God before the Annunciation is in fact implemented in the Catholic dogma). In reality, however, this logical arrangement must be refuted without fail: the accomplished incarnation, which already presupposes Divine Motherhood, is indispensable for the spiritual regeneration of the whole human race, and at its head, of the Mother of God herself. In this way the Virgin Mary must have become by the power of the Holy Spirit the Mother of God *prior to* her own particular salvation from original sin, which was accomplished only at Pentecost. Thus the Annunciation precedes Pentecost, which in its turn presupposes it. If the Entrance into the Temple is when the Most Holy Virgin herself becomes a temple, then the Annunciation is the realization of this transformation. The Virgin Mary becomes "a consecrated Temple, her womb is more spacious than the heavens."

But the incarnation, which is also a divine condescension, occurs in time. The pre-eternal God is born as a Child and only by degrees develops into the measure of perfect stature, passes through His earthly ministry, and accepts death on the cross, the resurrection and ascension. To each of these thresholds corresponds its own step in the realization of the work of salvation. So too Divine Motherhood in the Mother of God develops and happens along with the accomplishment of our salvation, and the Virgin Mary, by whom the Son of God was incarnated through the Holy Spirit, becomes the Mother of God, the Queen of heaven and earth only beyond the limits of time, after Pentecost and the Dormition. Therefore one can say that as in a seed there is a plant, so in the Annunciation is laid beforehand "the head of our salvation and the manifestation of the Mysteries from the ages," Divine Motherhood and Divine Humanity.

But grace does not compel and always leaves a place for human effort and freedom. Although the Annunciation imparted to the Mother of God such spiritual powers as were uncharacteristic of any human being, it leaves for her the possibility of heroic effort. Along with the earthly ministry of the Saviour the Most Holy Virgin performs her own ministry, remaining in humility, shadow, and obscurity the whole time, but undoubtedly co-participating maternally in the sacrificial ministry and sufferings of her Son and maturing in these sufferings. The Church, through innumerable "Staurotheotokion"[2] prayers, expresses this notion about the participation of the Mother of God in the sufferings of the Son. And the little that the Gospels contain, when the curtain of silence about Mary is opened slightly, bears witness precisely to her trials, struggles, temptations and sufferings. They are relevant here: the incident at the Presentation of the Lord — the prophecy of Simeon, the confusion about the loss of the Child and His discovery in the temple among the elders, the desire to be seen with Him during His ministry, the hurried address to Him with the petition concerning the miracle in Cana of Galilee, and the station at the foot of the cross, by which were expressed the Golgotha torments of the Mother over her Son's death on the cross. (Among Catholics a special memorial "of the seven sorrows" of the Theotokos is celebrated.) There are not and cannot be any indications that the Mother of God surrendered to the power of sin and temptation, but almost all these indications bear witness to her sufferings and struggles. This was the sacrificial ministry of the Mother of God, Divine Motherhood in progress, in the fullness of which followed its *perfection*.

But in order to remove the last and only obstacle to this process, which consists in original sin, reception of baptism at Pentecost, liberation from original sin, birth in the New Adam, and being clothed in Christ were necessary even for her who bore Him. With Pentecost, the work of Divine Motherhood can be considered completed: the ladder from earth to heaven is restored, the goal of the world's creation is realized, for the complete, divinized human has appeared. The Mother of God, personally sinless and cleansed of original sin, was the expression of Ever-virginity in a creature, the full revelation of Sophia in a human being. She was not freed from the law of death, which has its force for all the descendants of the old Adam: in her humility, the Mother of God did not refuse to pass through the common human path of death, in order to sanctify it. But death no longer had any power over her. Be that as it may, a prolonged period of existence on earth had to run its course before her departure. This was the time of the Mother of God's ministry for the militant church, for which she was the affirmation and focus.

The significance of the Ever-Virgin's sojourn on earth for the fortunes of the Church is written down nowhere and is not related in any books. No histories of early Christianity made a note of it, and yet the sojourn of the Mother of God on earth is the real *mystery* of early Christianity, of its power, its joy (in particular in the writings of St John the Theologian, the most new-testamental of all New Testament authors, it is impossible not to see, following on Origen, the pneumatophoric quality connected with his special proximity to the Mother of God). The earthly church needed this earthly ministry, although it was already unnecessary and could add nothing to the fullness of Divine Motherhood. The Most Pure was the perfect vessel of the Holy Spirit, almost His personal incarnation. Not only was the fullness of His gifts revealed in her, but also His personal hypostasis shines in her most pure countenance. In order to comprehend fully what has been said, it will be necessary to linger over the significance of her Dormition.

Realized Divine Motherhood presupposes the glorification of the Mother of God, which is in fact her Dormition. But the first impression arising from this event is not glorification but a certain humiliation. Why was the Mother of God, the most holy of all creatures, condemned to taste death when even in the Old Testament Elijah and Enoch escaped this fate? Why did she, who was the living temple, the throne of heaven, prove to be guilty of the debt of death? One can introduce here a religious-practical motif involuntarily suggesting itself: by means of her death, the Most Holy Virgin, following in the steps of her Son, passed through the gates of death, which all humanity is doomed to pass through. She sanctified this path and did not wish to be separated from the whole human race, whose Mother she became when she adopted it at the foot of the cross in the person of John. And according to the teaching of the Church, the Mother of God meets the departing soul on this dread path, and to her are addressed its last pre-death prayers (cf. the Canon of Prayer to the Most Holy Theotokos at the departure of a soul). The Universal Mother is faithful and close to the human race even in the hour of death.

Together with this limitless *love* of the Mother of God towards people it is appropriate to recall here her limitless *humility* as well, to which she remained faithful until the end. "All glory to the Daughter of the King inside, clothed in humility" is said about her in a prophetic psalm (Ps. 45). Is it possible not to be astonished that the Mother of God in her very great humility (like her relative the Forerunner) did not perform miracles on earth, at least, in the confines of the gospel narrative, and only once asked her Son (and there even indirectly) to perform a miracle in Cana of Galilee (Jn 2.1ff)? And if her Son humbled himself to a freely-accepted death out of love for the human race, could His most pure Mother have been separated from Him in this? Why the Mother of God did not escape death by some sort of special extraordinary path receives here at least a partial answer.

But it is essential to establish the difference between the death of the Lord Jesus Christ and of His mother. The first death was *freely chosen,* but not natural. Therefore, as a death contrary to nature it could only be violent, and the Lord showed no opposition to this violence, in keeping with His self-abasement. The Godman, because of His seedless conception from the Holy Spirit and the Virgin Mary, was free from original sin, and hence the new Adam was not subject to death, at least not in a lesser degree than was the old Adam *before* the fall. If the new Adam freely accepted death reigning in the world after the transgression of old Adam, with the purpose of abolishing death, then this unnatural death's powerlessness over Him was exposed by His glorious resurrection. Death was able "to seize but not to confine" Him and it turned out to be only the particular condition of His divine-human life, which had the task of joining everyone in itself and holding sway over the living and the dead ("in the grave bodily, in Hades with a soul as God, in paradise with the criminal, and on the throne you were with the Father and the Spirit, fulfilling all things, uncircumscribable one"). As the Lord assumed not a mortal body burdened by sin but only *the likeness* of the flesh of sin, so also His death was not a true or usual human death but only *the likeness* of death. On the other hand, the Dormition of the Mother of God — and it is important to assimilate this dogmatically — was a true, real, death in conformity with natural law, to which she was subject as a human being; for this reason her end was not violent, but natural. Divine Providence purposely preserved her from the cruelty of the synagogue of the Judaizers, although it treated the Mother of the Lord with hatred, in order to reveal with particular clarity the entire naturalness of her end. According to ancient tradition, the latter is accompanied even with some confusion: The Mother of God asks that her spirit be accepted by her Son, and the demonic shapes clustering around the path of death were pushed aside by Him. The obvious practical refutation of the Catholic dogma of the Immaculate Conception of Mary, in the sense of her removal from original sin, follows from this. If this is how it was, then the restoration of the *donum superadditum* to the Virgin Mary in the same measure as Adam possessed it before the fall, i.e., liberation from original sin, would unavoidably have to mean liberation from the power of death as well. The latter entered into the composition of *donum superadditum,* presenting in this sense a type of violence against human nature, created mortal by nature. The Dormition of the Mother of God is the obvious proof of the falsity of this whole theological construction.

True, Catholic theologians can object that immortality was still a particular, special gift, connected with the eating of the fruits from the tree of life, which was no longer accessible to the Most Holy Virgin because of its absence from the world. Such apologetics would seem to be theologically insincere, because the direct and positive link of death with sin is established with perfect clarity in both the Old and the New Testaments: the judgment of God upon the primogenitors in paradise and the word of the Apostle Paul in Rom 5. And eating from the tree of life, which Christ is, according to the explanation of some fathers, surely would not be compensated for by having God in the womb, would it? But the most holy Virgin tasted death as one subject to original sin and owing to the law of that sin. She therefore did not overcome death by her personal power; death was defeated for her by the power of Christ. Having fallen asleep the Mother of God was awakened from her Dormition by her Son. She was resurrected by Him and was, in this manner, the first fruits of the resurrection of the whole creation. But this resurrection only confirms the power and authenticity of death.

Catholics, beginning already with the Vatican Council, as far as is known, have the draft of a dogma concerning the resurrection and ascension of the Mother of God. It is hard to understand what stirs up this need to formulate dogmas concerning the Mother of God whose humility makes her more readily the object of quiet, particularly intimate and chaste respect (except, perhaps, the necessity to realize Vatican infallibility). But if it is necessary for some reason to name this mystery with its own name, one must unreservedly recognize that for Orthodox consciousness there is absolutely nothing new in this projected dogma in its substance besides its possible formulation, to which, one must imagine, will be added the usual portion of Latin theology. In fact Orthodoxy contains the doctrine of the resurrection, ascension into heaven and heavenly glorification of the Mother of God (that which corresponds to the motif of *le couronnement de la vierge* in Catholic iconography, which by the way is not foreign to Orthodoxy). All of this represents the content of the feast of the Dormition, in as much as its essence is disclosed in its liturgical interpretation, as it is established through iconography and liturgy, which in the given case are the sole church sources for theologizing about this subject.

Information about the celebration of the Dormition of the Mother of God arises only towards the fourth century and we know that earlier there are no traces in church tradition. It is the same with regard to the tradition itself concerning the events of the Dormition, which are preserved in an account of Ps. Melito of Sardis from the end of the fourth century clearly embellished with legend, "on the end of the Mother of God."[3] By the way, the legendary quality of the *style* of this account is in no way an objection against its *truthfulness* and so to say its religious realism. For historical naturalism, toward which "religious-historical" investigation strives, is completely out of place where events occur that happen simultaneously in all worlds and even beyond the limits of the world: here the language of legend alone is appropriate, which is entirely like the symbolism of iconography likewise distancing itself from naturalism.

In any case the absence of information about the honouring of the Dormition of the Mother of God corresponds to the general absence of direct indications about her veneration in the first centuries of Christianity, vested with the shroud of pious silence. For unbelief and rationalism this seems sufficient grounds to reject this veneration. But for reverential comprehension and faith it is clear that here we are dealing with a particular mysterious dispensation of Providence, which presented the veneration of the Most Holy Virgin *to free* inspiration, not to one bound by "history," to faith and love. The remarkable feature in this matter is that the veneration of the Mother of God appears with such axiomatic self-evidence, and takes root with such invincible force in the Christian heart to the extent of its ecclesialization; at the same time, with its increase, with the degree of veneration is determined the measure of ecclesiality.

The Gospels tell us about the Saviour, His image stands before our eyes, sculpted by the fourfold gospel narrative and apostolic witness. The image of the Mother of God, nowhere imprinted except for some disconnected features, enters the heart by itself, somehow being reconstructed in it as if out of its own cloth — in conformity with the fact that the Mother of God belongs to the human race and that in this sense the whole Christian church is the Mother of God. Therefore this same veneration of the Mother of God is connected with the church and it is born in individual souls as a later fruit than love and veneration for Christ the Saviour: love for the Son teaches love for the Mother, and not the other way around. If we ponder all this rhythm and harmony, which are inherent in the revelation about the Mother of God, that lack of earlier information about her and generally speaking the thick shadow concealing her become natural and cease to confuse.

According to church tradition, which finds full confirmation in the liturgy and iconography, when the Ever-Virgin passed away, she handed her spirit over to her Son who had appeared in order to receive it in glory with all the holy angels. This is as it were the anticipation of the second glorious coming, which nevertheless is not the Dread Judgment, for she who is presented does not come for judgment, but has passed from death to life. However, this is death as separation of the soul from the body which spends three days in the grave incorrupt. It differs from the Saviour's three-day Sabbath rest in the grave, which was *an active* condition beyond the grave, a preaching in Hades, a necessary part of the Saviour's effort. In her case death is the human *lot,* which is impossible to escape in order to be liberated from the body of death and clothed in the body of resurrection. After the three days had run their course the Mother of God was resurrected with her body and with it taken out of the world, to the marvel of the angels: "the angels saw the Dormition of the Most Pure and marvelled at how the Virgin ascends from earth into heaven" (antiphon for the feast).[4]

Here is established first of all the ascension into heaven of the resurrected Mother of God, not by the Godhead's own power, like the Ascension of the Saviour, but by Divine power. This retreat from earth does not signify a complete removal from it with the termination of every link to it; on the contrary, as is sung in the troparion of the feast, "in your Dormition you did not leave the world, Theotokos," but still she did indeed leave the world, for she was raised up from the world into heaven. In her and with her the world itself has already tasted or foretasted that odour of resurrection by the reception of which it ceases to be "the world" in the sense of defection from God and enmity towards God and becomes anew the world-cosmos, "the good thing," "the new heaven and new earth where truth lives." The Mother of God in her resurrected and glorified body is already the completed glory of the world and its resurrection. With the resurrection and ascension of the Mother of God the world is completed in its creation, *the goal of the world is attained,* "wisdom is justified in her children," for the Mother of God is already that glorified world which is divinized and open for the reception of Divinity. Mary is the heart of the world and the spiritual focus of all humanity, of every creature. She is already the perfectly and absolutely divinized creature, the one who begets God, who bears God and receives God. She, a human and a creature, sits in the heavens with her Son, who is seated at the right hand of the Father. She is the Queen of Heaven and Earth, or, more briefly, the Heavenly Queen.

The glorification of the Mother of God, her elevation from creatureliness, as if already into a super-creaturely condition of perfect divinization, into the dignity of Heavenly Queen, corresponds to some particular moment or event, almost completely invisible for the creaturely sinful eye, that also belongs to her Dormition, although it already lies beyond the limits of earthly life and of this very world itself. This is namely what is symbolically depicted in iconography as the imposition of a corona, the crowning with the royal crown of the Mother of God, a motif equally present in Orthodoxy and Catholicism. *Verbally* it is expressed in the naming of the Mother of God "Heavenly Queen," which is, of course, not only a verbal embellishment, but expresses in itself a certain reality, a spiritual essence. In the days of her earthly humility and abasement, there is no doubt, the Most Pure was not named Queen, although she is pre-eternally elected to this and after the Annunciation she became as much in the pre-conception.[5] She became Queen after her Dormition, which was in this sense a certain limit. What is this limit and what does it consist in? Here an analogy with her Son suggests itself first of all, who only after His resurrection bears witness about Himself to the apostles, *all authority in heaven and on earth is given to me,* as if earlier, at least in His humanity, He did not have yet that fullness of authority which is given to Him in the glorification of His body. The Lord in His perfect Humanity receives even for this humanity the glory won by Him through perfect obedience to the Father's will. Jn 17.4-5, "I have glorified you on earth; I have completed the work which you entrusted to Me to fulfil. And now glorify me, Father, with the glory you have yourself, which I had near you before the existence of the world." The Lord pre-eternally possesses this Glory in His Divinity and receives it from the Father in His humanity, so that in His person, the person of the perfect Godman, in which the divine and human nature were joined indivisibly and unmingled, Creator and creature, glory and power and might rested on His creaturely human nature. The Lord has the glory which He receives from the Father; this is His proper glory, the glory belonging to Him from all ages, radiating in His most pure flesh, the glory of Transfiguration. He is therefore God in both His natures (owing to what is called *perichoresis* by John Damascene, *communicatio idiomatum*).

On the contrary, in her glorification the Mother of God receives through the Son from the Father the glory and power which *are not* inherently hers according to human nature. This is *divinization* in the precise sense, a canopy of divine graced life unfurling over that being in which it is not inherent and which it transcends. Because of this the whole difference between the Son and the Mother, between His and her power and glory, remains. The first is boundless and unlimited, absolute, as the power of God in creation. The second is derivative, a graced givenness, and in virtue of this derivativeness it is not unlimited, not absolute. In other words, the Lord is God by nature, the Mother of God *is not God by nature,* but only by grace, no matter how full and complete her divinization is. In her person is fulfilled only what is foreordained for all humans: "I said, you are gods" (Ps 82.6; cf. Jn 10.34-35). Hence the well-known *antinomialness* in determining the measure of the Mother of God's power, as this is done in prayers addressed to the Mother of God. On the one hand she is magnified as "the heavenly all-sovereign queen," "all the elements, heaven and earth, air and sea obey you, and all the contrary spirits tremble seized by dread, fearing your holy name," "for you can do what ever you want";[6] to her Christians cry out with the same address as they do to the Saviour: "most holy Theotokos, *save* us" (whereas to all the saints we appeal "pray God for us"). But at the same time it is indicated perfectly clearly that this power of the Mother of God is derivative, conditioned by her "holy and almighty prayers," with which she "unceasingly" "prays to Christ our God for all, and works for all to be saved." And in this capacity, the Mother of God is only *the first* in a series of holy intercessors, as this is fixed, for example, in all prayers of dismissal: "Christ, our true God, by the prayers of Your Most Pure Mother," etc.

A similar place for the Mother of God is set aside in the order of the Proskomedia. She is the *petitioner* on behalf of the human race and *the mediator* between God and human beings as a glorified and divinized human. If the Lord is the petitioner and high priest in His capacity as the one offering Himself in sacrifice, she is the petitioner before Him and, in keeping with the vision of St Andrew the Fool, wears in that capacity the episcopal omophorion[7] as an intercessor before the Son, as the humanity of His divine humanity. He *joins* in Himself two natures, but she raises up in herself, *elevates* to God humanity and all creatures. As a creature, she does not participate in the divine life of the Most Holy Trinity according to nature, as does her Son; she only partakes of it by the grace of divinization. But this grace is given to her already in a maximum and definitive degree, so that by its power she is the Heavenly Queen. Between her and all the saints, no matter how exalted, angels or men, there remains an impenetrable border, for to none of them does the Church cry out *save* us, but only *pray to God* for us. With respect to the whole human race she is already found *on the other side* of resurrection and last judgement; neither the one nor the other has any force for her. She only attends the Last Judgment at the right hand of her Son, again as that unfailing *intercessor* just as St Andrew saw her in Blachernae[8] "praying for us in the air." She is the already glorified creation before its general resurrection and glorification; she is the already accomplished Kingdom of Glory, while the world still remains "in the kingdom of grace."

For this reason it is necessary to recognise the important, principal difference between the present-day state of the glorified saints beyond the grave who gaze on the face of God, and the glory of the Mother of God, for the saints are not yet found in the kingdom of glory. They pass through a certain graced increase from strength to strength, or a still ongoing sanctification. In this sense, although they have been liberated from the evil power of the sinful world, they remain in this world and are not above the world, not higher than the world, not in the heavens, as is the Mother of God. The resurrection and joining with the body still *stands ahead of* them; although their body abides as a holy "relic" and does not finally lose its link with their soul, it remains separated from the soul until the time of the universal resurrection. Of course, the world of the saints is permeable from above, it is accessible for the Mother of God, who therefore appears to her chosen ones accompanied by the apostles and saints. But all the same, the distance between heaven and earth remains in force. The Mother of God dwells in the heavens as the Heavenly Queen; the saints, although they stand before the throne of the Almighty, do not enter the intellectual heaven, which is more exalted than every creation. They experience eternal life by gazing on the Lord's face, but they keep their bond with the life of the world too, which the Heavenly Queen has surpassed. For this reason, she no longer increases from glory to glory, she does not ascend from strength to strength, for there is nowhere and nothing more to grow into or ascend to. She participates, though by grace, in the life of the Divinity itself, in the Most Holy Trinity of the true God. "Behold, people, and marvel: for the mountain holy to God and manifest is taken up into the heavenly habitations on high, the earthly heaven comes to reside in the heavenly and imperishable dwelling place."[9] This difference is expressed externally too in that the saints always have their sacred relics, no matter if they are revealed or buried and unknown to the world. They have in the world their consecrated body enveloped by their spirit, the body which is now the place of their graced presence in the world and of their link with it, and at the same time, is the seed of the future body of resurrection. The sacred relics are the pledge of the body of resurrection in this world, but only the pledge, since they belong precisely to this world. The Dormition of the Mother of God is evidence that as applied to her there can be no thought about relics. Even the very idea appears abusive and blasphemous, similar to how the same thought about the Saviour's relics would also appear. The Most Pure body of the Lord was in a state *similar to* sacred relics,[10] for three days in the grave, until the resurrection. After this, the Lord remained in His glorified body in this world, prefiguring with it the future bodies of resurrected humanity. After the Ascension, He raised His Most Pure flesh from this world, bestowing it only in the mysteries of the body and blood. But the resurrected body of the Mother of God was also taken from this world up into heaven; it is not in this world, which cannot accommodate its sanctity. The Heavenly Queen with her body is in the heavens, together with her Son, who is seated at the right hand of the Father.

The Supra-worldliness of the Mother of God is expressed not only by her removal from the earthly and human world, but also by her being "more honourable than the cherubim and more glorious without comparison (i.e. essentially, principally) than the seraphim." This praise of the Mother of God extolling her above the whole angelic world, not in degree alone but in essence, not quantitatively but qualitatively, yields only with difficulty to the concept or view that the life of the angelic world is inaccessible to us. Angels have no bodies, consequently there can be no question about a distinction, connected with a relation to a body. The angels who were steadfast and who cast Satan down from heaven (Rev 12.7-9) were definitively established on the path of good, and for them there exists no distinction between the kingdom of nature and grace, of grace and glory, which does exist for humans. They do not know death or resurrection, there is no Last Judgment for them or a second glorious coming, for their lot is already finally decided (the Last Judgment exists only for the spirits of evil, the devil and his angels who did not stand in their vocation). Regarding them, it is impossible to say that they are found *on the other side* of the world's transfiguration and universal resurrection, for even without this they are found on the other side of the world, generally speaking. Nevertheless, the ministry of angels is somehow connected with the destinies of the world, and in some sense its perfection and transfiguration has significance for the angelic world as well. The Last Judgment upon humankind, the head of this world, will be some sort of judgment on the angels too, about which the apostle Paul spoke the mysterious words, "do you not know that we will judge the angels?" (1 Cor 6.3). We know nothing about the judgment of the angels, but the judgment of the demons is already completed in heaven and will be fulfilled definitively along with the Last Judgment of the whole world, when the authority "of the prince of this world" is completely abolished.

The loftiness of the angels and their proximity to God, like "second lights standing before the first light," of course exceed that of human beings, but this does not change the ontological difference of their natures and does not remove the superiority of human beings over them. Only to humankind does *the plenitude* of creation belong, even in comparison with the angels. Humanity is the centre of the world and king of the world, the microcosm. This cannot be said of the angels who are only God's servants in this world. Here they occupy an intermediate place between the world and God, having in themselves the force of hypostatic being but not the force of cosmic being, which they serve. In this sense, in accordance with the explanation of St Gregory Palamas, to have a body constitutes the ontological advantage of a human being, connecting him with the whole world, although precisely this limits him in his present condition. The incorporeality of the angels is not so much an advantage as a *property,* inherent in the angelic world. It is impossible to imagine, following Origen, the Neoplatonists and contemporary theosophists and reincarnationists, that our natural, "material" or embodied world appeared as the result of some fall of originally incorporeal spirits equal to the angels, for a time imprisoned in earthly bodies for the sake of correction. On the contrary, the world with humankind was created by God at the end, i.e., in the fullness of creation. It already supposes the angelic world as "servants" of creation.[11] That which is later in time takes precedence with respect to fullness: humankind, created after the angelic world, thanks to predestination stands higher than it. The divine incarnation, which was precisely the hominization of the Logos, provides the most obvious evidence that it is so. He did not assume an angelic nature, although it might seem to be even more natural to assume the nature of the incorporeal. And the Virgin Mary, in whose person human nature was raised up to contain God, to divine motherhood, is in the same way — in her glorification — more glorious *without comparison* than the seraphim, i.e., essentially, hierarchically, she is more exalted than they. "Because the Word, who with the Father and the Spirit is without beginning, was conceived through the archangelic voice in your womb, O Theotokos, you were higher than the cherubim, seraphim and thrones" (Service for archangels and angels, sticheron for the "Lord, I have cried").

Thus, in the Dormition of the Mother of God we praise the glorification of human nature. The latter, having been resurrected, divinized and raised to the right hand of the Father, as the flesh of the Son, now is being glorified in itself, as such, in the person of His Most Pure Mother. The ladder which Jacob saw is realized in all its fullness, for heaven and earth have been reunited and made one.

The Mother of God is the Glory of the world, a world glorified in God and with God, having in itself and giving birth to God. One needs to understand this in all its ontological meaningfulness, to be fully theologically aware of the dogmatic sense of the veneration of the one more honourable than the cherubim and more glorious beyond compare than the seraphim. In the glory of the Mother of God the glory of creation has been revealed. The Mother of God is the personal manifestation of Divine Wisdom, Sophia,[12] which in *another* sense is Christ, the power of God and the wisdom of God. In this way there are two personal images of Sophia: the creaturely and the divine humanly, and two human images in the heavens: the Godman and the Mother of God. This must be understood in connection with the doctrine of the Most Holy Trinity, of God and the world. The Divine image in humankind is disclosed and realized in the heavens as the image of two: of Christ and of His Mother. The Son of God contains in himself the whole fullness of Divinity proper to the whole Most Holy Trinity, one in essence and undivided. And as the New Adam, having been incarnated and made human, the Son of God is the preeternal Human, who imaged himself in Adam. Only on the basis of this ontological affinity with the image and prototype are the incarnation and the hominization of the Second Hypostasis possible. The human image as the Divine image and the Divine image as the human image are glorified in both the first and second Adam. And yet in the heavens there is still one human image which obviously also pertains to the fullness of the human prototype, namely, the Mother of God, "the second Eve." The first Eve had been created out of the rib of the first Adam. Her origin proved possible only in connection with him, as his necessary disclosure and complement; the Divine image in humankind was realized in fullness only in the two of them (Gen 1.27, "And God created humankind after His image, after the Divine image he created him, man and woman he created them"). Both the first Adam and the first Eve are wholly the creation of God although a hierarchy of genesis is established between them: "Adam is of God," Eve is from Adam. The Second Adam is very Lord, who assumed flesh, i.e., His own creature; the second Eve is a creature, a human being belonging to the creaturely world. In this sense she originates from the Second Adam, i.e., from God, although she gives Him human flesh.

Further, Christ is the human image of the Second Hypostasis, the Logos. A human image of the First Hypostasis does not exist, for God the Father is revealed in the Son generated by Him; only in Him and through His instrumentality does He appear to the world and is He shown to humans. But in His hypostatic being the Father is transcendent. (This is why there was and can be a dispute about whether it is correct to depict the Father in human form in icons of the Most Holy Trinity, even in the form of the Ancient of Days. It is in itself clear that a proper icon of God the Father outside the Most Holy Trinity, i.e., outside the relationship to the incarnate Son, is completely impossible.)

The Father reveals Himself not only in the begotten Son, but also in the Holy Spirit proceeding from Him, acting in the world from its very beginning. He hovered over the abyss, in the Old Testament "he spoke through the prophets," anointed kings and in general hallowed the members of the Old Testament Church. Further He descended on the holy apostles and every creature in the New Testament. Does a human image belong to the Holy Spirit? Does He have for Himself a personal incarnation? The Holy Spirit is revealed to creation only through action, His gifts. His depiction is clearly symbolic, and does not disclose His Hypostasis: "in the guise of a dove" or "in the vision of fiery tongues," or in the form of one of the angels in the appearance to Abraham, though it is not known which one. A personal incarnation, a hominization of the Third Hypostasis, does not exist. Still, if there is no personal incarnation of the Third Hypostasis, no hominization in the same sense in which the Son of God became human, there can all the same be such a human, creaturely hypostasis, such a being which is the vessel of the fulfilment of the Holy Spirit. It completely surrenders its human hypostatic life, makes it transparent for the Holy Spirit, by bearing witness about itself: *behold the handmaid of the Lord.* Such a being, the Most Holy Virgin, is not a personal incarnation of the Holy Spirit, but she becomes His personal, animate receptacle, an absolutely spirit-born creature, the Pneumatophoric Human. For, if there is no hypostatic spirit-incarnation, there can be a hypostatic pneumatophoricity, by which the creaturely hypostasis in its creatureliness completely surrenders itself and as it were dissolves in the Holy Spirit. In this complete penetration by Him it becomes a different nature for its own self, i.e., *divinized,* a creature thoroughly blessed by grace, "a quickened ark of God," a living "consecrated temple." Such a pneumatophoric person radically differs from the Godman, for it is a creature, but it differs just as much from a creature in its creatureliness, for it has been elevated and made a partaker of divine life. In this pneumatophoricity God's image in the human is likewise realized.[13] Hence it is incumbent on us to consider that the human essence of the Mother of God in heaven together with the Godman Jesus displays the full image of humankind. *The Icon of the Mother of God with Child,* the Logos and the creature receiving Him, filled with the Holy Spirit, in unity and its indivisibility, is *the full image* of humankind. The Godman and the Pneumatophore, the Son and the Mother, displaying the revelation of the Father through the Second and Third Hypostases, also display the fullness of the Divine image in humankind or, to put it another way, of the human image in God.

In the Divine image in humankind, as it is said in Gen 1.27, are joined the male and female principle,[14] Adam and Eve. The male and the female in and of themselves, outside the fall, are in no way already *sex,* although afterwards they provide the foundations for the two sexual modes of human nature. Originally they are *spiritual* principles, some sort of spiritual qualifications. In as much as the male principle is determined by the primacy of reason and will over sense, as the power of immediate experience, so the primacy of feeling, of experience over reason and will is manifested in the female principle. The male is truth in beauty, the female is beauty in truth: truth and beauty are indivisible and of one essence, but at the same time they are differentiated as two images of the one principle, the revelation of the one Father, who begets the Son and issues the Holy Spirit. Both these images belong to the fullness of the Divine image in humankind. In the Holy Trinity the Father begets the Son and issues the Holy Spirit; He reveals Himself in a single and eternal act of hypostatic triunity. In monohypostatic humankind this dual image is disclosed as a dyunity, as two possibilities, two images of the human essence, neither one of which expresses it separately in fullness. Humankind is not only a male or only a female principle, but contains in itself the one and the other, and besides *not as sex,* i.e., half-and-half, non-fullness, but precisely as *the fullness* of its own existence.[15]

Hence the Lord Jesus Christ, perfect God and perfect human, truly became human and assumed all human nature; in *the image* of His humanity He is joined inseparably with His Most Pure Mother and is *Son* not only thanks to His Divinity, as the Only-Begotten of the Father, but also thanks to His humanity as Son of the Mother, born of her by the Holy Spirit. In this manner *in His human nature* His male principle is joined inseparably with the female principle of the Mother of God, and the fullness of the Divine image in humankind, or to put it another way, of the human image in God, is expressed through these two, through "the new Adam" and "the new Eve." As God, Christ assumed all the fullness of human nature in order to save it and resurrect it. In this sense the apostle Paul says, "there is neither male nor female, for you all are one in Christ Jesus" (Galatians 3.28). But He expresses the fullness *of the image* of human nature only together with the Mother of God, who thus has found her place in the heavens beside the glorified human nature of her Son, so that not only the male but also the female nature is glorified and divinized (though *in a different way*). Here there can be no chance, no caprice; there can be only a single strict, unwavering ontology. One must reverently press close against the mysterious meaning of the Dormition of the Mother of God and her heavenly glorification precisely as *Mother of God,* mother of the Godman and to that extent inseparable from Him. One ought to understand this unity not as an accident or a temporary condition, but as a revelation and realization of the fullness of the human image in the Godman and His Mother, which is given in any icon of the Mother of God.

The male principle in humankind is found in correlation with the Logos who is born as "a child of the male sex" (Lk 2.23), "a first-born son" (Mt 1.25; Lk 2.5). The female principle stands in correlation with the Holy Spirit, who descends upon the Mother of God. Motherhood proper to the female principle of Eve, "as the mother of all the living" (Gen 3.20), is united here with the visitation of the Holy Spirit. If it is said in the creed that the Son of God took flesh by the Holy Spirit and the Virgin Mary, this in no way signifies a fatherhood of the Holy Spirit with respect to the Godman. The Holy Spirit is never called father of Jesus in ecclesiastical literature — this thought would be a heretical profanity,[16] for the Son has only one heavenly Father (just like the first "Adam who is of God" Lk 3.38). The Holy Spirit through His overshadowing of the Virgin Mary creates her motherhood, the possession of the Infant in the womb.[17] The Father eternally generates the Son and the Son is begotten from the Father — the mystery of *fatherhood* and *sonship.* But the Father, in proceeding towards the begotten Son, issues the Holy Spirit, Who is the hypostatic love of the Father towards the Son and of the Son towards the Father. The Holy Spirit is not begotten and does not beget, but He finds the already begotten Son and joins Him anew, hypostatically, with the Father, and is the living hypostatic bond of the Father and the Son. In the same way as the *third* Hypostasis, as the hypostatic Love of the Two among themselves,

He closes the tri-hypostatic essence. This special place of the Holy Spirit as the *Third* hypostasis already having before Himself the Father and the Son, is determined by the correlation of all three hypostases.

In ecclesiastical literature (in the disputes about the *filioque*) principally from the Catholic side, the opinion has sometimes been expressed that if the Holy Spirit only proceeds from the Father and not *filioque* then He is the brother of the Son (others go even further and say sister), and in this way it comes out that the Son has a brother or a sister. But one must completely dismiss such considerations, for sonship is established only *by the generation* of the Only-Begotten Son. Although comprehension of the mystery of generation and procession is for the human inaccessible, still, as St Gregory the Theologian said, what does remain accessible to us is that they are not one and the same. The sole positive indication which is given to us about the nature of these relations is not based on human conjectures. It is given in the Virgin Mary, who becomes the Mother by virtue of receiving the Holy Spirit.

What is particular to motherhood that distinguishes it from fatherhood? We now know motherhood only through the prism of sex, i.e., we do not really know it according to essence. For us generation is entirely a function of sex, presupposing the joining of male and female, and through this there is a certain abolition of fatherhood and motherhood in their particularities. Fatherhood, *as generation,* is in general unknown to fallen humankind. It knows only the sexual act, a certain ecstasy of the flesh in which is contained only the *possibility* of conception, and besides not as the goal but only as the result, the unintended and in the majority of cases even unwanted or unexpected result. Spiritual fatherhood, as the revelation of the self in the other, and sonship, as the revelation in the self of the other — spiritual generation in the proper sense, is for fallen humankind unknown. And however paradoxically, the spiritual nature of generation shows through more clearly not in physical fatherhood, accomplished so to say through the head of humankind, but rather in spiritual fatherhood. For example, the apostle Paul begets in torments spiritual offspring (Gal 4.19) and preserves a bond with those begotten. Hence spiritual bonds, relations of spiritual kinship, frequently are more concrete, closer, more tangible, and what is most important, more human, than fleshly bonds in which the self-love of blood often is entangled.

Motherhood as a having in the womb, however, as pregnancy, is given much more immediately in the experience of fallen humankind, namely, in the female experience, although it too is darkened in it by pains, according to God's sentence upon Eve: "I will greatly increase your torment in your pregnancy and in pain you shall bear children" (Gen 3.16). Motherhood is a having in the womb prior to birth, by which the immediate bond between mother and what is born from her is later created. This immediate bond does not exist in fatherhood, for it is not established through conception alone: the father can even not know his child, which is not possible for the mother. The bond with the father has a mystical basis in the indistinct voice of blood, as a certain sociological fact, which can be quite absent, and in thousands of cases among both civilized and uncivilized peoples, it is virtually absent. On the contrary, for motherhood this bond is not eliminated and can be only weakened or paralysed by the influence of sociological and psychological factors. Motherhood is *the tangibleness of what is being begotten or already born* and the joy over this begottenness. The mother as such does not conceive, she contains in herself the already begotten, but she has it in herself as her own, her own and at the same time not her own, herself and the other. Generally speaking fatherhood is the immediate discovery of the self in the other, the revelation of the self through the other, of the Father in the Son ("no one knows the Son except the Father, and no one knows the Father except the Son," Mt 11.27). In motherhood this immediacy is mediated; for the mother the already given, the already engendered, is made *her own*, is borne in the womb.

The Father in His fatherhood generates the Son, and the Father issues the Holy Spirit, not owing to fatherhood, *but in connection with* fatherhood. The Father, namely as Father of the Son, the Second Hypostasis, is the issuer, *proboleus* of the Holy Spirit, the Third Hypostasis, which already supposes (of course not chronologically but ontologically) a First and Second Hypostasis. The Holy Spirit who proceeds from the Father towards the Son, finds the already generated Son, but by Himself He realizes Him for the Father. In this sense He is, as it were, hypostatic motherhood, proceeding from the Father towards the Son, "life-creation," as the intentional property of the Holy Spirit.[18]

The Father is the first principle, the first cause, from which is sonship, but later inseparably linked with it as with begottenness is motherhood. At the same time the features of the Divine image inscribed in humankind appear as the dyunity of male and female. The First Cause, the Father, Himself abides *outside* this dyunity, remaining transcendent to it. He in Himself grounds it as the First Principle, but is revealed, as Father and as Issuer, in both principles. The Son is the male principle, and this indisputably comes to light in His incarnation as a child of the male sex. The Holy Spirit is revealed by His visiting the Most Holy Virgin, in divine motherhood. The Mother of God bears a Son, who is pre-eternally begotten by the Father. This Son does not have an earthly father, only a Father who is in the heavens: "even before Abraham was, I am" (John 8.58). Hence in divine motherhood we have the exact image of true motherhood: the mother herself does not beget, she possesses in the womb the one already begotten before all the ages, for in truth only the Father begets. But she bears in the womb, shows the one begotten, creates life. On the divine-spiritual side of her motherhood, in relation to the Logos, she is the receptacle of the Holy Spirit; on the human side she herself gives to the Son what she has and what she can give: human flesh, which henceforth is single, common, and at the same time separate in her and the Son, in the human and God. This is what the text of the creed means: "was incarnate by the Holy Spirit and the Virgin Mary and became human." It does not mean that the Holy Spirit by His own power compensates for the absence of a physical father, but that He gave power to Mary the human being to be the true Mother of God, Theotokos, and not only Christotokos, according to the vain wisdom of Nestorius.

The heretical temptation of Nestorius consisted namely in this, that he was confused by the mystery of divine motherhood in general and in Mary in particular.[19] This temptation lies in that externally mechanical understanding of divine-begetting which was rejected and condemned in its Nestorian deductions by the Council of Ephesus, but continues to be upheld in its premises. In accordance with this understanding, which is essentially Nestorian even though it has a superficially orthodox aspect, the power and operation of the Holy Spirit lie precisely in a begetting without a male and a conceiving without seed; only the physical side of the miracle, so to say, attracts attention, unisexual or extra-sexual generation, virginal conception. The act is imagined in this way: flesh is formed in Mary's womb by the power of the Holy Spirit, and in that flesh the Logos dwelled as the soul. But this understanding represents the same heresy of Nestorius, only in another exposition. That which Nestorius attributes by comparison to the later (though generally undefined moment) here applies to generation itself: the body is assumed by the Logos as an external garment.[20] The Church, in condemning the doctrine of the "Christotokos" in Nestorianism, condemned it in *every one* of its forms, and one must accept and make one's own the dogma of the Theotokos in all its significance. The generation of a human being is his *full* generation, inseparably, with both body and soul, together and once only. However one understands as proximate means the mode of the soul's origination (i.e., in the spirit either of creationism or of traducianism), undoubtedly the soul in some way is co-generated with the body, and is not clothed with it, post factum. Therefore this is how parents are in actual fact, their role is not limited to the preparation of a body, and the generative power is implanted in them by the word of God: "be fruitful and multiply." Likewise, the begetting of the Divine Infant was in some sense a full, authentic God-begetting (which is precisely what Nestorius tripped up on), and for this reason *holy Church unceasingly confesses the Virgin Mary truly to be the Theotokos.* Mary is not the Mother of the Lord only according to the flesh, but also with respect to His soul. This "renowned and most glorious mystery," this inexpressible miracle, of course, is incomprehensible for both humans and angels in its *realization,* as indeed are all events of the economy of our salvation: the resurrection, the ascension and the second coming. But their dogmatic foundations we confess firmly and without question and must therefore accurately make them known.

How in actual fact can Mary, a human being, become and be called Theotokos, inquires Nestorius. But obviously as a human being she could not become Theotokos, but at the very most only Christotokos, i.e., Mother not of the Divine Infant the Logos but only His corporeal garment; as Nestorius correctly pointed out, like can beget only like. In addition to this she did not become even for an instant the Godman, such as only the Lord Jesus Christ is. How generally speaking did it prove *possible* for the Virgin to be Theotokos, while at the same time remaining a human being? The clear answer to this is given in the angel's words, "the Holy Spirit will come upon You and the power of the Most High will overshadow You; for this reason the Holy One being born shall be called Son of God" (Lk 1.35). "The Holy One being born" "shall be called" (i.e., will be) the Son of God because the Holy Spirit will come upon Mary and with Him, in Him and through Him the power of the Most High will overshadow her. According to the opinion of the exegetes (e.g. John of Damascus), by "the power of the Most High" one can understand directly the one born, the Second Hypostasis, the Logos, inseparably co-inhering with the Holy Spirit, the Third Hypostasis. But even if one does not resort to this somewhat more wide-ranging interpretation and understands the phrase "by the power of the Most High" simply as the gifts and action of the Holy Spirit, the meaning is not altered. Mary becomes the Theotokos precisely as a result of her overshadowing by the Holy Spirit (in icons of the Annunciation this interpretation is emphasized by the fact that the descending Holy Spirit is depicted in the guise of a dove as at Epiphany when he descends upon the Lord). It was not possible that this overshadowing, appropriate to the task, was not full and complete. Mary did not and could not become from this *the hypostatic* Godman, because she was already a human being, possessing a creaturely human hypostasis, and she could not lose it, but also because hominization is proper only to the Second and not the Third Hypostasis.

The influence of the Holy Spirit on humankind and the world is *different;* in no way is it the hypostatic hominization of the Logos. It consists in *divinization,* in the communication of divine life to the creature. This divinization occurs to the extent of the creature's ability to accommodate it. In the Virgin Mary a special, singular and exclusive instance of the relationship of the Holy Spirit with a creature, was manifested, namely, His dwelling in her as in His temple, as in a body. At the Annunciation Mary became the Pneumatophore. The Holy Spirit dwelled in her in that sense which is proper to Him, distinct from the hypostatic hominization of the Logos, the Second Hypostasis. The indwelling of the Holy Spirit in the human does not consist in *the replacement* of the human hypostasis by His Hypostasis, as occurred in Christ where the one divine hypostasis reunited two natures, divine and human. It manifests itself when the human hypostasis chosen from all generations becomes transparent for the Holy Spirit. By remaining a creaturely, human hypostasis in and of itself, it acquires a dyadic life, human and divine, i.e., it is completely divinized, which is why in its own hypostatic being it is the living creaturely revelation of the Holy Spirit. Although not itself the hypostasis of the Holy Spirit, this pneumatophoric hypostasis is His hypostatic revelation in the measure and in the sense possible for the Third Hypostasis. In the divine incarnation of the Logos the single *divine* hypostasis reunites two natures, divine and human, and has in them the dyadic life of the Godman, a "complex" (according to the expression of St John of Damascus) nature. In the Holy Spirit's visiting of the Mother of God a single *all-human* hypostasis has the dyadic life of divinized, pneumatophoric human nature in which the elements of human nature are illuminated by divine grace. A difference of natures appropriate to the difference of hypostases is established. For the divine hypostasis of the Logos divine nature is His proper nature, and the human nature is appropriated and assumed by Him from Mary "for our sake and on account of our salvation"; for the human hypostasis of Mary her proper nature is human nature, and divine life is communicated to her by the grace of divinization, in keeping with the visitation of the Holy Spirit. Therefore in no manner can the Mother of God be venerated as the Godman. But her pneumatophoricity, which makes her an animate temple of God and the Mother of God, elevates her higher than human nature and higher even than any creaturely nature.

Mary the pneumatophoric[21] human is more exalted than any creature and thus "every creature, the angelic choir and the human race, rejoices" on account of the Graced One. This is the Pneumatophore: though human by nature she is already higher than humankind. Although she is not the Godman, who is only One, Jesus, yet with respect to the Godman she stands in the necessary, essential and indissoluble relation of motherhood, precisely in that relation which has its foundation in the mutual relation of the Second and Third Hypostases. On the strength of this essential relation the Godman, God's Son incarnate, sits at the right hand of the Father in the heavens, but beside Him at His right hand is His glorified Mother, the abode of the Holy Spirit, not Godman, but God-bearer, Pneumatophore, *in truth* "the real" Theotokos.

Thus, the descent of the Holy Spirit on Mary caused her to *become* the Mother of God already in this very descending. Elizabeth expressed this in prophetic illumination, saying "and how does it happen to me that the Mother of my Lord should come to me?" (Lk 1.43). Mary became "in truth the Theotokos" not because she was physically carrying in the womb for a while; this happened because she was joined in her spirit with the Holy Spirit and thus became the Mother of God. Divine Motherhood was the expression that her own life "of the servant of the Lord" was suffused with the Holy Spirit, as though it was identified with Him, and thus she made her own that relation essential to the Logos which is proper to the Third Hypostasis. The Holy Spirit proceeds from the Father to the Son *dia ton huion* — on account of the Son, onto the Son, for the Son. He embraces, has in Himself and reveals to the Father the Begotten of the Father. This mystery of divine generation is imprinted in the image "of the truly Theotokos." By receiving the Holy Spirit, Mary was made into the receptacle of divine motherhood. She was made Mother of God *spiritually*, and in virtue of this she conceived in her womb a Son, Emmanuel. She conceived Him in the Holy Spirit, Who has Him in Himself, while resting on Him, and precisely for this reason she became in truth the Theotokos. Here and only here is the answer to Nestorius and simultaneously the repudiation of his blasphemy: by what means could Mary, a human being, give birth to the Godman and not merely to a human being, in whom consequently the Logos had to dwell? By what means is Mary *in truth* the Theotokos? As a human being, this would not be possible for Mary, but as Pneumatophore, i.e., already more than a human, namely as the hypostatic shrine of the Holy Spirit, not only is it possible but natural. It is necessary to accept what constitutes the very hypostatic nature, the property of the Third Hypostasis: to proceed from the Father to the Son, to possess the Son for the Father, not generating Him but quickening Him. And thus Mary, in receiving the Holy Spirit — not only His gifts, or power, but the very Holy Spirit — becomes the Mother of God. That is the direct and exact sense of the words of the Archangel: "hence, *dio*" (Lk 1.35), i.e., in virtue of the visitation of the Holy Spirit, the holy fruit will be none other than the Son of God, whom the Holy Spirit has hypostatically.

Although the Holy Spirit in the pre-eternal order does not beget but only has the already begotten, in the temporal order the Mother gives birth by His power. She conceives the Pre-Eternal Begotten One. Pre-eternally only the Father begets, which is why fatherhood is a synonym for generation, and in pre-eternal *generation there is no place* for motherhood.[22] Christ, as the Son of God, begotten of the Father, in His *generation* is without a mother, but as the Son of Man He does not know a father, and has only a Mother. In this way in the Godman, *sonship* in His Divinity is addressed only to the Father, in his humanity only to His Mother. And for this sonship fatherhood proves to be essential, independent of motherhood, and motherhood, independent of fatherhood. At the same time both of these determinations are identical, they coincide with and are in accordance with what was said above. The Holy Spirit does not beget, but only has the already Begotten One, but for this reason precisely the visitation of the Holy Spirit brings generative power to the Pneumatophore, and therefore also generation — without father or without a husband. If there were no pre-eternal motherless begetting from the Father, there would also be no husbandless generation from the Mother. The Holy Spirit is the one who connects both generations in His relation to the Son, whom He pre-eternally carries as the Only Begotten of the Father and in virtue of this communicates the power of generation to His Mother. Thus the seedless conception is accomplished by the visitation of the Holy Spirit.

Each of the divine hypostases is inseparable from the others, but each realizes this inseparability by its own particular hypostatic means, which is why the order of revelation of the hypostases in creation differs. The Father, first initiator and first cause, is not revealed personally to creation at all other than in the Son and the Holy Spirit. Hence the full revelation of the Father refers to that fullness of time that has not set in for the world when God will be all in all, the Son will submit everything and hand it over to the Father (1 Cor 15.24), and the Spirit will fill all things with Himself. The Holy Trinity is revealed to the world in the Son and the Holy Spirit. Besides, these revelations, multipartite and multiform, at first anticipatory and imperfect, afterwards become complete in the

Godman in Whom the fullness of Divinity abides bodily, and in the Mother of God, who is the personal elect vessel of the Holy Spirit, the Pneumatophore.

The outpouring of gifts of the Holy Spirit, Pentecost, is in the well-known sense the consequence of the Divine incarnation of the Second Hypostasis. In addition to Himself, Christ offers to humanity, "he will send" and "he will pray the Father" concerning the sending of the Holy Spirit, the Comforter, Who will give power to experience Christ tangibly, to show the living divine incarnation for all creation. The Comforter will show namely *life* in Christ, not a new *content* of revelation, but its new *vital* perception. Thus He will speak not from Himself, but will say what He hears. . . . "He will glorify Me because He takes from Mine and announces it to you" (Jn 16.13-15). The revelation of the Holy Spirit is not a new word as content, for the pre-eternally begotten Word contains *everything* and thus fulfils everything himself ("all was through him, and without him there is nothing that is"). The Spirit will give a new sensation, a living knowledge, a vital adoption of this Word, a word-bearing, a universal cosmic divine motherhood. But the hominization of the Word Himself must necessarily precede this, His joining with human nature, inseparably and without mixing, in such a way that the Word became *his own* for the sake of humankind, for the Word *assimilated* to itself human nature and through the Holy Spirit is acquired by it. This is the *assimilation* of Christ by the creature, a living sensation of the universal Christophoricity of creation, and in this sense Christ-bearing or Divine Motherhood is the operation of the Holy Spirit, a world Pentecost.

But preceding this Zion Pentecost, which is revealed in the world Pentecost, there had to be a personal Pentecost, the Pentecost of Nazareth, the Annunciation, the indwelling of the Holy Spirit in a definite human personality, as the precondition for the Divine incarnation and universal Pentecost as well as another personal Pentecost, the descent of the Holy Spirit on Jesus at his baptism. In this way here we have the reverse order of relations: the descent of the Holy Spirit into humankind *precedes* Christ's descent into it, which becomes His birth from a human being. If the Holy Spirit, sent by Christ from the Father *after* His resurrection and ascension, *completes* the work of Christ, shows in the midst of people the Christ who has been revealed, already incarnated and present among them, then the Holy Spirit, descending before the descent of the Second Hypostasis, before the divine incarnation offers in Himself and with Himself the very Christ, accomplishes the divine conception by the Most Holy Virgin.

The first and direct consequence and disclosure of Pentecost turned out to be the sermon of the apostle Peter and the other apostles about Christ, with the manifestation of Christ's power in them as the clear and palpable gift of the Holy Spirit. The Annunciation with its descent of the Holy Spirit had as its direct and sole consequence not a sermon and not the cognition of the power of Christ, but the reception in the womb, the womb-bearing of Christ himself, personal Divine Motherhood, which only later, in the fullness of time, must be made universal and cosmic. Then creation will appear as Christ being born, while the human being will appear as the bosom giving birth to God, and the whole world as the Mother of God.[23]

In the same manner in the order of internal consistency the theophany of Christ precedes and conditions Pentecost as the theophany of the Holy Spirit. But in the order of the divine *economy* of our salvation the reverse occurs: the descent of the Holy Spirit upon the Virgin Mary *precedes* the hominization of the Second Hypostasis and brings it with itself. The question is, of course, not chronological but ontological consecutiveness. Chronologically it is inseparable; in that sacred incomprehensible and miraculous moment before which the cherubim and seraphim tremble, covering their faces, when the Virgin said, "behold the handmaid of the Lord, be it unto me according to your word," the descent of the Holy Spirit was at the same time the seedless conception. The Pneumatophore became the Mother of God; along with the Holy Spirit she received the Logos as a Son being generated. In that event was concluded the foundation for both the divine incarnation of the Word and the Pentecost of the Holy Spirit, for the *fulfilment* of the divine plan: "today the captain of our salvation and the manifestation of the mystery from the ages: The Son of God is the Son of the Virgin" (Troparion of the Annunciation).

The effect of the Holy Spirit's visitation of the Virgin Mary consists in the seedless conception of the Divine Infant. One need not understand this "mystery from the ages," this pre-eternal secret, as some physical miracle which consists of a supernatural or anti-natural, asexual or monosexual conception (parthenogenesis). Of course, with respect to human nature burdened and perverted by sin, here "the laws of natures are defeated," and the miracle of the virgin birth occurs, with the preservation of virginity *ante partum, in partu* and *post partum*: "the unutterable nativity of the seedless conception by a mother without husband." This miracle is incompatible with the contemporary physiology of the human being, it contradicts it and subverts it, and it is contrary to nature. And yet this conception does not in the least signify that in the given case human nature itself in its most essential and intimate disclosure, namely in the form of generating and multiplying, was abrogated, annihilated by an act of divine omnipotence. If it were so, it would scarcely be possible to speak about an authentic hominization of the Lord which has so paramount and decisive a meaning in the economy of our salvation, would it? In its own provenance His humanity then would be a non-human, inauthentic result of some sort of *deus ex machina,* of a completely new and particular act of creation. Was not the whole attack of Docetism rushing into that breech by having called in question precisely the authenticity of the human body of the Lord, desiring to understand it only as a veil of Divinity, essentially a ghostly decoration? Thus, affirming the miraculous nature of the seedless conception in the sense of its intentional graciousness, in conjunction with the visitation of the Holy Spirit, we at the same time must resolutely deny that it is contrary to nature and thus somehow non-human. On the contrary, we must deem it completely natural and in full accord with the laws of human nature uncorrupted by sin. Its miraculousness, along with its naturalness, consists precisely in its liberation from the captivity and power of sin, but in no way in its liberation from human nature itself (which is the reason that the Lord's body is called in the Word of God only "in the likeness of the flesh of sin," *not* in the sense of Docetism but precisely in the sense of its freedom from sinful nature). The Lord was, as the new Adam, a true human being in the sense that He alone was precisely the true Adam. The whole human race in the old Adam does not have in itself *true humanness,* being defeated by sin, and it receives it only in Christ. Thus His Nativity was in truth a birth, not abrogating but fulfilling the Divine command concerning Him. We must scrutinize this mystery all the more intently and distinguish what in it belongs to human nature and what to Divine pleasure.

Adam and Eve were created out of one flesh, as husband and wife; to them was given the command, "be fruitful and multiply and fill the earth," but this mode of procreation proper to them, had they not known sin, remains completely unknown to us. On the contrary, it is reliably known that the contemporary form of procreation is bound with sin: after the fall "God said to the wife, I shall greatly multiply your pain in your pregnancy, in painfulness shall you give birth to children; and your attraction will be for your husband and he will rule over you" (Gen 3.16). He will rule not by his hierarchical superiority which was given to him by God, but by the bad, enslaving, lordship of sexual desire. From this it follows that the painfulness of pregnancy and child-bearing is a direct consequence of sin and does not in the least belong to human nature; on the contrary, the painless bearing of children is natural. So too sexual attraction is somehow bound with the fall after which people have felt their nakedness and the shame of this nakedness. When they made for themselves a girdle out of fig leaves (Gen 3.7), they bore witness to an awakened sense of sexual shame. Therefore sexual feeling along with sexual desire *is not* properly normal, i.e., to the sinless human. Consequently, sexual conception inseparably connected with sexual lust ("in lawlessness was I conceived and in sins did my mother give me birth," Ps 51) is also not proper to the human. Hence one unavoidably concludes that a completely other mode of procreation, beyond the sexual or super-sexual, would be proper to Adam and Eve in keeping with their own nature, not distorted by the whisper of the serpent and not poisoned with his poison.

According to the interpretation of many fathers of the church (in particular John Chrysostom)[24] it was precisely *virginity* that was the norm for relations between a man and a woman, and physical marriage is already the garments of skin, lying on the body of sinful humankind. And so, although it is completely unknown by what manner, there would have existed a command of God concerning procreation.[25] But if carnal conception is ruled out, spiritual conception is not in the least ruled out, in which the wife would bear, giving her own flesh to an infant spiritually conceived by the father. Not entering further into this inaccessible region, unless it is revealed, we can nonetheless confidently say that asexual conception would be a virginal conception, not destroying the virginity and chastity of the human couple. In this way child-bearing would be connected with virginity in the sense of freedom from copulation, pregnancy and pain. Consequently, the seedless conception and painless birth, which we have in the Nativity of Christ, in *this* relation appear precisely natural and normal, not the abrogation of nature but the fulfilment of its laws. In this the Mother of God truly was the new Eve, who did not know sin. Generation ceases to be a function of sex. In seedless conception the Mother of God is completely healed of the power of sex, although, of course she does not lose her female nature because of this. From the Virgin she becomes the Ever-Virgin, *aei — parthenos*, i.e., essentially the Virgin. Therefore Virginity becomes inherent in her as her inalienable property, as her nature, which she can no longer ever forfeit.[26]

Virginity for Eve (together with Adam) was only *a state*, which still was subject to confirmation through trial. But they forfeited it after sin, having fallen into the captivity of sex. In the Ever-Virgin this became not only a state but her very nature. To say it another way, though a female being, Virgin and Mother, the Ever-Virgin *is not a woman* in the sense of sex.

So too her Son: although He has a male nature, of course, He also possesses the most perfect Ever-Virginity, and is not *a man* in the sense of sex. The Lord and the Mother of God, having male and female nature, nonetheless remain free *from sex, higher than sex,* ever-virginal. Sex, on the contrary, as the condition of man and woman turned towards each other, is the lot of the whole sinful human race.[27] From this it is understandable that we have a single instance of completely sinless ever-virginal generation from an Ever-Virgin being realized in complete ever-virginity, i.e., in a seedless and husbandless conception and a virginal painless nativity.

The question that emerges apropos of this can only be: in what way is the Virgin Mary, all the same guilty of original sin, suddenly liberated from it in its most essential consequence, i.e., liberated from sex? Are we not introducing *here* all the same, although unwittingly, the Catholic dogma of the Immaculate Conception of the Virgin Mary, which precisely liberates her in general from the power of original sin, and in so far makes her the Ever-Virgin? But apropos of such an objection it must be recalled that in harmony with Catholic understanding, the nature of the human in the fall *has not been altered* substantially. Humankind even before sin is not considered free from lust (and, as a result, from sex) in the least; it is only that *concupiscentia* has been held on a leash by virtue of *donum superadditum.* Thus freedom from original sin there is *not* brought into connection with seedless conception: Catholic dogma does not explain it and in any case in order to be utilized in this aspect it must be correspondingly altered, supplemented and made more precise. It contains in itself, although in an incorrect dogmatic formulation, a presentiment of the correct idea that the Ever-Virgin was placed in a completely special relationship to original sin by an extraordinary grace of the Holy Spirit. This relationship is not full freedom from original sin (which would signify freedom from human nature, i.e., Docetism), but consists in the overcoming of certain of its essential consequences, in particular in the overcoming of sex, which we have in seedless conception.

Conception and generation among humans is connected with sex, in other words, bisexual, and presupposes therefore father and mother. But all the same it is poisoned by sinful lust and guilty of death. ("Aphrodite and Hades are one and the same," which the ancient Greeks knew.) Every life is mortal, conceived "in lawlessness," in passion, in the ecstasy of the flesh. This law knows not a single exception, and the conception of the Most Holy Virgin, even in accord with Catholic dogma, is no exception either. She was given by her parents only mortal life. But she herself is in such a degree holy and pre-cleansed through the gracious influence of the Holy Spirit, beginning with her conception and continuing through-out her life, that in her the life of sex is completely paralysed, and receives *no kind of* development and expression. This barely imaginable supreme, paramount human holiness and purity proved to be such that the *Annunciation* became possible. The Virgin Mary was the vessel worthy to receive the Holy Spirit who with His visitation fashioned her simultaneously Ever-Virgin and Mother, the new Eve. She gives birth in accordance with the form of virginal conception foreordained for the progenitors before the fall. The Holy Spirit gives her *the power* of Ever-Virginity, and *in so far,* really, is she removed from under the dominion of original sin, not in her conception, but precisely in *the Annunciation.* In point of fact it is impious to allow that the contact of sin with the generation of the Lord, even in its most remote consequences, was possible in any degree at all. For its sake the sinless state of humankind in paradise before the fall must be com-pletely restored. This restoration was completed by the Holy Spirit in Mary, not mechanically or automatically, apart from her, before her birth, but with the participation of her freedom, personal heroic effort, and faith, her complete self-surrender to the Divine will: *behold the handmaid of the Lord.*

It is thus necessary to conclude that the original human nature of Eve before the fall is restored in the form of virginal, seedless conception in the Virgin Mary. But at the same time there is a substantial absence which makes this conception extraordinary, unique, namely that it is ac-complished husbandless, without a father, only by the mother alone. Pro-creation is entrusted by God to the human couple Adam and Eve, not in their separateness but in their togetherness. In this way, generation, initi-ated by the father, is completed in the mother. Only Adam in his origin es-caped this general lot: in place of a mother he receives the earth — *'adāmâ* — and in place of a father, God who created him and breathed into him a living soul: "Adam is of God" (Lk 3.38). In this sense Adam conceives by himself a race of sons of God, humans, although in distinction from the Only-begotten Son of God they are created sons of God.

Thus one has to ask why husbandless conception takes place for the Ever-Virgin. Of course one need not inquire into the very manner of the miracle's occurrence, but one can ask about its ontological foundation. This foundation consists in the Virgin conceiving not a human being coming into existence for the first time but the pre-eternally generated Only Begotten Son, the Second Hypostasis of the Most Holy Trinity. The Son of Mary has a Pre-Eternal Father, and hence he does not have a hu-man father. The begetting of Christ by the Holy Spirit and the Virgin

Mary does not indicate that the Holy Spirit here has taken the place of the father and as it were was the father of the Infant. But the same Holy Spirit, who as Third Hypostasis proceeds from the Father to the Son, in Himself and for Himself, along with His overshadowing brings the Son, having Him in Himself as one begotten by the Father. The Holy Spirit, in overshadowing the Mother, brings from the Father the Begotten Son, and this is a conception that is husbandless and seedless. He who is pre-eternally begotten is conceived spiritually in Mary by virtue of her over-shadowing by the Holy Spirit.

In sexual conception and birth the true essence of spiritual mother-hood is darkened, which is love for the one being conceived and still not born but already begotten, a voluntary, loving surrender of the self, a go-ing out from the self to the other, life simultaneously in the self and in the other. We have a certain reflection of true motherhood in spiritual cre-ativity. The mother gives her flesh because she loves the begotten one, she has the will towards its birth. In this sacrificial self-offering the bliss of maternal love is contained. In the current human condition it is mani-fested not as a spiritual act but as a phenomenon corresponding to the physiology of motherhood; besides, it is proper not only to the human but also to the animal world. In its essence motherhood is *the will to incar-nate* the already embryonic but not yet born fruit. As a psychosomatic act it is accomplished in the spirit and realized in the body. It would have been thus with the reproduction of Adam and Eve in the absence of sin and thus it became again in Mary, who was freed from the consequence of original sin, of the corporeality of sex, through the overshadowing of the Holy Spirit. Those characteristics of the pneumatophoric body of the pro-genitors were returned to the body of Mary, owing to which it was an obe-dient instrument of the spirit, but it did not show hostility towards the spirit and did not inflict its own law on it. Therefore it is erroneous to think that the conception of the Divine Infant is simply the influence of the Holy Spirit on the body of Mary, so to say, a physiological miracle, in abrogation of the laws of nature: here "the laws of nature are defeated," precisely in the abrogation of the limitedness of *sinful nature.*

The operation of the Holy Spirit was expressed in Mary's experience of herself in her spirit as Mother of the Only-Begotten Son of God, engen-dered in her through the indwelling of the Holy Spirit inseparable from Him. That spiritual plasticity was communicated to her body, owing to which it became capable of implementing the movement of the spirit. Therefore, when Mary felt herself as Mother in her spirit, she conceived bodily as well, for the spiritual is first, and then, the bodily conception,

97

not the reverse, as it is now. "Behold the handmaid of the Lord; *let it be* to me according to your word" (Lk 1.38). This *let it be* is not just a passive bowing down before an accomplished fact, rather it is its loving vital reception, it is *love* for the One being born that flares up and *the will* to motherhood. This answer is not only an expression of consent or submission, but bears witness to the already accomplished birth in Mary's spirit: in this moment, by saying these words, *she became the Mother of the Lord,* although the birth was realized only after the period of bodily womb-bearing had run its course. The righteous Elizabeth testifies about her in the Holy Spirit, "blessed *is she who came to believe,* because what was said to her by the Lord will be accomplished" (Lk 1.45). Coming to believe here is already fulfilment, the direct consequence of which is "the seedless conception, the ineffable nativity, the incorrupt fruit of a mother without a husband." And to the greeting of Elizabeth, in all her measureless humility, Mary answers "for *he has looked* (already accomplished action) on the humility of His handmaiden, for from now on all generations will bless me, for the Almighty has done·(the same thing) great things for me, and holy is His name" (Lk 1.48-49). She knows about what has been accomplished in her and·upon her and bears witness about it as if about a fact come true already in the very first moment of its execution. This signifies that Mary, in obeying with her body the omnipotent word of its Creator and submitting with her will to that omnipotence, *not only externally but also internally* became the Mother of the Lord in the mysterious moment of the Annunciation, and thus was shown to be Mother in the Nativity of Christ.

In her was accomplished a change that cannot be comprehended by human or angelic minds: her entire being changed from human into divine-motherly. For divine-motherly being is no longer human being, though inseparably connected with it and belonging to it, in the way the human essence of the Godman belongs to it and is connected with it. Mary is not a Godman, for in her a creaturely human nature with a creaturely hypostasis has been preserved, and the sole Godman is the Lord Jesus Christ, in two natures, divine and human, having a single divine hypostasis, whereas Mary has a human hypostasis. But Mary is not simply a human being in the manner she was before the Annunciation; she is Mother of God. This means that she received the Holy Spirit and was made inseparable from Him, and hence with Him the Only Begotten Son was implanted in her, as her Son. The Son is pre-eternally begotten by the Father, and this begetting cannot be subordinated to time. Mary became the Mother of God in time, because the whole existence of the human race flows in time. But this divine motherhood which was initiated in time, and is foreordained from the ages, has already an eternal nature, is accomplished for all times and for eternity. In this respect divine motherhood becomes completely like the divine humanity of the Saviour. It likewise is accomplished in time, in which flows the whole life of the creaturely world and of humankind, but it has force in eternity, for the Son of God, when he ascended into heaven, sits in His flesh at the right hand of the Father. His Mother, resurrected by Him, is borne into heaven. Every philosophical and theological difficulty that arises in the comprehension of this transition from time immediately into eternity, arises completely equally for the one and the other. Thus, Mary is no longer a human being but the Mother of God, though she remains a human being not only in her nature but also in her hypostasis. She is not the Godman, for whom it is not fitting to have a human hypostasis. But divine motherhood is inseparably connected with divine generation: where the Son is, from there the Mother cannot be removed. Divine motherhood belongs to divine incarnation, which having been realized once and for all in a temporal act, preserves its whole force, and in this sense eternally. For all times it is realized as the condition of a creature being divinized, as a ladder of divinization.

It is possible to express this idea in this way: although only the Second Hypostasis, the Son, was to be incarnated and become human, the personal indwelling of the Holy Spirit in a human being, in the Ever-Virgin, is inseparably connected with this divine incarnation. Through this, the human hypostasis and human nature in this being are not abolished, but filled by divine life. This human being, by becoming spiritual, but not being a godman, is *divine,* as the perfect dwelling of the Holy Spirit. There cannot be imagined a more complete indwelling of the Holy Spirit in creation, in a human being or an angel, than was accomplished in the Mother of God. Mary is therefore the perfect appearance of the Third Hypostasis; in creation her human countenance reflects on itself the hypostasis of the Holy Spirit, for it is transparent for Him. The hypostatic revelation of the Son was accomplished in the divine incarnation, in Christ Jesus. The hypostatic revelation of the Father is possible and exists only in the Son and through the Son in the Holy Spirit. The hypostatic revelation of the Holy Spirit was accomplished, is accomplished and will be accomplished in fullness in the future age, in the kingdom of the Holy Spirit, through Mary, the Heavenly Queen, the Mother of God. She is in heaven the Spiritual Human, sitting at the right hand of the Godman. Hence it is absurd and impious to expect a new, Third, Testament[28] with a personal revelation of the Third Hypostasis, for in a possible and appropriate form this revelation of the Third Hypostasis has already occurred in the Mother of God. In her is the personal revelation of the Holy Spirit, shown in creation. Therefore the steps in the revelation of the Holy Spirit are essentially and necessarily steps in the showing of the Mother of God to the world, which has not been completed and in fullness belongs only to the future age. The coming of Christ in glory will be also the appearance in glory of the Mother of God; along with the revelation of the Second Hypostasis the Third will be revealed. Hence the resurrection, ascension and heavenly glorification of the Mother of God become perfectly necessary and comprehensible. The Mother is inseparable from her own giving birth, and where the Son is, there too is it fitting for the Mother to be. They are indivisible, just as the Second and Third Hypostases are indivisible, eternally originating from the Father.[29]

On the path of her ascension toward full and complete pneumatophoricity, towards the spiritualization of her whole essence, and not only of separate powers and capabilities, but in a full and ultimate degree, the Mother of God, as also the Godman, had to pass through many temptations, sufferings and death. By His perfect obedience to the Father's will the Lord completely sanctified and divinized His human nature. For the Most Pure Virgin it was similar. In order to surrender herself fully and ultimately to the Spirit of God living in her, she too had to complete the heroic effort of her entire life, which was filled with the most heavy temptations, so that the hour of her most glorious Dormition might come. On this path, among other events, was the descent of the Holy Spirit, baptism by the Spirit and fire, along with all the apostles. It is possible to see in this a certain discrepancy and contradiction with what was said about the pneumatophoricity of Mary. In what manner can the temple of God, the receptacle of the Holy Spirit, need a new descent of the Holy Spirit? How is Pentecost possible for the Ever-Virgin after the Annunciation? And yet it will be just as incorrect to see in this a contradiction as it is when the Holy Spirit, who eternally rests on the Son and is indivisible from Him, descends upon the Son at his baptism in the form of a dove, in order to consecrate His human essence. The descent of the Holy Spirit on the apostles was also a baptism which was extended to the Mother of God who is higher than the whole apostolic choir and who stands ahead of the whole human race. With this in no way is weakened the fact that in the Annunciation the hypostatic visitation of the Holy Spirit occurred in the Virgin Mary. This visitation did not remove the possibility or the necessity of her ever greater self-offering, of His penetration of her human essence. On this path of increase at Pentecost the intended gifts of the Holy Spirit were sent to Mary, so that by baptism they would finally liberate her from the burden of original sin, and communicate the power of redemption to her human essence. The fullness of this ripening of the human essence into a heavenly abode was accomplished at the time *of the Dormition,* which is therefore the triumph of human holiness, pneumatophoricity and purity, the *glorification* of human nature. The Theotokos is the glory of humankind, the glory of the world. In the Annunciation the Mother of God became the Ever-Virgin and in this was freed from the burden of sex, the fundamental though not only result of original sin. She therefore could communicate to the Christ begotten by her the flesh of the New Adam, not weighed down by sex, ever-virginal (see above).

But another fundamental consequence of original sin remained in her without being eliminated, and that is death. She gave her Son a Body, though not subject to death, in consequence of freedom from the burden of sex and the absence of sin, yet capable of accepting death. The latter has been defeated by the Divinity of Christ, resurrected and in Himself co-resurrecting all humankind. That power of redemption — the victory over death and bodily resurrection — was communicated by Him to the Mother of God who herself did not possess this power, which is confirmed by her death. Hence she calls her Son her Saviour as well, not from personal sin which she did not have, but from inherited sin, the mortal infirmity of nature. The mother is redeemed and saved by the Son, because only the complete unity of Divine-human nature in Jesus Christ is capable of healing and restoring humankind to its original state of immortality. At the Lord's own baptism by the descent of the Holy Spirit His human nature was sanctified and those infirmities of nature were removed which could remain in it in keeping with His human origin, however much it would have been sinless. Similarly for the Virgin Mary Pentecost was the crowning sanctification of her human nature from every consequence and remnant of original sin and the communication to her of the redemptive power of Christ. Her personal Pentecost or Annunciation was supplemented here, or more correctly, was unveiled as the world Pentecost, the foundation of the earthly Church by the descent of the Holy Spirit. Participating in the assembly of the holy apostles, Mary was the invisible centre, the true ladder between earth and heaven. The significance of Pentecost was different for her and for the apostles. As the representative of the whole creation and more exalted than everyone, she is the personal incarnation of the Church: the head of the apostles, the focus of the whole creaturely world. Her significance for the Church leads us to new dimensions in the doctrine of the Mother of God.

In patristic literature the Mother of God is named *Hē Theopais, daughter of God*[30] the Theotokos. This name can be understood first of all in a general sense: of all the human sons who became children of God, the Mother of God is the first and most elect Daughter, foretold from the ages, according to the word of St Gregory Palamas. She alone joins *(methorion)* creaturely and non-creaturely nature.[31] It is, however, necessary to remove from this notion an incorrect interpretation: by likening the Mother of God much too closely to the Son of God, it would bring her into the divine-generating heart of the Holy Trinity. According to this understanding, the Father has in addition to a Son a Daughter on whom the Holy Spirit rests, and daughterhood is appropriated to Him in relation to the Father. In that case the relation of the Son and the Holy Spirit is understood likewise as that of brother and sister. Such a doctrine (not foreign, by the way, to certain Eastern theologians) must be rejected as perverting the very concept of fatherhood in the Holy Trinity and abolishing the "only-begottenness" of the Son. The procession of the Holy Spirit, although connected to fatherhood (He proceeds from the Father), is not generation[32] and consequently is not daughterhood. The latter in general has no particular independent place for itself in generation, but must be regarded as its simple variety, for in Christ Jesus "there is neither male nor female": "for you all are one in Christ Jesus" (Gal 3.28), "for you are all sons of God, you are one by faith in Christ Jesus" (Gal 3.26), "As many of you as received Him He gave them power to become children of God, believing in His Name: who is born not from blood, not from fleshly desire, not from male desire, but from God" (Jn 1.12-13). Generation from God into sons of God happens in this way only in Christ, the only-begotten Son of God, the only Saviour and Redeemer *without distinction* of human sex. In as much as the Mother of God has participated in redemption, she will receive adoption to God in His Son, whom she herself names "My God and My Saviour" (Lk 1.47). And so, there is nothing to be said about divine daughterhood with respect to *divine* generation from the Father; it can be applied exclusively to *the human* image of the Mother of God.

Here it is incumbent upon us to return afresh to that notion that *the fullness* of the image of God in humankind is expressed not in one but in two, in Adam and Eve, in the son and daughter of God. For the fullness of its restoration, participation in it is required not only of the New Adam but also of the New Eve (one of the constant titles for the Mother of God). Only the New Adam, as head of the Church (Eph 5.22-23; 1 Cor 11.3), is the Saviour, the completer of the work of redemption. But the immaculate "new Eve" must share the path "of the one sinless" new Adam with Him, *and in the two* in heaven and on earth the fullness of the human image, as the image of God, begins to shine, the power of redemption is revealed. In the person of the Mother of God divine sonship for the whole female part of the human race is realized, which in human speech can be called divine daughterhood.

In this standing before the Father in her humanity the Mother of God is sometimes called by the name *sister-bride* (in the Song of Songs, see below). In Catholic theology this relation not infrequently receives an exaggerated and one-sided character, under the influence of the 1854 dogma.[33] The Virgin as Mother, Theotokos, is honoured in sacred hymnody also as *the Unwed Bride*, i.e., as the Eternal Bride. In other words, ever-virginity is combined with the condition of mother and bride, and obviously, is not found in contradiction to this. Such expressions we encounter in St Ephrem the Syrian[34] and St John of Damascus,[35] et al.[36]

In iconography the Mother of God is not always depicted with the Infant, as Mother, but simply as Virgin: examples are the icon of Tender Compassion before which St Seraphim prayed, the Indestructible Wall, et al. These depictions express not so much the idea of Mother of God as the idea of Bride of God. In a corresponding manner, the Bride from the Song of Songs[37] and the Mother of God are closely likened and even identified in iconography, in church hymns and in patristic literature. (See for example Song 1.8-16; 2.2, 10; 3.6, 4; 4.3-9; also the second half of the Theotokos psalm 44.10-16. It is customary to take from these passages the prokeimena for Theotokos services and the text used at the excision of the particle from the Theotokos prosphora at the Proskomedia.) Finally, for interpreters the image of the woman clothed in the sun from Rev 12.1-6 relates to this point. One must still add that sometimes in the Word of God no distinction is made between *bride and wife,* for example Rev 19.7; 22.17. In this manner the Church applies very different terms like "Mother" and "Bride" to Mary as the personal incarnation of the Church. Of course, these terms are incompatible if one translates them in the language of sex and sexual relations, but this incompatibility is eliminated in spiritual relations. The Mother of God, as the abode of the Holy Spirit, bears in herself the Logos, conceives and gives birth to Him, and is the Theotokos. But as a creaturely, human being, as the representative of the human race, she is the handmaid of the Lord. As the Church she belongs to the Logos, to Christ as ecclesial Bridegroom and Head of the Church, and she loves Him with the love of an Ever-Virgin.

The Song of Songs is also a song about Mary and the Logos, as about every soul seeking its heavenly Groom and joining with Him. The

Virgin Mary, Mother of God and Bride of God, is the image of every soul in its relation to the Logos, in its ecclesialization. The soul loves, seeks and finds Christ and is united with Him; it gives birth to Him within. This motherhood and betrothal are joined indivisibly, and one without the other is impossible.[38] In the Song of Songs the bridegroom calls the beloved "my sister the bride" (Song 4.9, 10), and this does *not* refer to physical kinship, of which there is none (Song 8.1-2). The Logos who becomes human becomes the Brother of the whole human race, which He taught to invoke the Heavenly Father in the Lord's Prayer; hence humans are His brothers and sisters. ("I shall declare Your Name to My brethren, in the midst of the assembly I will sing of you," Ps 22.22; Heb 2.12; cf. Jn 20.17: "go to My brothers and say to them.") In this way it turns out that in divine motherhood such relations of love are contained which prove to be incompatible in fallen humankind living not an integral life but a life *of half-measure* and brokenness.

All of these definitions are at the same time definitions of the Church. The Church is the Body of Christ. In a broad sense this means that it is animated by Christ and will surrender itself to Him as obedient, loving and inseparably united with Him. The Mother of God, not having in herself another life except Christ's, is His Body both in a general and a particular sense. She gives Him her own body, having Him in her womb and bearing Him as the fruit of her womb: the unity of Christ with the Church, as with His Body, has here a fully patent expression. But the Mother of God, being the Mother of Christ, is in virtue of this the Mother of the whole human race which was adopted by her at the cross in the person of the Apostle John. Through this, in her and with her, the whole human race becomes not only His "brother" but also His body. Further, the Church is the Bride or Wife of the Logos, in as much as marriage is performed "in Christ and in the church." The bride and wife are spiritually one and the same relation, taken only in two different aspects which are nonetheless connected with each other: searching and discovering, striving and attaining, thirsting and slaking. The relation between Christ and the Church in corresponding texts (Eph 5 et al.) and in particular in the Song of Songs is depicted as love and the bliss of love, replacing the languor of searching. Love is the joining of two lives into one life, a *common* life, a new life; in this joining are revelation and bliss, and the torments of love which are experienced when for some reason this unity is not realized (the searching by the beloved for her beloved in the city squares, Song 3.1-3, 5.6-7). In this light the sense and power of the Song of Songs, and the whole importance of this mysterious hymn of love for the New Testament doctrine of the church, become understandable, for truly this Old Testament Song contains the most New Testament part of the whole canon.[39] Mary, as the personal dwelling of the Holy Spirit, is in truth the personal heading up of the Church, the heart of the Church, the Head of which is Christ. Overshadowed by the Holy Spirit she becomes the Mother of God, she gives birth to the Logos, and this divine motherhood, in her and with her, is the possession of the whole Church. The Logos who was born of the Virgin is born in the souls of the faithful, for every church soul participates in the divine motherhood of the Mother-Church, the Mother of God.[40]

Thus, what is said about the Church is also said about Mary. It will be incorrect to say in a general form that Mary is the Church, and yet it is possible to say that the Church is represented by Mary, in as much as in her person are united all the properties of the Church, in a personal incarnation that is sublime and ultimate. For if the Church lives and is moved by the power and gifts of the Holy Spirit, then He abides in her; if the Church effects the image of Christ in her offspring and as it were begets Him in them, then in the Mother of God He was born and became human as His own Hypostasis. That which is Church is the very essence of Mary, who is the dwelling place of the Holy Spirit, both Mother of God and Divine Bride.

The divine maternal principle is symbolized by the blue of church vestments, by heavenly azure. This azure is a hymn of creation to the Lord and about the Lord, glory and doxology. The Mother of God is the exalted, glorified, divinized creature: the darkness of creaturely non-existence is overcome and illuminated by Divine Sophia and it has lighted up in receptive feminine blue. If the fullness of creation, its truth and beauty, its rational glory, is divine Sophia, as *the revelation* of the Holy Trinity, then it is necessary to repeat this when applied to the Mother of God. The Mother of God is *sophianic* in the utmost degree. She is the fullness of Sophia in creation and in this sense is creaturely Sophia.

The Lord's words at the end of His discourse on the Forerunner: "Wisdom Σοφία is justified by her children" (Mt 11.19) first of all relate precisely to the Mother of God. Sophia is the foundation, pillar and ground of the truth,[41] the fulfilment of which is the Mother of God, and in this sense she is as it were the personal expression of Sophia in creation, the personal image of the earthly Church. Divine Sophia is the pre-eternal self-revelation of the Most Holy Trinity, the Glory of God, the Divine world of eternal essences, the Divine All, the Revelation of the Father in the Only-Begotten Son and in the Holy Spirit. The Father shows Himself in the Son and proceeds towards Him by the Holy Spirit; the Word of God, filled with the Holy Spirit, contains the All: "all was through him and without Him there is nothing that is." The Word of God determines the ideal content of the pre-eternal idea; the Thought of God, the Holy Spirit quickens it and makes it tangible, clothes it in beauty. Hence Wisdom is the Logos in its ideal content, but this does not mean that its essence is exhausted only by one ideal content, for it is also the Holy Spirit in its existence, it is the living, concrete tangibility of this ideal content, beauty, God's Glory. The thought-images of Truth are revealed in her by the images of Beauty. "The Lord is king, he is clothed in splendour." This divine world of God's Glory is the basis and also the utmost goal of the universe.

The world is created by the Wisdom of God and for her sake[42] it is creaturely Wisdom, and in the fullness of time must be transformed according to the image of Divine Wisdom.[43] The biblical doctrine about Wisdom, principally from the Old Testament, amounts to this too (see the second excursus at the end of the book). Wisdom is the Church: in the heavens, it is pre-eternal, in creation, it has growth and development, it is the earthly Church. The ecclesialization of the world is also its penetration by Wisdom. The divine incarnation is the foundation of ecclesialization: Christ, the Power of God and Wisdom of God, was made human, and in Him the sophianic unity of the divine and creaturely world was established. But the fullness of sophianic revelation includes the appearance not only of the Son but also of the Holy Spirit, and on the other hand, the hominization of the Logos supposes a corresponding brightening of human nature, the triumph in it of the sophianic principle. We find this triumph of the earthly appearance of Sophia in humankind, and with it the revelation of the Holy Spirit, in the Mother of God who remains inseparably with her Son. The fullness of the sophianic image in the creaturely world or in humankind is Christ and the Mother of God, as this is depicted on our usual icons of the Mother of God, most clearly of all in the icon of the Sign. But in essence *every* icon of the Mother of God according to its deepest sense is a sophianic icon. In the Mother of God heavenly and creaturely Wisdom were united, the Holy Spirit living in her was joined with the creaturely human hypostasis. Her flesh was made completely spiritual and translucent for heaven, in her was fulfilled the goal of the creation of the world. She is its justification, goal and meaning; she is also in this sense the Glory of the world. In her the revelation of the Son, born of her and of the Holy Spirit by whose power this birth is accomplished, is united with the creaturely nature in which it is accomplished. Therefore the Mother of God substantially belongs to this world and at the same time is exalted above it, surpasses it. This is creaturely Wisdom, glorified in heaven and crowned as heavenly Queen. The meaning of the Dormition of the Mother of God is disclosed here in a new light.

Glorified Mary, Heavenly Queen, is a creature and no longer a creature, for she made room in herself for the fullness of divine life. In her God is already "all in all," for her there no longer exists a further development or perfecting, as is still true for all creation, angelic and human. This is eternal life, if not of the Godhead itself, then eternal life in the Godhead, in the unfathomable deep of the ocean of the absolute. Creation became here perfectly transparent for the Creator.

Through all this the Theotokos has not ceased preserving her creaturely nature, she has not been detached from the world, which she has glorified through herself and in herself. She is the world, for she remains in union with it: "in your Dormition you did not abandon the world, Theotokos," sings the Church. Bearing witness to this are all the appearances of the Mother of God to the saints, her Veil over the world, her miraculous icons and the whole sea of prayers of the church which flow unceasingly towards her in the firm faith and hope that there is no human being with a heart more loving and responsive to all than the all-hymned Mother, the holy Patroness of the Christian race.

The *Russian* Orthodox Church has confirmed this idea of sophianic reverence for the Mother of God, which crowns orthodox theologizing about her as with a cupola, by liturgically connecting the celebration of Sophia with the commemoration of the Mother of God. This differs from the *Byzantine* church where the Christological aspect was singled out in Sophiology and sophianic festivals were united with dominical ones (Nativity of Christ, Resurrection). The one and the other have their own indisputable foundation; sometimes the one and the other merge so as to be indistinguishable. Divine incarnation is inseparably connected with divine motherhood, the one implies the other, hence dominical festivals implicitly or explicitly suppose festivals of the Theotokos. In certain ones this connection comes to light in such an obvious way that it becomes difficult to comprehend how to understand, for example, such a festival as the Nativity of Christ or the Presentation. In the one case heavenly, uncreated Wisdom is emphasized, and in the other, Sophia in a creature, the Mother of God. This, in its turn, corresponds to how the one or the other hypostasis revealed in Sophia, the Logos or the Holy Spirit, is primarily singled out: the first corresponds to Christ-Sophia, the second to the Mother of God as Sophia. In an analogous way a distinction of nuances is obtained in the understanding of the text Wisdom 9.1, "Wisdom has built herself a house and established seven pillars," which is read as the lesson on festivals of the Theotokos. In the Christ-sophianic interpretation, this will mean: Wisdom — Christ — built for himself (in the act of creating the world) a house — his Body, the Church with seven gifts of the Holy Spirit and seven sacraments. In the Theotokos-sophianic interpretation this same text will mean: Wisdom — the Holy Spirit,[44] built for himself (in the act of divine incarnation) a house — the Mother of God and established seven pillars (the Kievan depiction of St Sophia corresponds to this where she is depicted as a seven-columned temple with the Mother of God at the center).[45]

Russian Orthodoxy preferred primarily the second, Theotokos-Sophianic interpretation, and therefore the festival of Sophia here became that of the Theotokos: it is combined either with the Nativity of the Theotokos or with her Dormition (analogously with the celebration on the day of the Nativity or Resurrection of Christ). In the north, in Moscow and Novgorod, the celebration was most widely held on the Dormition which is why the temples in honour of the Dormition of the Theotokos much loved here are essentially Sophianic temples in their design,[46] as for example Dormition cathedral in Moscow. We have liturgical evidence for such a Theotokos-Sophia memorial in "the service of Sophia Wisdom of God which is sung in Great Novgorod" on 15 August.[47] This didactic service, a more detailed analysis of which does not pertain to our task, represents a service of the Dormition of the Theotokos that is simultaneously referred "to most eminent Sophia the Wisdom of God," and is correspondingly supplemented and made more complex by stikhira and canons dedicated to her. Here in a series of hymns is expressed the close likening of Sophia to the Mother of God.

The Mother of God is the universal intercessor and advocate: "pray your Son and our God for us all." She is the personified prayer of the Church. Why and in what sense is this deliberate task appropriated to her, to be the High Priestess in her capacity as Advocate of the Church, a sign of which is her adoption of the bishop's omophorion (in the festival and in the icon of the Veil of the Most Holy Theotokos)? Here we approach the mystery of our redemption, though from a new and unaccustomed side. Christ is the High Priest and Advocate of the New Testament (letter to the Hebrews), "in the order of Melchizedek." He offered God the sacrifice which replaces all sacrifices, His Body, His very self. He is the sacrifice and sacrificer, "the one offering and the offering" (Liturgy of John

Chrysostom). He has passed through the heavens and has raised glorified human flesh into heaven. His sacrifice has redemptive meaning, both in the sense that by it we are given the remission of sins, and in the sense that by His incarnation and resurrection new life is given to the human race in the new Adam and death is defeated. In the death, resurrection and ascension of Christ our redemption was accomplished, i.e., a general, objective foundation was laid for us, it became *givenness.* However, its *to-be-doneness* for the creature, its realization is still not fulfilled in this.

The descent of the Holy Spirit on the apostles, and in their person on all people, was required so that the New Testament church might be founded as realized redemption, as the ark of *salvation.* In this manner, although the salvation of humankind is brought about once and for all in a certain absolute way on Golgotha and by the Resurrection of the Son of God, nonetheless *salvation,* the assimilation of salvation by creatureliness and creaturely freedom, is accomplished by the Holy Spirit. In this the participation of the Holy Spirit in the salvation of humankind is manifested, a participation which became possible only after the completion of the redemptive work of Christ, after His ascension (as He said to his disciples: "it is better for you that I go; for if I do not go, the Comforter will not come to you; and if I go, I will send Him to you, Jn 16.7). The descent of the Holy Spirit and His indwelling in human beings and creation founds the Church on the rock of Christ, and in this sense it is rightly said that the Church is the Holy Spirit, and those saved in it are saved by the Holy Spirit.

The Mother of God, as the personal revelation of the Holy Spirit, is the heart of the Church, its so to say personal expression, the Representative of the Church. Of course, this judgment must not be understood collectively, i.e., not in the sense that the Mother of God is the Church as a totality of all or many believers, for such a judgment would be frankly incorrect; rather it is to be understood qualitatively or dynamically. That which comprises the essence and power of the Church in a perfect degree is contained in the Mother of God through the Holy Spirit. As the Church in its personal realization the Mother of God is above every sin. She is a perfectly divinized and saved creature. The Mother of God is no longer being saved, for her unconditional salvation was accomplished by the visitation of the Holy Spirit. She *is not being saved but saves.* Here the particular participation of the Holy Spirit in our salvation is revealed and afterwards, that of the Mother of God, not as a saviour, for there is only one Saviour of the whole human race and of her as well, He about whom she speaks as "God and my Saviour," but as an advocate and intercessor for the human race.

The meaning of the Mother of God in this respect is twofold: on the one hand as a human being she represents in herself the whole creaturely world, the whole human race, every human soul. With her and in her in heaven *nature (natura naturata* inseparably from *natura naturans)* remains and bears witness through her about itself, about its creaturely impotence and its hunger for divine existence. On the other hand, in her the whole creation prays to God with a prayer formed by the Holy Spirit himself, "who intercedes for us with inexpressible sighs" (Rom 8.26). Every prayer of a weak and sinful human is powerless and limited in as much as it belongs to him, but when done in the Spirit and completed by the church it finds churchly wings which make it a prayer of the Church and raise it up to the very throne of God. Then, its might, power and authenticity bear no relation to its creaturely limitation any longer. But as much as it is a church prayer and in it there is something personal, by outstripping itself it grows into something universal, it becomes necessarily also the prayer of the Mother of God who, according to the testimony of church hymns, prays without ceasing to her Son for all people and all things. None of our prayers, not only one directed immediately to her but also one addressed directly to God, passes her by; rather, it becomes her own prayer, it is offered in and by her. Our words are both coarse and imprecise for the expression of this ontological dynamism: nothing ecclesial in the Church exists in separation or isolation or is composed of separate components like an aggregate or simple sum. But there is a certain dynamic sum where one is multiplied into all, combining with it, being interlaced in it like sound in music, and this unity of prayer, this soul of prayer belongs to her, who generally speaking is the soul of the church, spirit-bearing, glorified Mary, Mother of God.

The Mother of God does not need prayers for herself, for in her divinized state she possesses everything. As the glory of God and the glory of the world, as the love of God for the world and the love of the world for God put on view, she glorifies God with her prayer. Her *proper* prayer is doxology, i.e., love pre-eternally being realized, flaming and triumphing in perfect joy — the love of God for Himself in His creation. But the Mother of God, as head and representative of the world and the whole creation, also has a *non-proper* prayer which in virtue of the stated correlation is also her own prayer, is the prayer of every creature. She provides the wings for this prayer by lifting it to the throne of God, she gives power to this prayer, she is the intercessor, the one who raises her hands to God in high-priestly fashion over the world *(oranta)* and overshadows the world with her omophorion.

The Mother of God is the praying Church itself in a personal incarnation, in this sense she is the universal Mother, patroness and representative. She is personal, incarnated mercy and pity for the world in its creaturely limitation and sinful perverseness. Being Herself already absolutely free from this limitation and the power of sin, she is the gilded summit of this very world for she belongs to it. The saints and the prayers of the saints are a bright cloud encircling this summit and drawing near to it. However, the most exalted saints and even the angelic world are distinguished from the Mother of God not only by her perfect holiness but also by the perfect overcoming in her of creaturely limitation, by her divinization. Her own graced life is the hypostatic life of the Holy Spirit, who dwells in her, and at the same time her non-proper life is the life of the creaturely world, to which she belongs. Her mediatory significance consists in this: she brings to her Son, the Saviour of the world, the world saved by Him; its salvation is realized through and in her, and outside her and past her nothing is accomplished in the world. She gave flesh to her Son, and she is this God-bearing and theophoric flesh through which the flesh of the world is brought to Him for salvation. In humility before the will of God she offered the life of her Son to God in sacrifice, and as she stood by the cross she silently continued to say what was spoken once but forever: "behold the handmaid of the Lord."[48]

One must take a final step on this path, after recognizing that the outpouring of the Holy Spirit on all flesh is not accomplished without the participation of the Mother of God, who therefore was present at Pentecost. For her central place in the Church removes the possibility that anything might happen in the life of the Church apart from her and without her knowledge. Her significance as the abode of the Holy Spirit makes the activity of the Holy Spirit in creation also her co-activity. Hence, that striking fact becomes understandable, that the vast majority of miraculous and revealed icons are Mother of God icons, and many appearances of the heavenly world to the servants of God are appearances of the Mother of God. In the Mother of God are concentrated the *ecclesiality* of the Church and the power of ecclesialization, and those who make room for this power in themselves become the particular associates of the Mother of God, from "her race," as she herself was pleased to say about the wondrous Seraphim, who were made worthy of such repeated appearances of her. This is why reverence of the Mother of God is the measure of ecclesiality. The Church is the Holy Spirit, who gives life, and the revelation of the Holy Spirit grants comprehension and reverence of the Most Exalted Queen of heaven and earth.

From her innate nature flows out her sophianic significance as guardian of all creation, Queen of heaven and earth. Appropriate titles include sovereign of the seas, abundant provider of grains, fragrant flower, protector of cities and realms, and guardian of the vegetable kingdom. In general there is no creature which would not be subject to the Queen of heaven and earth. In *this* sense — but of course only in this sense — she can be called the soul of creation, more precisely the soul of the soul: for humankind as Adam, as lord of creation, is the soul of the world, and the Mother of God is the soul of the human race. As the pardoning heart, as maternal mercy and pity, not judging but only grieving and forgiving all things, the Mother of God appears at the Last Judgment where according to the iconographic witness of the Church, she prays the King on behalf of the human race and serves as advocate for sinners before the One who came to save sinners.

What does this advocacy signify, how it is to be understood? Is it not out of place before the One Who offered Himself for the salvation of many and accomplished this salvation with His blood? Here is the mystery and antinomy of redemption. It could be accomplished only by Christ's power, and yet Christ as God and at the same time the Son of Man, to Whom the Father has given all judgment, judges at His Last Judgment with a righteous judgment; but before the righteous judgment of God no flesh will be justified and all are subject to condemnation. Judgment was given by God the Father to the Son precisely because "he is the Son of Man" (Jn 5.27). The humanness of the Son is in the eyes of the Father the foundation upon which He may pass judgment on human beings. This foundation consists in this: by His hominization the New Adam saved the human race and was shown to be the true Human among all humans (as this is disclosed at the Last Judgment). He shared a common fate with humanity, and He raises it on the last day. But the Godman judges as *King,* with the impartial judgment of divine justice before which no one can stand, no creature. "Behold He does not trust even his holy ones and in His eyes the heavens are impure" (Job 15.15), "and he perceives deficiencies in His angels" (Job 4.18). "And do not enter into judgment with your servant (cries the psalmist) for no living thing shall be justified before you" (Ps 143.2). According to the judgment of justice who shall be shown justified? The judgment of justice can sound "depart from me, accursed, into eternal fire." The One who in His abasement will not snuff out a smouldering wick and will not shatter a fractured reed judges and condemns for ever according to the judgment of God's justice.[49]

But this justice is paradoxically attended by *mercy,* and the judgment of God is inseparably combined with forgiveness of infirmity: "have mercy on me, Lord, for not only am I infirm, but I am also your creature" (Prayer in preparation for Holy Communion).[50] This condescension towards infirmity, determining the very nature of creation summoned out of nonbeing, this mercy of forgiveness seemingly in spite of justice, the Mother of God manifests at the Last Judgment, praying her Son to have mercy on sinners. The humanness of the Godman, who appears here at the Last Judgment as God the Divine Judge replacing the Father, is represented here by the Mother of God who gave to Him that humanness: in her and through her He is "the Son of Man." The very fact that the Mother of God herself belongs to the creaturely world, and is connected with it by an ontological unity, although in a divinized state, gives her boldness for this advocacy at the dread hour for all creation. In the Last Judgment the twofold nature of the Godman, united out of divine and human nature indivisibly and without mingling, here presents itself as seemingly dyhypostatic, yet without being divided; for the divine hypostasis of the Logos performs the divine judgment of the Father and delivers to the creature the final determination of the whole Holy Trinity, while His humanity is hypostatically represented here in the person of His Mother.

The advocacy of Mary at the Last Judgment, in itself so mysterious, points to still a further mystery concealed here concerning the participation of the Third Hypostasis, the Holy Spirit, in this final tribunal, as well as beyond its bounds. There are no direct indications about this in church teaching, while indirect ones are connected with the general teaching about the transfiguration of the world, the creation of a new heaven and a new earth, the Heavenly Jerusalem coming down to earth. Of course all of this is accomplished by the power and operation of the Holy Spirit. The justice of God condemns the sinful world to fire: "the day of the Lord will come like a thief in the night, on that day the heavens will pass away with a clamour, the elements set on fire will be destroyed and the earth and the deeds that are on it will perish in flames" (2 Pet 3.10). The mercy of God, however, bears witness that "we expect a new heaven and a new earth according to his promise, in which justice lives" (2 Pet 3.13). This justice and the judgment of justice are entrusted by the Father to the Son of Man, the Word of God, who is the Truth of the world which exposes its sin. Mercy and the healing of the world's sores are entrusted to the Holy Spirit, who quickens every soul. The Mother of God at the Last Judgment shows not only the Humanity of the Son but the hypostatic revelation of the Holy Spirit through the human hypostasis of Mary as well. In Mary the Mother of God is revealed the participation of the Holy Spirit both at the judgment itself, determining the result of the world process, and beyond its limits in creation, in *the final* transfiguration of the world, which is already glorified in its summit, the Queen of heaven and earth.

That word which the Theotokos sang about herself in her hymn is being fulfilled in all times but will be fulfilled definitively at the Last Judgment of Christ: *for he has regarded the lowliness of his handmaiden, behold from this day forth all generations will call me blessed.* "O the depth of the riches and wisdom and knowledge of God! How unsearchable are His judgments, how inscrutable His ways! For from Him and through Him and in Him are all things. To Him be glory for ever. Amen" (Rom 11.33, 36).

Most Holy Theotokos, save us!

Prague.
Summer 1924

Appendix 2
From the Akathist of the Dormition of the Theotokos

"Rejoice, you whose all-bright soul takes up residence in the highest all-radiant Zion, rejoice, you whose uncorrupted body is glorified there together with your soul, rejoice you who entered the capital city of the Almighty Himself, rejoice you who are raised up to the beautiful paradise of the most high gardener" (Ikos 8). "Wanting to save the world, the Lord of all chose you from the earthly to be His mother . . . and He led you with Him to dwell in eternal glory and co-reign with Him without end" (Kontakion 10). With particular vividness the idea of the resurrection of the Mother of God and her bodily ascension into heaven is expressed in the service for the burial of the Mother of God performed in Gethsemane skete:

> "The praises or sacred service for the holy death of our Most Pure Lady the Theotokos and Ever-Virgin Mary"

Stikhera on the "Lord I have cried" (from the Jerusalem service)

This is the blessed Sabbath, this is the divine day of rest on which the mother who is life rested from life; by her gazing on death, she took Sabbath rest in the flesh and passed away and *entered into heaven* by the power of Christ our God who was incarnate of her; *and she abides with Him eternally in the ages of ages and bestows eternal life on us who with love honour her holy Dormition.*

When she who is life and who gave birth to the life of all, the Son of God in the flesh, was taken up ascending to the divine entrances, the pure one to the heavenly, then the miracle occurred which the Holy Spirit proclaimed: as she now is ascending from the wilderness, they sang with fear: glory to your ascending, beloved lady.

To the "God is the Lord," When you went down to death, immortal mother of life, then Hades marvelled and was filled with dread: when you were beheld appearing in heaven, Mary, all the heavenly powers cried from the grave: life-bearing Mother of our life, glory to you.

Praises from the first stasis

Your honourable body, virgin, did not see corruption in the grave, but with your body you passed from earth to heaven.

Now heaven gloriously receives the queen of the universe and is glad, beholding her reigning with God. The God of Glory, Your Son, pure one, with glory receives you as a Mother and seats you at his right hand.

O inexpressible joys! O unfathomable honours! Mary reigns with Jesus her Son in heaven and on earth.

O you who gained the Holy Spirit, divine bride of the one who took up lodging in you, seeing you without breath our spirit grows faint.

Even if you received burial, virgin, because you are mortal, as Mother of God you rise by the all-active Spirit of God.

The body which received God, although it lodges in the grave, does not grow accustomed to remain in the grave, and rises by divine power.

From the heavens the fruitless tree fell bitterly: now wondrously above the heavens is the fruit-bearing Virgin Mary.

Third stasis

Come near my Father, my dear one, having risen from the earth.
Come my Lovely one, and delight in the beauty of your Son and Creator.
Come, My Mother, to divine joy and the kingdom.
Come, Mary, where Father, Son and Spirit are worshipped.

What now shall I offer you in heaven, My God, if not the soul and body of
the Blessed One?

. . . see the sash and understand, the Virgin has risen from the grave.

. . . the time for sobbing has ceased, do not weep, tell the resurrection of
the Virgin.

. . . why do you think with the dead she who lives, for she rose as the parent of God?

Having born the Giver of Life, you passed over to the life that does
not grow old: joy in place of sorrow, O Virgin, you have given to the
disciples by rising from the grave, Virgin, like the Lord.

In the Akathist of the Dormition of the Most Holy Theotokos we read:

Kontakion 3: (Thomas) who knelt down to see her departing, understood
that she had been borne up to heaven with her body, and having come to
believe in this he shouted out: Alleluia.

Ikos 7: Rejoice, Thomas, after your burial by the power of God she
intercedes even more excellently; rejoice, through him having come to believe in your translation in the flesh into heaven. . . .

Ikos 8: Rejoice, you whose all holy soul takes up residence in the
highest all-radiant Zion; rejoice, you who entered into the capital city of
the Almighty Himself, rejoice, you who are raised up to beautiful paradise
of the gardener himself. Rejoice, you are brought to the city founded of
all-lustrous stones, rejoice, you who are led into the wall encircling the
warriors of the most high powers. Rejoice, taken above the heavens in the
reverence of God, rejoice honoured more than all immaterial minds. . . .

Kontakion 10: . . . (the Lord) came up to heaven from earth without
leaving anywhere and brought you with Him to abide in eternal glory and
to reign with Him without end. . . .

Ikos 10: The creator of heaven and earth proceeded from you in the
flesh, Most Pure One, He translated you spirit and body into the heavens
to be the most dear intercessor on all our behalf.

On the Glory of God in the Old Testament

The entire Old Testament speaks about the Mother of God and her race both as a whole and in particulars, beginning with the very creation of the world which, according to the interpretation of St John of Damascus, prefigured the birth of the Most Holy Virgin.[1] She is the new earth and heaven, created in place of the former ones defiled by sin. She is paradise and the woman promised by God in paradise whose seed would trample the head of the serpent (Gen 3.15). She is Noah's ark of salvation and the ladder seen in a dream by Jacob. She is the Burning Bush, seen by Moses, the Red Sea in which Israel was saved. She is the tabernacle and temple, both as a whole and in its parts, the Ark of the Covenant, the urn, the tablets, the incense stand and rod of Aaron. She is Gideon's fleece. She is the Queen of the psalm (Ps. 45) and the bride of the *Song of Songs* (St John of Damascus in his discourse on the Nativity of the Theotokos). She is the Virgin foretold by the prophet Isaiah (7.14) and the closed gates seen by the prophet Ezekiel (44.1-4). She is the mountain not hewn seen by the prophet Daniel,[2] the mountain overshadowed by a thicket[3] seen by the prophet Habakkuk. These prototypes and prophecies, attested in their relation to the Mother of God in church hymns and patristic literature, present no special difficulty for comprehension. But there is one group of prophetic visions which requires an interpretation and which refers to the Mother of God as well, namely the appearances of the Glory of God, and it is necessary to unveil the mysterious meaning which has these substantial images of the Glory of God in the Old Testament. It is our conviction this disclosure is possible only in conjunction with a general doctrine of divine Wisdom. The Glory of God is Sophia, or if one speaks with the expressions of St Gregory Palamas already received in Orthodoxy, the Glory of God is *the energy of God's energies* which alone are accessible to the creature, given the complete inaccessibleness (transcendentalness) of God's very essence. One way or the other, every Theophany arises in connection with the divine incarnation, and the principle of divine motherhood is inalienable from it. We propose to analyze and trace precisely this.

The first appearance of the *Glory of God* is described in Ex 16.7, 10: "and in the morning you shall see the Glory of God . . . they looked in the wilderness and there the Glory of God appeared *in a cloud.*" In this first appearance there is already present one feature which is repeated more frequently than any other in further *doxophanies* or appearances of Glory, namely the appearance in a cloud. The cloud signifies a kind of device which for weak eyes simultaneously covers and uncovers God's presence within that cloud. But in this very signification the prototype of the Mother of God is understood as the Church in the appearance of the cloud — such, for example, is the pillar of fire and cloud which led Israel in the wilderness.[4] Thus, already the first appearance of the Glory of God speaks about human Glory too, about the Mother of God. (Evidently in a series of passages where it is simply said "and the Glory of God appeared," Lev 9.6, 23; Num 14.10; 16.19, 42; 20.6 the appearance of a cloud is to be understood; it is directly said only in Num 16.42.)

The cloud appears at the consecration of the two places of divine worship: initially, at the consecration of the tent (Ex 40.34-35: "and a cloud covered the tent of assembly and the Glory of the Lord filled the tent. Moses could not enter the tent of assembly because a cloud overshadowed it, and the Glory of the Lord filled the tent"), and then at the consecration of Solomon's temple (1 Kg 8.10-11: "when the priests came out of the sanctuary a cloud filled the house of the Lord. And the priests could not stand in their service by reason of the cloud, for the Glory of the Lord filled the Lord's temple"; cf. 2 Chr 5.13-14). In connection with this one needs also to recall Num 9.15-23, which speaks about the cloud halting above the tent during encampments, and about its movements when underway. The tent and the temple in themselves are prototypes of the Mother of God, but the tent-temple, overhung with the cloud of God's glory, is already a double sign for her. She is the dwelling place of the Glory of God but is herself glorified; she is the dwelling place of the God who cannot be contained, but is herself divinized. In a word, where the Glory of God is spoken about undoubtedly the Mother of God is spoken of as well.

Let us turn now to the theophany to Moses, which also was an appearance of the Glory of God. Moses' climb up Mount Sinai is connected with the appearance of a cloud: "and Moses went up the mountain and a cloud covered the mountain. And the Glory of the Lord hung over Mount Sinai; and the cloud covered it for six days, but on the seventh day the Lord summoned Moses from the midst of the cloud. The appearance of the Lord's Glory on the summit of the mountain was like a devouring fire in the sight of the sons of Israel. Moses stepped into the middle of the cloud and went up the mountain; and Moses was on the mountain forty days and forty nights" (Ex 24.15-18). Here are united two revelations of the Glory of God: through a divine incarnation — a principle of divine motherhood, *a cloud,* and through a theophany — *a devouring fire,* and both are inseparably united to each other, for without the cloud cover the sight of the devouring fire would be unbearable for human eyes; a human cannot see the face of God and remain among the living (Ex 33.20). The revelation of the Glory of God in a form accessible for a human being is linked with the principle of divine motherhood. "Does not Moses delay a long time on the mountain because he had to learn the unknown mysteries of the Theotokos?" exclaimed one of the fathers (St Methodios of Patara).[5] "Moses said, show me your glory. And the Lord said, I shall pass all my glory before you and I shall utter my name before you; and on whom I am to have mercy I will have mercy, and whom I am to pity, I shall pity. And then He said: you may not see my face, because a human cannot see me and remain among the living" (Ex 33.18-20). These words of the Lord represent a direct explanation and supplement of the foregoing. They contain an indication that the vision of the Glory of God *is not* a vision of the Lord's Face, doxophany is not theophany. It is a revelation of God accessible and bearable for humans but not the vision of the Face of God, God's essence. This is confirmed by the witness of the apostle John, which refers of course to Moses as well: "No one has ever seen God" (Jn 1.18; 1 Jn 4.12. Cf. 1 Tim 6.16). In further words of the Lord this conclusion is expressed in anthropomorphous images: "The Lord said, here is a place by me. Stand on this rock. When my glory passes by, I will place you in a cleft of the rock and cover you with my hand, until I shall have passed by. When I remove my hand you will see me from behind, but my face will not be visible" (Ex 33.21-23). The premeditated and seemingly exaggerated anthropomorphic concreteness of these images covers rather than uncovers the mystery of God's operation in a human being who accommodates from God only what is feasible. But thereby the distinction established above receives even greater emphasis as in a certain sense does the contrasting of God's hypostatic essence, "God's Face," and His Glory. In Ex 34.5-6 the very appearance of Glory is described in such features: "the Lord came down *in a cloud* and remained there near it and proclaimed the Name of Yahweh, and the Lord passed before his face and exclaimed: The Lord, the Lord, a God who loves humankind and is gracious, long-suffering, abounding in kindness and true." There two features startle. First, the appearance of Glory is depicted here as the descent of God in a cloud, which is, as we already know, one of the Old Testament images of the Mother of God. The appearance of Glory here is divine motherhood and divine incarnation. Glory is the Mother of God in whom the Lord descends, from whom the Lord is born by the visitation of the Holy Spirit; it is the Sophia of the Theotokos. But proclaimed at the same time is the Name of Yahweh which is the Word who reveals, speaks and names the Father. This proclamation of the Name also speaks about the divine incarnation, expressed no longer with respect to the principle of receptive divine motherhood, but to the incarnating Logos Himself. The Glory of God is here in this sense the Godman, Christ-Sophia.

In such a combination the text concerning the Glory of God mysteriously contains in itself a verbal icon of the Mother of God, of the Mother with Infant, the Cloud and the Name (the term itself points to the divine incarnation: *"God who loves humankind and is merciful"*).

And so *the first* appearance of the Glory of God to the holy prophet Moses contains in itself the mystery of divine motherhood and the mystery of divine incarnation. This mystery is shown by God prior to its fulfilment in time by virtue of its pre-eternal design. A further detail of the narrative, namely, that "Moses' face began to shine with rays because God was speaking with him" (Ex 34.29), indicates the divine power present in the appearance of the Glory of God, and Ex 34.34 directly says that "Moses entered before the Face of the Lord in order to speak with Him," thereby affirming, so to say, the divine authenticity of this appearance, i.e., that for Moses within the limits of his human possibility the vision of Glory was also an entrance before the Face of God, although it was not a vision of God according to His essence. At the same time the glorification of Moses has a relation to the illumination of Mount Tabor in which Moses also took part: this is the light of the Glory of God, which the Lord showed to His disciples on Mount Tabor.

The appearance of the Glory of God was, in accord with what has been said, the appearance of Wisdom simultaneously in its Christological and Theotokos aspects. This makes the God-seer Moses the chosen mystagogue of the divine incarnation, which corresponds to his place in the history of the church as the establisher of the law and, in this sense, the founder of the Old Testament church. In the law, liturgical and ritual, the advent of grace in the world, the incarnation of the Son of God from the Virgin Mary, was promised covertly — like "the canopy of the law" — and the whole ritual law, the temple and the sacrifices are elucidated in this sense in the letter to the Hebrews. Therefore extraordinary revelations concerning the Mother of God, which become accessible in the light of the achievements and revelations of the New Testament, were given to Moses the prophet of God. God revealed His Name to him and made him a God-seer, friend and confidant. Moses wore a veil on his face because weak human eyes could not endure the radiance, the reflection of God's Glory. But in the New Testament God was incarnated and "lived among humans" and "we have seen His Glory as of the Only-Begotten of the Father, full of grace and truth" (Jn 1.14). This veil, according to the explanation of the apostle Paul (2 Cor 3.13-16), lies also on the hearts of Israel for it can only be removed by Christ, so that they "might not gaze on the end of what was passing." But for Christians this veil is removed, and it is clear how overflowing Moses the God-seer was *with the vision of the Mother of God*[6] who is prefigured and prepared by the whole of Old Testament piety.

Particularly deserving attention among the revelations of the Mother of God to Moses, besides the revelation of the Glory of God, is the first theophany to him — the Burning Bush, which is invariably explained by the Church as an image of the Holy Virgin.[7] Thus there exists a special icon of the Most Holy Virgin, called "The Burning Bush." (The depiction of the Mother of God with cosmic symbols in the centre of a four-pointed star, inscribed in a rational heaven, filled with angels; on the corner of the four points are four animals from the vision of Ezekiel and Revelation, corresponding to the four Gospels; there is, by the way, under this same name a depiction of the Mother of God in a circle of fire like the shrub seen by Moses.)

Ex 3.2: "and the Angel of the Lord appeared to him (Moses) in the flame of fire from the midst of the blackthorn bush. And he saw that the blackthorn bush was burning with fire but the bush was not burning up." The Angel of the Lord, here as in other cases of theophany (e.g. Gen 18;[8] Num 22.31, 5.1; Judg 2.1-4), is used with obvious indifference in place of God Himself (compare the speech of the protomartyr Stephen in Acts 7.30-31, 35). The general patristic understanding sees here in each instance a certain portent of the divine incarnation; sometimes it likens the angel directly to the Son of God, sometimes it sees a manifestation of the triune God (an allusion to trinitarity is perceived in the threefold naming: "the God of your father, the God of Abraham, the God of Isaac and the God of Jacob," Ex 3.6).

The appearance of the angel in the bush must be understood in comparison with the vision of the Glory of God. As in the latter, with the impossibility of seeing God Himself, "the Face of God," Moses nonetheless is made worthy to see His Glory, so also here Moses "turned away his face for he was blessed to look on God" (Ex 3.6). And yet in this dread he does gaze on God, he carries on a conversation with His angel. In other words, he receives a theophany feasible for him, which, more precisely, is a doxophany, an appearance of Divine Sophia in the form of the divine incarnation foretold. Two moments of this sophiophany are present: on the one hand the Burning Bush itself, a shrub enveloped by fire, blazing and not being consumed, "holy ground" (Ex 3.5). This is the Mother of God, overshadowed by the Holy Spirit. On the other hand, the appearance of the Angel of God in the flames of fire from the midst of the blackthorn bush (Ex 3.2), the very "Lord who calls out to Moses from the midst of the bush" (Ex 3.4). This is the Son of God being incarnated. Hence this vision is a shadowy icon of the Mother of God seen by the prophet Moses, an image of divine incarnation in which the fire of divinity penetrates and divinizes creaturely nature without burning it up. Divine Sophia is united with the creaturely, whence it has two forms of appearance, in Christ and in the Mother of God. In other words, the vision of the Burning Bush given to Moses is identical in essence to the vision of the Glory of God requested by him of God. There is one feature, which corroborates and discloses this likening: we saw that the appearance of Glory was connected with the proclamation of God's Name (Ex 33.19, 34.5, 6). But here too the proclamation of the Name, requested by Moses (Ex 3.13), also occurs in the phenomenon of the bush. From the blazing bush, God reveals to him His Name, mighty and dread, which was surrounded with great veneration in Old Testament piety.[9] God's Name — Jehovah, Yahweh — is usually considered an Old Testament revelation concerning the Divinity and refers to the *hypostatic* self-existence of Divinity: *The One who is, I am who I am, I AM BEING.* In this sense this Name can also refer to the whole Most Holy Trinity, in unity of essence, to the triune hypostatic God. But the Holy Trinity is named and has its own Name in the Son. He is the Name of the Father (as in the Lord's Prayer we read, *Our Father* — the First Hypostasis, hallowed by *Thy Name* — the Second Hypostasis). The Name of the Father revealed to Moses — *The One Who Is, ho on,* is also the Name of the Son. He gives direct testimony to this Himself in the New Testament: "I am the alpha and the omega, the beginning and the end, says the Lord, the One Who Is and who was and who is to come, the Almighty" (Rev 1.8, cf. 1.10; 2.8). The immediate relation of this text to the Logos can be called into question although it is obvious from the text and parallels that the name *ho on* refers to Christ, along with the names that indisputably belong to Him: alpha and omega, beginning and end. This interpretation of the text of Rev 1.8 is corroborated by iconography where customarily the depiction of the Saviour as the Logos, the Pre-eternal Child, is inscribed with the Greek *ho on,* which is the Greek translation of the Hebrew Yahweh. In this manner the joining of the Name with the theophany, the pronouncing of the Name from the midst of the flaming blackthorn bush, directly speaks about the incarnation of the second Person of the Holy Trinity from the Virgin Mary, and the most sweet *Name of Jesus* is the new-testamental, divine human *Name of Yahweh* (and is here not the reason that before the advent of Christ respect for the Name *of Yahweh* is lost and forgotten?).

The appearance of God to Moses on Mount Horeb supposes the beginning of a new epoch of divine worship, preparatory-educational and under the law, which continues until John the Forerunner; it is revealed through the vision of the Mother of God in the bush but is brought to an end and exhausted by her appearance in the world and the divine incarnation accomplished through this. This exceptional knowledge of the mystery of divine incarnation by Moses receives its corroboration (besides the direct prophecy concerning the prophet in Deut 18.15-19) in the appearance of Moses and Elijah beside the Lord Himself on the mountain of Transfiguration, revealing their special penetration into the mystery of redemption. "When they appeared in glory, they spoke about His departure which He was to complete in Jerusalem" (Lk 9.31).

Next to Moses is the prophet Elijah as a sage of the mystery of redemption. Here that theophany unavoidably comes to mind of which this great zealot for true divine worship was found worthy in the days of the great trials for the faith. "And He (the Lord) said to him, go out and stand on the mountain before the face of the Lord. And there the Lord will pass by, and there will be a great and powerful wind rending mountains and shattering rocks before the Lord, but the Lord will not be in the wind. After the wind there will be an earthquake, but the Lord will not be in the earthquake. After the earthquake there will be fire, but the Lord will not be in the fire. After the fire there will be the blowing of a gentle wind (inbreathing of a thin cold)."[10] The mysterious meaning of this theophany is disclosed through a comparison with the theophany to Moses together with whom Elijah was present on Mount Tabor, as one privy to the redemption and theophany. The appearance of God in the phenomena of nature — not in menacing and stupendous ones that seemingly were more appropriate to the flaming zeal of Elijah and to his entire ministry, but in meek and caressing ones — corresponds to divine condescension, the abasement of the Lord in His incarnation. The very blowing of a gentle wind by such an interpretation receives the same meaning that the cloud has for Moses; it refers to the Mother of God as to a living medium between God and human beings, bearing the God who cannot be contained. Such an interpretation finds for itself its chief support in that place which is given to Elijah along with Moses on the mountain of Transfiguration. (Also when the Lord indicates that the Forerunner, whose whole ministry is connected with the coming of the Saviour on earth, comes in the spirit and power of Elijah, it is Elijah who must come: Mt 11.14, 17.11-12; Mk 9.12; Lk 1.17.)

The prophet Isaiah to whom was given the *second* appearance of the Glory of God is an Old Testament evangelist, prophesying the divine incarnation, and he also had prophetic knowledge about the Mother of God. A direct prophecy of the birth of Emmanuel by the Virgin (Is 7) belongs to him, unique among the prophets.

The Church sees her image also in "the swift cloud" on which the Lord comes to Egypt (Is 19.1). It is also contained in the vision of God's Glory to which we now turn in Is 6.1-7: "In the year of the death of King Uzziah I saw the Lord Adonai sitting on a throne high and lofty and the hems of his garment (in the LXX translation: and His Glory; in the Slavonic translation: the house is full of his glory) filled the whole temple" (Is 6.1). This variant reading of the LXX translation from the Masoretic text is decisive. "No one sees God anywhere," and, if it is said that Isaiah "saw God" this obviously refers to a vision not of God Himself but of His Glory, as this is directly said by John the Evangelist: "Isaiah . . . saw His Glory . . . *tēn doxan autou* and spoke about Him (Jn 12.41); according to the apostle Paul, he heard the Holy Spirit (Acts 28.25). From a comparison of these clues it follows that in his vision of the Glory, Isaiah was given a triple revelation of Father, Son and Holy Spirit, of the whole Holy Trinity, and this is evident as well from the threefold exclamation of the seraphim: "holy, holy, holy is the Lord of Hosts, the whole earth is full of His Glory" (Is 6.3). (This is also indicated in the use of the pronoun: "whom shall I send and who will go for Us?" Is 6.8.) This vision of the Glory, compared with that of Moses, is notable for how a revelation of trinitarity comes much more plainly to the fore. Here the appearance of Glory, turned both towards the divine world as well as towards the creaturely world, refers not only to the Glory of God but also to the Glory of the world, to the Mother of God. The Church in particular interprets the tongs with the burning coals held in the hands of the seraphim as an image of the Mother of God receiving the fire of Divinity.[11]

But according to the fundamental meaning, the vision of the Mother of God is that high and lofty throne on which Christ is seated.[12] She is more glorious beyond compare than the seraphim who, covering their faces and feet with their wings and flying around the throne, cry out to the holy Trinity "holy, holy, holy is the Lord of hosts," but already with reference to the Mother of God, "the whole earth is full of Your Glory." For, she is that earth which is the receptacle of God's Glory, the fulfilled Glory of the world. Such is the meaning of Isaiah's vision with reference to the Theotokos.

It now is incumbent upon us to pass over to the third and final Old Testament vision of the Glory, the most mysterious, namely that of the prophet Ezekiel. A revelation about the Mother of God was made known to the prophet above all in the image of the closed eastern gates through which no one passes except the Lord (Ezek 44.1-4). The Church, by selecting this excerpt for a liturgical reading in services honouring the Theotokos, interprets this vision as applying to the Mother of God. And indeed the whole second part of the book of the prophet Ezekiel (chapters 40–48), referring to the organization of the temple and the sacrifices, mysteriously refers to the Mother of God as well, prefigured by the temple and the tent.

But *the Glory of God* is a special revelation given to the prophet Ezekiel and which singles him out from all the prophets. Through the vision of the Glory, Ezekiel is summoned to prophetic ministry (Ezek 1–2) and it accompanies him on all his ways. Ezekiel himself nowhere gives a definition of Glory; he speaks about it in concrete religious images, as about an appearance that occurs at a definite time and place, shifting, arriving and departing (Ezek 3.12-13, 23; 8.4; 9.3; 10.4; 10.22;[13] 11.22-23; 43.2-5). The appearance of Glory is no longer connected with the temple as it was at the time of Moses and Solomon (Ex 16.10; 1 Kg 8.11; 2 Chron 5.14). It is distinguished from the essence of God, "the Face of God," for of it is said "such was the vision of the image of the Lord God's Glory" (Ezek 1.28), and it is not identified with the Lord Himself who speaks to the prophet (Ezek 1.28–2.3), although the revelation of God is connected with this appearance.

It is not part of our task to provide a detailed explanation of the mysterious vision of Ezekiel's chariot (chapter 1), all the details of which scarcely submit to an interpretation in the limits of the present age. But all the more important is it to note some of its features. From the midst of fire was seen "a likeness of four living creatures" and "their face was like that of a human" (Ezek 1.5). "The likeness of their faces was the face of a human and the face of a lion on the right side of all four, and on the left side, the face of a calf on all four and the face of an eagle on all four" (Ezek 1.10). (This vision is repeated in Rev 4.7.) These living creatures correspond to the symbols of the four evangelists who represent the Man Christ as a human, a calf, a lion and an eagle. The human being combines in itself the power, wisdom and meekness of the animal kingdom, for it is a cosmic being, a microcosm. These mysterious symbols of the four evangelists, referring to different images of Christ's ministry, contain in themselves a mysterious indication of the relation of humankind to the pre-human world and its transformation, brightening and humanization into a human being. In a word, in the four living creatures of the fourfold Gospel is contained the mysterious revelation that the human being is anthropo-cosmos, heading up the whole creaturely world, and that all creation is in a certain sense a Human Being (just as Moses' account of the six days, which concludes with the creation of the human being, is in essence a narrative about his creation).

The vision of Ezekiel is at the same time a revelation concerning the heavenly and eternal nature of humankind, about "the heavenly human being" (and in this sense there is as it were an explanation of the words of Proverbs 8.31 concerning the Wisdom of God: "and my joy is in human sons"). In the Glory of God an image of humankind is present, created after the image of God. Nonetheless, one must point out that a human countenance is ascribed also to the cherubim (Ezek 10.20-22), who carry the Lord's throne above the firmament stretching over them (Ezek 1.22, 26), and yet they belong not to the human but to the angelic world. To this one can reply that the fullness of human, and generally speaking cosmic, nature is not ascribed to the cherubim here; they are *the likeness* of the four living creatures," they have a countenance "as humans have" (Ezek 1.5). The nature of the spiritual world, the angelic, remains other than that of the human world. Nonetheless a *ministering* relation to this world is proper to the angels, and thus a certain ontological kinship with it and correlation: in order to serve humankind, they need to have a human likeness (this correlation is impressed in the doctrine that everyone has a personal guardian angel who is their heavenly image). In other words, the Glory of the heavenly world corresponds to the Glory of the human world and is — in this sense — human. This explains why the highest ranks of angels on which the Lord rests, "seated on the cherubim," exhibit both animal and human qualities.

This idea about the heavenly image of humankind, a reflection of which lies on the angelic world, receives a new confirmation in the further details of the vision: above the vault over their heads was the likeness of a throne, but "above the likeness of the throne was something like a human on top of it" (Ezek 1.26). This likeness of a human on a throne bears direct witness to the heavenly pre-eternity of the human image, visible not only in the creaturely spiritual world of the cherubim carrying the throne on themselves, but also on the throne itself (this represents an analogy to Daniel's vision of the Son of Man, Dan 7.9, 13-14; cf. Rev 4-5).

The Church sees in the human likeness seated on the throne an image of the incarnation of the Son of God.[14] This vision, however, which was before the incarnation, bears witness to the pre-eternity of the human image in the heavens, by virtue of which the creation of the human and, as its new creation, the divine incarnation, was possible. If we are to understand the vision in relation to the divine incarnation and see in it only a prophecy about Christ, then in that case we unavoidably arrive at the conclusion that the human creaturely nature, glorified in Him, likewise participates in the Glory of God. The Glory of God embraces in itself both the eternal world and the world created according to its image, in their ontological unity, Divine Sophia which is revealed in the Son of Man.

The revelation of Sophia, of the Glory of God, inalienably contains in itself the principle of divine motherhood, which is why Ezekiel's vision, similar to that of Moses and Isaiah, refers also to the Mother of God. "The throne of the cherubim is the Virgin," more honourable than the cherubim and more glorious beyond compare than the seraphim — this is indicated in the vision of the throne with the One Seated on it, and the whole wondrous chariot signifies the Most Holy Virgin who in church hymns is called "the chariot of the rational Sun," "the fiery chariot of the Word." The allusions to the Theotokos characterizing Ezekiel's vision are corroborated in his vision of the rainbow that also appeared to Noah after the flood and that signifies the Church and the Most Holy Virgin (Ezek 1.28).

And so, Ezekiel's vision, containing an insight into the mystery of the divine incarnation conceals in itself an insight about the Mother of God as the Glory of the world.[15] Therefore a comparison of Ezekiel's vision with the teaching about the Wisdom of God in Proverbs 8, Wisdom 7.22-30, 8, 10-12, and Sirach 1.24, suggests itself. Generally speaking the Glory of God is only another image of the Wisdom of God. As does Sophia, so does Glory have two faces: a Christ-Sophianic and a Theotokos-Sophianic, a divine and a creaturely face. Prophecy about the divine incarnation has as its content simultaneously Christ and the Mother of God, the appearance of Christ and the outpouring of the Holy Spirit.

Thus the vision of God's Glory shown to Ezekiel signifies both the Theotokos and Sophia: God in creation and creation in God, a creature being divinized. Only in conjunction with this is it possible to understand that peculiarity of Ezekiel's doxophany, where the Glory of God arrives and departs, enters the temple and leaves the temple. In a word, it seems to have an earthly history, and enters into a reciprocal relation with the human race. This is completely incomprehensible in relation to the pre-eternal Glory of God which exists before the creation of the world (Jn 17.5), but is fully applicable to the Glory that is revealed in creation and possesses therefore a history. This is the history of the Old Testament Church which the prophet Ezekiel has in mind, i.e., *before* the Mother of God, and also the New Testament Church *after her and with her.* In her the history of the world and of the Church interiorly comes to an end for it reaches its culmination. She is the already accomplished Glory of creation, creaturely Sophia. However, in the human world the history of the church continues until the end of this age. The miraculous icon of the Mother of God and her merciful appearances to the saints are new-testamental likenesses of the Glory seen by Ezekiel as it draws near and withdraws from the temple, appearing or stealing away from human beings.

Thus, all three doxophanies include in themselves a revelation about the Mother of God as the Glory of the world and the Throne of God. The appearances of God's Glory are up to a certain degree prototypes and prophecies about what is coming, predictions of future events. Their meaning, however, is not exhausted by this temporal fulfilment, for in the temporal is disclosed what exists from the ages, and in God everything temporal is eternal. In time the Son of God was incarnated and He was taken up into heaven with His most pure flesh, but even for eternity He remains the Godman, sitting on the throne of Glory as He was seen by the prophet Ezekiel. Here is an antinomy for reason, which is not capable of uniting the temporal and the eternal, and a sweet mystery of faith: what is for us temporal is eternal in God. But what refers to the divine incarnation, to the Son, refers also to the Source of the incarnation, the Ever-Virgin. Her life begins and flows in time. Only since a familiar fixed period of time does she become Mother of God, and the power and grace of divine motherhood enters the world as if for the first time. However, divine motherhood exists for God pre-eternally, as it was given to be perceived in the appearances of Glory to the holy prophets of God. The creation of the world, accomplished in time, like the whole life of the creature, exists in God in an eternal manner. The heart of creation and its glory is the Mother of God. And if, according to the sage word of Tertullian,[16] "when He formed each feature of Adam's body out of clay, God was thinking of Christ who someday would become human," then in creating Eve, the Lord built a temple of the body of the coming Mother of God. Similarly, just as the place in the heavens for the Godman, who ascended and is seated at the right hand of the Father, is pre-eternal, for there is no change in God, so too a place in the heavens for the Mother of God who is seated at the right hand of the Son, is prepared pre-eternally as the foundation for the creation of the world; the world is created for the sake of the Mother of God as Her dwelling-place. One cannot imagine in the world anything absolutely accidental, or such that it could be and not be, and this impious thought is all the more inappropriate with respect to the Mother of God. The divine incarnation is usually connected with redemption from sin and subordinated, consequently, to the accomplished fall. In this conception the notion *implicite* creeps in that the appearance of the Mother of God is connected with the fall of the progenitors, for without this, it would have been unnecessary and therefore accidental. Such a thought is completely subverted by the biblical narratives about the appearance of God's Glory which refer to God Himself and not to a human being and which reveal a divine world. In this world an inalienable place belongs to the divine incarnation and divine motherhood. These appearances comprise as it were the heavenly prologue to the New Testament. They bear witness about the Mother of God as the pre-eternal Glory of the world, visible in God earlier than the Virgin Mary appeared in the history of humanity. As the Lord in His Glory sits on the cherubim and is adored by the seraphim, by these second but all the same creaturely lights, so too the Throne of the One Sitting in the likeness of human form is glorified creation, the Mother of God, more honourable than the cherubim and more glorious beyond compare than the seraphim. She along with the angel hosts has a share in Divine Glory as "the Church of God is all-radiant."[17]

This does not mean in any way or in any sense that the Mother of God has entered the core of the Holy Trinity as a special fourth hypostasis (such a tendency is sometimes observed in Catholic theology), just as the angelic "second lights" do not enter into this core. But without entering into the Holy Trinity, the Mother of God through the blessing of grace participates as *the Blessed One* in divine life by virtue of her perfect divinization. She is Wisdom in creation, and in her is revealed the fullness of Divine triunity. She lives the life of the Holy Trinity and is the first of creaturely hypostases, the beloved Daughter of God and also Mother of the whole human race. She is the Glory of the world, the Burning Bush, creaturely nature, burning and not being burned up in the divine flame of the Holy and Life-giving Trinity.

The Old Testament Doctrine
of the Wisdom of God

In the Old Testament, the doctrine of Wisdom *(Sophia, chokma)* is set forth in one of the canonical books, *the Proverbs of Solomon,* and in two uncanonical books, *the Wisdom of Solomon* and *the Wisdom of Jesus ben Sirach.* (To this can be added Job 28.12-28.)

Proverbs 1-9 sets forth an integral theological doctrine about Wisdom (which is why among early Christian authors the book itself bore the title *hē panaretos sophia* — all-good Wisdom, as did the book of Jesus ben Sirach; other titles are *hē sophē biblos* or *hē paidagōgikē Sophia,* in the Talmud, "the book of wisdom"). The word *wisdom* is used here undoubtedly in a double sense: in a metaphysical and a moral-practical sense, signifying at one time a certain rational essence, at another time a human quality, now Wisdom itself, now a participation in it or its works. Both shades of meaning of course are connected and mutually conditioned; however, in individual cases they can be particularized and differentiated as Wisdom and simply as understanding.[1]

From the Book of Proverbs the following texts undoubtedly speak *about wisdom as understanding:*

1.7 — the beginning of wisdom is the fear of the Lord; 9.10 — only fools despise wisdom and admonition.

2.6 — The Lord gives wisdom; 2.10 — when wisdom enters your heart (the Slavonic translation reads "your thought"), and knowledge (Slavonic "the feeling of your soul") will be pleasant to you.

3.13 — blessed is the man who has found wisdom, and the man who has gained understanding (see further 3.14-18).

4.5 — gain wisdom, gain understanding; 4.7 — the chief thing is wisdom: gain wisdom and with all your possessions acquire understanding.

5.1 — Son! Pay heed to my wisdom.

7.4 — Say to wisdom: "you are my sister," and call reason your darling.

There are instances when the meaning of the term "wisdom" is twofold and can be interpreted in one and the other way. To this point we relate the first speech in the name of wisdom, Proverbs 1.20-33, "Wisdom cries out in the street," etc. According to the content of this speech there is no necessity to see here a direct indication of Divine Wisdom itself; it is more natural to understand *wise men,* bearers of wisdom and preachers (Old Testament prophets and teachers), although the first, metaphysical, interpretation is not excluded. 3.19-20 is also notable for the same duality, "The Lord founded the earth by Wisdom, He established the heavens by understanding, by His Wisdom (Slavonic, "in His feeling") the depths broke open and the clouds sprinkle with dew." Here, however, both a descriptive interpretation (together: *wisely, reasonably*) and an ontological one are appropriate, in connection with the content of chapter 8.

There is no doubt that Wisdom receives an ontological meaning in her second speech, in the second half of chapter 8. The first half, Proverbs 8.4-21, is little different from the moral-practical teaching of chapter 1.22-33. But suddenly, beginning with 8.22, a sharp transition of thought is made and the speech begins not about wisdom but about Wisdom as a pre-worldly principle. We will cite this passage according to the Russian text, indicating variant readings.

22. The Lord *possessed* me as the beginning of His paths, before His creations from time immemorial (Slavonic, "the Lord *created* me the beginning of his paths in his works"). ("Possessed" corresponds to the Greek reading *ektēsato, created* to *ektise.* On this point the Slavonic and Russian texts represent *two different redactions.* According to the reading of the Slavonic text, which appears to be the more ancient, Wisdom *is created;* according to the Russian reading, corresponding to a more correct text, nothing is said here about its origin; the text only testifies to its presence.)[2]

23. From the ages *I was anointed prokecheirisma* (Symmachus), from the beginning, before the existence of the earth (Slavonic, "before the ages *he founded me — ethemeliōse me* in the beginning before he created the earth").[3]

24. *I was born (Slavonic, "he gave me birth") when the depths still did not exist, when there were still no fountains abundant with water.*[4]

25. *I was born before even the mountains were raised, before the hills.*

26. *When He had not created either the earth or fields or the elementary*

specks of dust of the universe (Slavonic, "The Lord created uninhabited lands and districts inhabited beneath the skies").

27. *When He prepared the heavens, I was there, when He drew a circular tracing on the face of the deep.*

28. *When He made firm the clouds above, when He strengthened the fountains of the deep.*

29. *When He gave the sea its law, so that the waters would not overstep its bounds, when He laid the foundations of the world.*

30. *Then I was in His presence **as an artisan** (lacking in the Slavonic) and I was joy every day, making merry before His face for all time.*

31. *Making merry on His earthly sphere, my joy was with the sons of men* (Slavonic, "when I made merry, the universe having been made, I made merry on account of the sons of men").

Afterwards, from 8.32 until the end of the chapter, 8.36, the speech about Wisdom ceases and once again the wisdom that the sons of men discover is spoken of.

As we see, Wisdom is defined here as a beginning, existing before the creation of the world; and placed by God in its foundation.[5] Her origin from God, like her relation to God, is described in indefinite terms, which is why various interpretations prove possible. According to one of these interpretations, Wisdom is created and is *the creaturely principle* of the universe, as it were an instrument in God's hands or a creaturely mediator between God and the world (understood this way, these texts were very suitable for the conception of Arianism). However, this interpretation is supported by only *one* of the variants of 8.22, preserved in our Slavonic translation: *the Lord created me.* Currently, this reading is not considered to correspond to the precise meaning (not *created* but *possessed*). This Arian notion does not fit in any Orthodox doctrine whatsoever and it must be unconditionally rejected; however, it is generally erroneous to see here any sort of definite teaching about *the origin* of Wisdom in this series of expressions: *possessed me, I am anointed, I was born (summoned into existence), I was.* These descriptive expressions contain the general idea that Wisdom is pre-worldly with God and that she is a world-creating principle. But it would do violence to the text to affirm that it here establishes a definite teaching on the provenance of Wisdom only by means of generation and on this basis to understand here a hidden teaching about the generation of the Son from the Father (the use of a term of the feminine gender — *chokmah, Sophia, Premudrost'* — and not one corresponding to Son, hinders this interpretation).

There are also no grounds which would require us to understand the term Wisdom to mean without fail and exclusively the Second Hypostasis, the Son of God, although such an interpretation, Arian in its initial derivation, received a broad dissemination in the writings of the church fathers too (See Excursus 3). Primarily on the basis of 1 Cor 1.24, Christ is usually called in those writings "the power of God and the wisdom of God," but even this rule admits of exceptions, and some very important ones at that: in two of the most ancient authors it is not the Second but the Third Hypostasis, the Holy Spirit, who is called Wisdom, namely in St Theophilus of Antioch[6] and St Irenaeus[7] bishop of Lyons.

Before settling on our own conclusion, faced with the whole contentiousness and vagueness of this question even in patristic literature, we must search for an interpretation of this text on the basis of the Word of God itself by comparing the doctrine of Wisdom in the *Wisdom of Solomon* and the *Wisdom of Jesus ben Sirach*. True, both books are uncanonical (deuterocanonical according to Catholic terminology) but the authority even of uncanonical books found in the Bible is so great that this interpretation ought to be accepted in the first instance.[8] And so, what doctrine of Wisdom do we have, first of all, in the book of the *Wisdom of Solomon,* which represents as it were a commentary on Prov 8.22-35?

In its teaching about Wisdom, the book of the *Wisdom of Solomon* (*hē panaretos, hē theia sophia* among the Greek fathers, *hē sophia Salomonos* among the Alexandrians) partially differs from and partially resembles the corresponding teaching of Proverbs.

A first difference is that the author of *Wisdom* speaks not only about Wisdom as such but also about the spirit of Wisdom: 1.5 — "the holy spirit of Wisdom" (Slavonic, "for the holy spirit of instruction"), "the philanthropic spirit of Wisdom" (1.7). (In the following verse, contextually in connection with the teaching about the spirit of Wisdom it says "The Spirit of the Lord fills the universe and as an all-encompassing spirit, knows every word" 1.8.) In chapter 7 this teaching about the spirit of Wisdom continues: "I have come to know everything, what is hidden and what is plain, for Wisdom taught me, the artisan of everything *(hē gar pantōn technitēs)*. For in it there is[9] a spirit, fine, mobile, bright, pure, not harmful, loving the good, quick, irrepressible, beneficent, philanthropic, firm, unwavering, peaceful, unoriginate, all-seeing and penetrating all intelligent, pure and most fine souls" (7.22-23). (The quantity of epithets is $21 = 3 \times 7$, the product of two perfect numbers, which, according to the opinion of commentators, was intentionally chosen.) The author of the book of Wisdom "prayed and understanding was given me, I cried out and the spirit of Wisdom came down upon me" (7.7). In connection with this, so we think, we ought to understand the text: "who would come to know your will unless you gave them Wisdom (*sophian,* without the article, and consequently without a definite interpretation) and sent down from on high your Holy Spirit?" (9.17).[10]

Along side of this teaching *about the spirit of Wisdom* the author also speaks about Wisdom itself, though without making a clear distinction between it and the spirit of Wisdom. Thus in the same chapter 7 the text of verses 22-23 known to us continues without any transition in this manner: "for Wisdom is more mobile than any motion and by her purity she passes through and penetrates everything. She is the breathing of God's power and the pure outpouring of the Glory of the Almighty *(tēs tou Pantokratoros doxēs).* She is the reflection of eternal light and the pure mirror of God's operation — *tēs tou theou energeias* — the image of His goodness. She is one but can do all and while remaining in herself she renews all and passing from generation to generation in holy souls she prepares the friends of God and the prophets, for God loves nothing except those who live with Wisdom" (7.24-28).

All of these expressions are undoubtedly evidence for an ontological understanding of Wisdom, as some kind of intelligent essence, shown in Divine revelation, but they offer no possibility of referring her entirely, so to say, to the domain of the Second Hypostasis or of directly equating her with It (as is understood by some interpreters). If such expressions as "reflection of eternal light" (recalling "light from light" in the creed) or "pure outpouring of the glory of the Almighty" (cf. Heb 1.3, "who is the shining of glory and the image of his hypostasis") favour this, the words "passing from generation to generation in holy souls she prepares the friends of God and the prophets" (Wis 7.27) can be referred with considerable grounds to the gracious operation of the Holy Spirit. The following texts oppose even more so such a hypostatic interpretation in the sense of designating any one of them as the Second or even the Third Hypostasis: "I have loved her (Wisdom) from my youth and desired *to take her as my bride* and I became an admirer of her beauty. She glorifies her nobility, *having a life together with God.* She is an initiate of the knowledge of God — *mustis gar esti tes tou theou epistemes*" (8.2-4). "Thus I determined to take her to live with me knowing that she would be for me a counsellor for the good and a comfort in labours and sorrows" (8.9. Cf. 8.10-18). "O God of our fathers and Lord of Mercy, who created all things by Your Word *en logoi sou,* and with Your Wisdom you established humankind *kai tēi sophiai sou kataskeuasas anthrōpon* to rule over all creatures created by you and govern the world in holiness and justice, and to pronounce judgment in uprightness of soul.[11] Grant me Wisdom that is seated before your throne — *dos moi tēn ton thronon paredron sophian* — and do not reject me from among your children. . . . Were anyone perfect among the sons of men, without Wisdom he would be acknowledged as nothing" (9.4, 6). "With you is Wisdom *kai meta sou hē sophia* who knows Your works and was present — *parousa* — when You created the world and she knows what is pleasing before your eyes and what is right according to Your commandments: *send her down from the holy heavens and from the throne of Your glory send her down* so that she may accompany me in my labours."

These texts (particularly the italicized passages) are in our eyes incompatible with the understanding of Wisdom as the Second Hypostasis because neither the desire to take her as a bride or to receive her in cohabitation, nor the prayer for bestowing gifts and sending her down from the heights of the Throne of God's glory to a human being[12] can in any way be referred to It. This prayer refers namely to Wisdom who knows the works of God and was present when God created the world. It is generally clear that these texts are speaking about the revelation of God in the world through His operations (*energeiai* 7.26), about the divine foundation of the world or the foundation of the world in God, and about the power that preserves and directs the world in and through humankind. They speak about reason to which a human being can be conformed or not conformed, and which can be solicited in prayer, thus appearing sophianic to a greater or lesser degree, but they do not speak about one definite divine Hypostasis and in particular not about the Second. On the contrary, according to the *Wisdom of Solomon,* it becomes necessary rather quickly to distinguish first of all Wisdom and the spirit of Wisdom, as the disclosure of one and the same essence, and secondly to combine Wisdom not only with the Word but also with the Holy Spirit, omnipresent and fulfilling all things, and also with God the Father to whom undoubtedly the prayer for the sending down of Wisdom is addressed. In a word, one has to conclude that Wisdom is a divine principle in which and through which are revealed all three (and not only one) hypostases in unity and distinction, the consubstantial, life-giving and undivided Trinity, God the Father, God the Son and God the Holy Spirit. Sophia is the single life, the single essence, the single content of life of the whole Most Holy Trinity; and with respect to the world and humankind (more precisely, to the world-human), she is the divine world, its foundation or idea in God, the world in God prior to its creation (prior not, of course, in a chronological but in an ontological sense). In the created world Wisdom is not only the world-establishing but also the world-preserving power, operating in humankind through the sophianicity present in it by virtue of the Divine image. This side of Divine Sophia is disclosed with the greatest clarity precisely in chapters 10–12 of the *Wisdom of Solomon*.

Here human history, more precisely the history of the economy of salvation, and even more precisely, the history of the Church in the history of the human race, is depicted as the work of Sophia, as the making and preserving of the sophianicity of a human being, beginning with its very creation. "She preserved the first-formed father of the world, who was created alone and she saved him from his own fall" (10.1). It is remarkable that first-formed Adam is here called *father of the world . . . patera kosmou,* by which is indicated his mediatory significance for the whole world precisely in virtue of his sophianicity. "Wisdom saved again the flooded earth" . . . she is between nations confused in the unanimity of evil, "she found a righteous man and kept him irreproachable before God. . . . She saved the righteous man at the time of the destruction of the impious" (10.4-6ff). "She freed the holy people and spotless seed from the people that oppressed them; she entered the soul of the Lord's servant and opposed frightful kings with wonders and signs. She gave the saints a reward for their labours, and led them on a marvellous path; and by day she was for them a cover, by night a starry light. She led them through the Red Sea and brought them through mighty waters" (10.15-18ff).

Chapters 11–12 describe how Wisdom "prospered their works by the hand of the holy prophet in the time of their wandering in the wilderness and after this." What is particularly remarkable is that those works which in the books of Moses and in the historical books are said to be accomplished by God Himself (and "by His Angel") are here evidently ascribed to Wisdom. Even in the confines of the eleventh chapter the author with apparent and significant indifference substitutes the pronoun "she" for "You," that is, having begun to speak about God's works, he as it were equates the Wisdom of God and the very Lord. "You deliver all, because you can do everything and you cover the sins of the people for the sake of repentance. You love all that exists and shun nothing that You created, for You would not have created had You not desired them. Or how would it be preserved if it were not summoned by You? But You spare all because all is Yours, soul-loving Lord. Your imperishable spirit dwells in them all" (11.24-12.1). The entire twelfth chapter continues the exposition of the works of Wisdom and in this sense immediately joins chapters 10 and 11. Of course one cannot see in this the alternation of chance; on the contrary, one must discern here a hidden theological meaning and instruction.

Nor is it possible to have done with this question by simply equating

Wisdom to the Second Hypostasis and recognizing that chapters 10–11 speak precisely about her. For this equation there is no basis, neither is there in the corresponding parallels from the Pentateuch. In fact what grounds are there for thinking that Yahweh of the book of Genesis or Exodus is the Logos and not the consubstantial Trinity which has a common Wisdom and operates and speaks by her to humans? In any case in dogmatics it is held firmly and indisputably that the world is created not by one Person of the Holy Trinity but with the participation of all Three Hypostases: the Father spoke by His Word and accomplished by the Holy Spirit. Likewise too the economic activity as it is here depicted inheres in the whole Holy Trinity. Therefore in the alternation of names indicated above — Wisdom and God — we see a new corroboration that Wisdom is not only the Second Hypostasis, as is plain from all the foregoing, and that generally speaking she is not a divine hypostasis at all, but is proper to the whole Holy Trinity and all Three Hypostases; she is God in His self-revelation and disclosure to the world.

With respect to the world she is "energy," if we use a term from the Palamite controversies, God's operation in creation. But the energy of God, according to the doctrine of St Gregory Palamas, cannot be tied to any single Person of the Holy Trinity but can refer to all of them individually and to the Holy Trinity in its entirety. At the same time, if we recall the fundamental notion of Palamas' theologizing about the Divine Energies, namely that "energy is God" (although not the contrary: it is impossible to hold that God *is* energy, for an unknowable transcendent essence belongs to Him), it becomes comprehensible by analogy why and in what sense the *Book of Wisdom* says with evident indifference now "Wisdom," now "God," for Wisdom is God in the world, not according to essence and not according to hypostatic existence, but according to life-causing revelation.[13]

On the basis of our examination of chapters 11–12 we obtain a striking commentary for understanding the words of the Saviour about Wisdom in both of the accounts: *and Wisdom is justified by her works* (Mt 11.19), *and by all her children* (Lk 7.35). These chapters explain "the justification" of Wisdom in the human race through those who sought her and found a place for her in the Old Testament church. Those words are said about John the Forerunner who thereby is counted among those righteous ones; by exceeding them in righteousness he thereby exceeds them in his sophianicity.

Chapters 1 and 24 of the book of *Wisdom of Jesus ben Sirach* are a new commentary on Proverbs 8.22f. "All Wisdom — *pasa sophia* — is with the Lord *para tou kuriou* and it is with Him for ever" (Sir 1.1), so begins Sirach, who gives evidence by this that he wants to speak about pre-eternal universal Wisdom and not about a human property. The abiding character of Wisdom in her simultaneous distinction from God with Whom she abides — such are her chief features. "Before all things Wisdom arose (properly: was created, *ektisthē*) and prudent understanding from eternity."[14] "There is one who is wise — *sophos* — greatly fearful, sitting on His throne. The Lord Himself produced *ektisen* her and saw and measured her out and poured her out on all His works and on all flesh in keeping with His gift, and specially endowed with her those who love Him" (Sir 1.1-10). In this text it is difficult to find an indication of Hypostatic Wisdom as the Second Person of the Holy Trinity: in such a case, the contrasting of "the Wise One" with "Wisdom" would have to refer to the First and Second Person of the Holy Trinity, to the Father and the Son, while in the text the contrast is clearly made between the Lord sitting on the throne (which of course equally refers to the Son too) and Wisdom whom God possesses as the Wise One; however, He is not identified with her, as would be the case if she were the Second Hypostasis (never mind that the expression *ektise* — produced does not correspond to this understanding). Therefore Sir 1.10 must be understood in the same sense as the teaching of the *Wisdom of Solomon*. Later on in the first chapter, ben Sirach moves to the practical doctrine more akin to him about the *acquisition* of wisdom: "love for the Lord is glorious wisdom" (14), "the beginning of wisdom is to fear God" (15), "the fullness of wisdom is to fear the Lord" (16), "the crown of wisdom is dread of the Lord" (18), "the root of wisdom is to fear the Lord" (20).

In chapter 24 ben Sirach once again returns to the doctrine about Wisdom. This chapter has a particular heading, *Ainesis sophias* — Praise of Wisdom. 1. "Wisdom will glorify her soul *psuchēn autēs* and among the people she will be extolled. 2. In the assembly of the Most High she will open her lips and before His host she will be extolled. 3. I came out of the mouth of the Most High and like a cloud covered the earth; 4. I set up a tent and my throne on a cloudy pillar; 5. I alone have gone around the heavenly circle and among every people and tribe I had dominion; 6. Among them all (peoples and tribes) I sought calm and in what heritage I was to settle. 7. Then the Creator of all commanded me and He who produced me *(ho ktisas me)* pointed out to me a peaceful dwelling and said. 9. Dwell among Jacob and receive a heritage in Israel. 10. Before the ages from the beginning He produced me — *ektisen me* — and I shall never pass away." (The continuation of this speech, verses 14-36, presents the lauding of wisdom and expresses her relation to the Law of Moses.) The texts of ben Sirach bear witness to Wisdom as a world-creative principle, but they do not at all propose seeing in her the Second Hypostasis. Rather the description of Wisdom here speaks about the operation in and through her of the gracious power of the Holy Spirit,[15] operating in the Church (in particular in the Old Testament Church). Likewise here the difference is established between the Lord who produces or has Wisdom and Wisdom herself as *a divine* principle, being with God and inseparable from God, but not being identified with His hypostases.

Thus, these commentaries on Proverbs 8.22-31, although found in uncanonical books which nevertheless entered into the composition of the Bible and were highly esteemed by the Church, not only do not support the widespread patristic interpretation of the text about Wisdom that the hypostatic Word of God is to be understood here, but, it must be directly stated, are incompatible with it. If it had been necessary to choose between the two witnesses according to their proportion, preference would have to be given to the uncanonical books of the Bible. But fortunately such a choice does not have to be made, for the patristic opinions are sufficiently accounted for by their derivation in the struggle with Arianism; clearly coloured by this struggle their historical conditionality and relativeness are adequately revealed. They do not contain a direct positive disclosure of a doctrine of Wisdom, but only a polemic with Arianism, although in this polemic in the works of St Athanasius the Great (see the following excursus) features of both aspects of the doctrine of Wisdom are outlined, namely the pre-eternal and the creaturely. Besides, we suppose, the latter aspect in general favours the interpretation which we have adopted on biblical and theological foundations. As an organic part of church tradition the facts of iconographical and liturgical theology, which definitely do not favour the understanding of Wisdom as the Second Hypostasis, must be noted. Neither the fiery angel sitting on the throne holding over itself a separate image of Christ, nor the Mother of God on icons of Sophia, leaves any possibility of understanding Sophia as the Second Hypostasis. The same must be said about the content of the service for Sophia the Wisdom of God in which she is likened at one time to Christ, at another to the Mother of God as the bearer of the Holy Spirit; however, she is not fully identified with the one or the other. At the same time, of course, not for a single instant does she acquire the character of a special Hypostasis, thereby turning the Holy Trinity into a quadrinity. May this blasphemy not exist!

*   *   *

Until now we have left without examination Proverbs 9 where a doctrine about Wisdom is also set out.[16] This text is remarkable in that it is read as one of the three lessons (in fact, the third) in all feasts of the Theotokos and by this very fact is interpreted as being applicable to the Theotokos. Here is the text: "Wisdom has built for herself a house and set up seven pillars. She has slaughtered her animals and mixed wine in her cup and prepared her table. She has sent her servant-girls, inviting to the cup with a great proclamation and saying," etc. (Prov 9.1-2). The house of Wisdom spoken about here is clearly the Mother of God and in a wider sense the Church in general. The seven pillars which correspond to the seven lamp stands of the Apocalypse (Rev 1.12, 13; 4.5, "which are the seven spirits of God" [Rev 4.5] and further the seven seals, the seven trumpets, seven cups, in general the mysterious number seven indicating fullness) can refer to the seven sacraments of the church (unless it has yet another secret meaning now unknown), just as the slaughter of the sacrifice and the mixing of the wine can point to the Holy Eucharist.

A fundamental question of exegesis here is how to understand the words *"Wisdom has built herself a house."* Obviously their meaning depends on the already established meaning contained in the word *Wisdom*. In any interpretation, *the House* built by Wisdom points to the Mother of God, which is entirely clear from the text's use as a reading in services honouring the Theotokos. If one sticks to the understanding of Wisdom as the Second Hypostasis then such a meaning is obtained: The Word of God Jesus Christ built himself a house, that is, His Mother. It is clear to what sorts of difficulties such an interpretation leads. How and in what sense can one correctly state that the Word built for Himself a Mother? One can understand this in the general sense that "all things came to be" by the Word and that counted among all these creatures is the Mother of God. First of all, this general sense by itself is too little to be an intentional instruction concerning the building of Wisdom's house. Secondly, it would be imprecise to say that the world or humankind were created by the Word alone, for the whole Holy Trinity participates in their creation — the Father as "Maker of heaven and earth," as First Principle, the Son "through whom all things came to be," and the Holy Spirit the giver of life who completes all things. On the other hand, in particular the preparation "of a house" for Wisdom in the Mother of God was accomplished by the Holy Spirit, sent by the Father, and only as a result of the Holy Spirit's visitation does the hypostatic Word born of Her come to dwell in Her: "The Holy Spirit will come upon you and the Power of the Most High (the Word) will overshadow You" (Lk 1.35). It is precisely the Word who participates least directly of all in the preparation "of a house" for Himself. The gospel account of the Annunciation teaches us this, which an interpretation of Proverbs 9 with reference to the Second Hypostasis directly contradicts.[17]

If one equates Wisdom in Proverbs 9 with the Third Hypostasis, for which in any case there is a greater foundation than for the Second, then it would follow from this that the content of Wisdom's actions would refer in some cases primarily to the Second Hypostasis while in other cases to the Third, and consequently its equation to any *one* of the divine Hypostases is dogmatically incorrect.[18]

But as we have tried to show, the idea of such an equation generally speaking cannot be supported exegetically. Wisdom generally speaking *is not* a Divine Hypostasis, she is the life, action, revelation, "energy" of the Divinity, which is worshipped in the Holy Trinity and has been revealed to creation at one time in Its all-divine unity and oneness of essence, at another time in the trinitarity of Persons. On the basis of inner-trinitarian relations the Father reveals Himself in the Son by the Holy Spirit. Therefore the Wisdom of God with respect to distinctiveness of Hypostases appears at one time as the operation of the Son or directly as the Son in creation (which is why He is called then "God's power and wisdom") and at another time as the Holy Spirit, "the Spirit of wisdom" (Is 11.2), (who is for this reason called Wisdom by several church authors), living in the Church. And further — in the same sense — Wisdom is ascribed to her own children in whom she "is justified" by her works, that is, above all to the Most Pure, and then to the first of those born of woman, the Forerunner of Christ, and then to the world of angels and humans, to glorified creation, to the City of God, the new heaven and earth in which justice lives, to the revelation of the Holy Spirit in creation about which the Church sings, "you have made all things with Wisdom" (Ps 104.24).

In the New Testament the most important passage about the Wisdom of God is found in the saying of the Saviour about John the Forerunner, which concludes with the following words: *and Wisdom — hē Sophia — is justified — edikaiōthē — by her works* (Mt 11.19) *and by all her children* (Lk 7.35). The expression "wisdom" must be clearly understood in connection with the Old Testament doctrine of Wisdom, set forth above.[19] For other instances of an ontological meaning of this expression see Lk 11.49 and 1 Cor 1.24 (though not uncontested). In all other cases "wisdom" indisputably signifies only a property with reference to God or to people. Relevant here are Mt 13.54; Mk 6.2; Lk 2.52; 21.15; 2 Pet 3.15; Rom 11.33; 1 Cor 1.17, 19, 20, 21, 30; Eph 1.8; 3.10; Col 1.9, 28; 2.3; 3.16; Rev 5.12; 7.12.

The Doctrine of the Wisdom of God in
St Athanasius the Great and Other Church Fathers

A twofold question was raised by Arianism, drawn from two sources of doubt. The first concerned the doctrine of the Holy Trinity, the second, the doctrine of God as Creator of the world. With respect to the first, Arianism is essentially anti-trinitarianism. It thinks God as monohypostatic and the thought of a trihypostatic God seems strange and unacceptable to it. Only the Father is properly God, and the Son and Holy Spirit represent His powers, degrees of His revelation. This is the trinity of Neoplatonism with its progressive gradation: the One — Mind — Soul, but not three equally honoured and equally divine hypostases. Arianism thinks God as one in the sense of a monohypostatic monad: the monohypostaseity and monadity of the Godhead are for it the initial premise. The doctrine of the creatureliness of the Son and His origin in time out of non-being is only a direct conclusion of this premise. And as much as the struggle of St Athanasius was directed in defence and confirmation of the doctrine of the Trihypostatic God, and in particular, of the pre-eternal generation of the Son from the essence of the Father, the debate essentially concerned the doctrine of trinitarity even though a Christological theme was its immediate subject. In proving the pre-eternity of the Son, St Athanasius overthrew monohypostaseity and confirmed the trinitarity of Divinity. This was the main line around which the battle was waged, which ended with the Nicene victory of Orthodoxy. All the decisions of Nicaea, expressed in both positive and negative form, as a creed and as anathemas, concern the question of the trinitarity of the Godhead, and confirm this fundamental dogma. The formula *homoousios,* that Nicene gonfalon of Orthodoxy, confirms it: *one essence* of three hypostases — not likeness, not difference, not repetition, not identity but unity, coinherence and compatibility. By his victory over Arianism, St Athanasius saved the Church from injury in this most fundamental and essential doctrine.

The other side of the question posed in Arianism was connected with the first and even flowed out of it. It concerned the relation of God to the world. How can one imagine this relation without diminution of Divinity in its absoluteness and without diminution of the world in its self-existence? In Greek speculation this question already arose in Platonism where it received a preliminary resolution in the doctrine of the *demiurge* as the mediator between God and the world, a servant of God during the creation of the world *(Timaeus)*. Philo apprehended this statement of the question and applied it to Jewish theology and the interpretation of the Old Testament. Here it was converted into the doctrine of *logos endiathetos,* the inner word of God, His immanent wisdom and power, and *logos prophorikos,* His manifested, instrumental word, wisdom in the creation of the world. Arius and Asterius accepted this formulation of the question.[1]

The difficulties in defining the relation of God to the world, especially when conceiving Him abstractly as a monad, a monohypostatic Godhead, are not fabricated; they really exist and are great. The philosophical genius of Hellenism brought to light here the question's natural dialectic. Actually, if we allow that God and the world are *immediately* related to each other, a radical difference between them is lost. God in His solitude in such a case *needs* the world as His other (if not as other), He strives to come out of this isolation and overcome it by means of creation. He himself is incomplete, unrealized for Himself *without* creation, for a monopersonal egotistic knowledge does not satisfy itself or self-revelation, does not give absoluteness and self-sufficiency. The monohypostatic God *for His own sake needs* the world and thus the world enters as a necessary element into the divine life. God *before* creation is not *what He is after* creation, and on the other hand, the world becomes God, in so far as it enters into the inner life of the Godhead. In this way the sinister tints of *pantheism,* theocosmism, appear in the doctrine of monohypostatic theism.

At the same time the world placed in direct and immediate relation with God is powerless to endure this relation without losing its own self-existence. *No one anywhere has seen God;* a human cannot see God and not die; only the "hindmost parts of God," "the Glory of God," were revealed to Moses, the friend of God. Meanwhile here God and the world inescapably stand face to face without any mediation, flaming fire restrained by nothing and the dry straw of the world defended by nothing, the absolute losing its own absoluteness as a result of the absence of a proper inner life, and the relative being exhausted in the embraces of the absolute. The monohypostatic absolute subject is power which in itself has no manifestation and needs the creation of the world. It is the open embraces which are empty and need creation, but as for the world, it is the *sacrifice* of the hunger of the Absolute, doomed to combustion in Its fire.

Up to this point, before it is a question of a personal God, an absolute Subject, faceless divinity as a divine aggregate of the powers of the world willy-nilly dissolves in the world in the twilight of pantheism (or what is the same, atheism). But once an absolute Subject, the living God, pre-worldly and transcendent, is thought, in the limits of monohypostaseity the proposition becomes interminable and the cosmological problem irresolvable. The yearning to find a go-between, the attempt to place some super-creature *between* God and the world who will act as a shield for the world against God and combustion in scorching fire, naturally results from this. This super-creature, which is both not God and not the world but something in between — *metaxu* — is the demiurge by means of which God created the world. From here Arius develops completely logically the doctrine of a mediator between God and the world which, when joined to the church's doctrine of Jesus Christ, develops into a distinctive heretical Christology. However, the Arian doctrine of God and the world and of the necessity of a special intermediation and its possibility is internally contradictory, and this was shown by St Athanasius the Great. *Mediation* between God and the world as some sort of middle position is unthinkable and impossible. The mediator himself requires for himself a new mediator and so on *ad infinitum;* no matter by how much we increase the number of steps on the ladder it is all the same incapable of reaching heaven, of leading the creature into immediate contact with the Godhead. The thought of *a mediator* is impossible; it is to some extent the square root of negative one or a circular square. But the problem is sensed correctly and the disclosure of true Christian doctrine concerning this question was made unavoidable.

All the same, a *direct response* to the question about the true nature of the relations between God and the world, between the Creator and the creation, was not given this way. At the council of Nicaea this question evidently was not discussed from this aspect; at least there are no traces of such a discussion in its decisions. All energy was concentrated around the decisive question about the Holy Trinity whose correct resolution decided in advance this question too. Moreover we do not find a fully distinct formulation of the question even by St Athanasius who bore on his shoulders this titanic fight for Orthodoxy. Here we encounter in him incompleteness, imprecision, unfinished doctrines although *the general* direction of his thought was defined to a sufficient degree. With the victory of Orthodoxy, homoousianism, faith in the trihypostatic God, over the doctrine of the monadic monohypostaseity of the Godhead, the whole formulation of the question about the relations of God and the world is changed. It is now impossible to say about the trihypostatic God that which inescapably has to be said about the monohypostatic monad that *needs* the world: the life of the trihypostatic Godhead, as Love, as pre-eternal mutuality and self-revelation, is absolutely self-sufficient and complete, it needs no one and nothing and cannot have any supplementing. The trihypostatic God lives in Himself, i.e., in the Holy Trinity, and this Life is a pre-eternally realizing Fullness. Hence the world *is not necessary* for God himself and it is powerless to add any supplementing to the Fullness. The world is entirely a creation of the generous and magnanimous love of God, a love *which gives and which receives nothing*. God is necessary for the world as its foundation and goal, but not the reverse. By trihypostaseity *the solitude* of the Absolute subject, his aloneness, is overcome, and thanks to this victory the monohypostatic God is compelled as it were to create the world. The Trihypostatic God is one in His triunity, but not alone. . . .

The creation of the world for the sake of humankind, which is made according to the image of God, is only by the generosity of love, a set *repetition,* to be sure, in the creaturely life of the Prototype, His *self-repetition* as it were, which for Him does not contain and is not able to contain anything new. If it can be expressed this way, the divine necessity of self-revelation is fully satisfied by trihypostaseity, and the creation of the world is only an outpouring from the fullness of the divine ocean of love. Love is insatiable by nature and that is why divine trihypostatic love thirsts to extend itself in creation, by emptying itself into non-being, by creating the world; in this insatiableness of love is contained the basis of world creation. In its divine life, however, this love is completely satisfied, for God has in Himself by Himself the One He loves and to Whom He is revealed. He is absolutely self-loved and self-revealed and this eternity does not know any change or increase. God possesses His Very Self in an absolute manner as Person, owing to His trihypostaseity, as being, owing to His divine essence, and as consubstantial Trinity — in the indivisibility of His Personhood and essence. The life of God is a pre-eternal self-revelation, unconditional according to *the trihypostatic image* — as the Word of the Father being sealed by the Holy Spirit, and according to *content* — as the one eternal Wisdom of the Father being proved by the Holy Spirit, as the one life of the Holy Trinity, as the Glory of God.

Such is the relation of *God to the world:* it is not necessary for God, but its possibility is given in Him. The question of the relation of the world to God remains. Is this question fully dismissed by the doctrine of the trihypostatic God as Creator of the world? Or do the bewilderments and inquiries of the Arianizers demand an explanation all the same, even if in another formulation: is a direct, unmediated relation of God to the world, of Creator to creature, of the Absolute to the relative, possible? Is there and can there be some sort of *mediation* between God and the world, *metaxu,* whose necessity is not obviated even by the trihypostaseity of the Godhead? Actually, if we only comprehend the creation of the world by God as an unmediated *operation* of God somehow beyond the limits of His own being, as the foundation of something new and until then not existing and not being in God, we thereby inescapably erase the boundary between the Creator and the creature. This means that prior to creation, when God still had not created the world, *He did not have it with Himself;* this means that He received some sort of supplement in the world's creation; it means that the world is in a certain sense a special domain of the disclosure of Divinity, necessary for His Very Self; it means that God is not absolute fullness, that God Himself did not know the world before His act of creation and that this act was for His Very Self a self-revelation. All these bewilderments ought to have received a viable explanation, and they find it in the works of St Athanasius, although not yet a definitive one, as can be expected given his straightforward task.

The question arises here about Wisdom as the pre-eternal foundation of the world in God, as the pre-eternal world, the creaturely image of which, its projection in time, is the created world. The world is created by God through the Word.[2] St Athanasius tirelessly develops this idea (the participation of the Holy Spirit as a crowning and life-giving one is likewise implied by him but it remains outside his dogmatic attention which is absorbed by the question of the Logos).

But of course the role of the Logos in this is not instrumental, as Arius thought; the Logos is not *the instrument* of creation but its truth, its content, its *all.* In the Holy Trinity the Logos *reveals* the Father, and is the expressed Word of Divine Life, its content; it is received by the Holy Spirit who rests on the Word. The Word speaks Itself, reveals Itself not in the creation of the world, rather, It speaks Itself pre-eternally and, as Athanasius says, "not for our[3] sake did the Word of God receive existence, on the contrary, we received existence for His sake" (*Oratio II contra Arianos*, 31), for "to create is secondary for God, to beget is primary" (II, 2), and so the Logos is the Son and not a creature or an intermediary. In this manner, in the order of disclosure of the problems before St Athanasius and at the same time before the whole dogmatic consciousness of the Church, the following problem arose inescapably and naturally, which was not seen by Arius because of the limited nature and perverseness of his general point of view: how must one understand the relation between the pre-eternal Logos, the Son of God, and creation? Creation could very well not have been at all "if it had pleased God not to create creatures" (II, 31), and at the same time "it would have been impossible for creatures to receive existence without the Word" (II, 31). Obviously it is necessary to establish a direct correlation between the Word begotten by the Father and the Word in the act of creating. It is said of Him, "The Father, as with a hand, made everything with the Word and He creates nothing without It," "The Word of God creates and builds, and is God's will" (II, 31), "all is created by the Word and by Wisdom in which is contained the Father's will" (II, 31). St Athanasius stands up for both series of truths with equal energy: on the one hand, the Word is the pre-eternally begotten Son of God and not at all a creature fashioned to be an intermediary in creation, and on the other hand God creates everything by His Word Which is the Wisdom of God. Both of these ideas, of course, easily and naturally accord with each other in a general doctrine of God: it is understood that the pre-eternal Logos is the disclosure of Divinity in creation. But they are not understood this way in a doctrine of the world and its relation to God. Is the world some sort of creaturely Logos that exists according to the image and likeness of the pre-eternal Logos? One must still recall that St Athanasius, absorbed by Christological themes, leaves outside his attention the participation of the Holy Spirit in the world's creation which, according to the general patristic doctrine, was accomplished by the whole Holy Trinity with the corresponding participation of all three Persons. As a result of this, the very formulation of the question in the works of St Athanasius is one-sided. Nevertheless the problem did arise for him and even against his will he brushes against it in his doctrine of the Wisdom of God. The difficult exegesis of Prov 8.22f, which was interpreted by the Arians in their own favour, served as the occasion for it. *The Lord created me*. St Athanasius returns endlessly to his own apologetic interpretation of this text and neither he nor his opponents hesitated for a moment to refer it immediately to the Logos. (So far as the polemic rests simply on the unfaithful translation of *ektise* — *created*, where *ektēsato* — *had* must stand [Russian translation], the whole thing rests on a misunderstanding; but all the same it gives cause for broaching an important subject.) We shall first ascertain the interpretation of the text by St Athanasius.

St Athanasius reads Prov 8.22 as follows: *kurios ektise me archēn hodōn autou eis erga autou* (LXX) — *dominus creavit me initium viarum suarum in opera sua* (Vulgate), the Lord created me as the beginning of His ways in his works.[4]

A widespread interpretation among the fathers refers this text to the Logos principally on the basis of 1 Cor 1.24 where Christ is called the power and wisdom of God (although, on the contrary, Is 11.2 speaks about the Spirit of the Lord as the Spirit of Wisdom and understanding, the spirit of counsel and strength, of knowledge and piety). Among church authors St Theophilus and St Irenaeus ascribe the title of Sophia to the Holy Spirit (see the previous excursus).

The general idea of St Athanasius is that *the Lord created me* was said "proverbially" (*Oratio II contra Arianos,* 44) and thus is in need of an interpretation. The fundamental idea of St Athanasius' exegesis is that *created* refers not to pre-eternal Wisdom but to her creaturely incarnation, and the further *gave birth to me* refers to Wisdom itself. Therefore *created* indicates "not the essence of the Godhead and the Word and not His eternal origin from the Father but His humanity and economy" (II, 45, 46, 47). "The Word speaks about Itself figuratively, *He created me,* when It was clothed in created flesh. Although the Word is Son and Father, and has God as Its own generation, It now calls the Father Lord, not because the Son is a slave but because He took on Himself the mark of a slave" (II, 50; cf. 51). Here is indicated "not the principle of existence, not the creaturely essence of the Son but the renewal which by His favour is accomplished in us . . . the economy in works which He accomplished in the flesh" (II, 53, 55, 62, 66, 74). Proof for the correctness of this exegesis St Athanasius sees in the simultaneous use of the words *created* and *begets Me* (II, 60).

St Athanasius supposes a distinction between Wisdom as *created* (creaturely) and as begotten in two of its aspects: as the foundation and the imprinting. "As through Wisdom the Father creates and founds the earth, so that it would be unshakable and endure, so too is Wisdom herself founded in us, so that she may be made the beginning and the foundation of a new creature in us and of our renewal" (II, 73).

St Athanasius develops this thought in more detail in the following lines. "Although the only-begotten and original Wisdom of God makes and builds all things, for it is said: *you have created everything by Wisdom and the earth is filled with your creation* (Ps 104.24), still in order that what is created should have not only existence but also blessed existence, God deigned *to have his Wisdom descend to the creatures* so that in all creatures in general and in every nation there should be placed *a certain imprint and likeness of her image,* and so that what is brought into existence should prove to be a wise work worthy of God. For as our word is an image of the true Word, the Son of God, so again *is the image of true Divine Wisdom the wisdom which is being revealed in us,* in which, by possessing the power to think and reflect, we are made *fit to receive creative Wisdom,* and through her we arrive at the state of getting to know her Father. For it is said: *whoever has the Son in himself has the Father as well* (1 Jn 2.23[5]). The one who receives Me receives the One Who Sent Me (Mt 10.40). In as much as in us and in all works there is such *an impress of created Wisdom,* true and creative Wisdom, apprehending in herself *what belongs to her impress,* rightly says of herself: *the Lord created Me in His works.* What *wisdom which is in us* would say, this the very Lord names His Own. He, as Creator, is uncreated, but *by reason of His created Image in His works* He says this as if about Himself. And as the Lord Himself said, *whoever receives you receives Me* (Mt 10.40), because His impress is in us, so, though He is not in the number of created things, in as much as *His image and impress* are created in the works, as if He himself were this Image, He says: the Lord created me the beginning of His ways in His works. The impress of Wisdom is placed in the works so that the world would recognize in Wisdom Its Creator — the Word, and through the Word, the Father. Paul said the same thing: *since he has made plain in them what can be understood of God, for God showed it to them. For His invisible things from the creation of the world are visible through the creations he has produced* (Rom 1.19, 20). Thus the Word is in essence not a creature, and what is said in Prov refers to *the Wisdom present and named in us*" (II, 78).

The text of Sir 1.10, *"He poured her (wisdom) out on all His works [she is] with all flesh according to His gift, and He bestowed her on those who love Him,"* is interpreted in this way: "such an outpouring is a sign of the essence not of Wisdom original and only-begotten, but *of the wisdom that is imaged in the world.* For in the world it is not creative Wisdom *but the one being created in the works* according to which *the heavens are telling the Glory of God and the firmament proclaims his handiwork* (Ps 19.1). But if people make room in themselves for this wisdom, they will acknowledge the true Wisdom of God, they will know that they are created really according to the image of God" (II, 79). He compares this with the tracing of the name of a king's son on each building of his father's town under construction. And the town, according to his words, will be constructed reliably, understanding under his name "not his own created essence but his image impressed in the name." Therefore these words *The Lord created me in his works* signify "My image is in them and to such an extent did I descend in the work of creation," so answers Wisdom (II, 79).

"Original Wisdom is active and creative, and her impress takes root in the work as *the image of the image.* The Word calls her 'the beginning *of ways' because such wisdom becomes a sort of beginning and as it were rudiments of the knowledge of God.* [. . .] He says: *before everything he established me,* because the works remain unshakeably and eternally affirmed in the image of this wisdom" (II, 80). Wisdom says as if of herself: "everything received being by me and through me. When there was need to implant wisdom in the works, although in my essence I remained with the Father, out of condescension to creatures *I impressed my image in the works in conformity with them* so that *the whole world would be one body not at variance but in concord with itself"* (II, 81). "And this same Wisdom which originally showed Herself and Her Father by means of Her image in creatures (according to which She is called created), afterwards this same Wisdom, that is the Word, *became flesh"* (II, 81). (*St Hilary* interprets Prov 8.22 in a similar fashion: "here is distinguished the Divine and human side, where 'creation' refers to the human body which Divine Wisdom received from the womb of the Virgin, but in such a way that it was created by God. *De trinitate,* 12.32, 37, 42.)[6]

St Athanasius' interpretation of Prov 8.22 carries an essentially apologetic character. It is directed entirely against the Arians who referred the text to the Son in order to prove His creatureliness. Without disputing the Arian exegesis of this passage on its merits (which would have been fully possible) St Athanasius tries to defend himself against their interpretation of the text, as far as the one-sided meaning pre-established by Arianism was imparted to him.

Reluctantly, as if against their will, both St Basil the Great and St Gregory the Theologian were compelled to address this text, among other texts brought by the Arians against the Orthodox. In St Basil (*Contra Eunomium,* book 5, III, 140)[7] we read concerning the words *the Lord created me* (Prov 8.22): "If the One who came in the flesh says *I am the way,* and if He said *no one comes to the Father except by Me* (Jn 14.6), it was also said by the Same One[8] *the Lord created Me the beginning of His ways.* But the words creation and creature are also used of begetting, e.g., *I have made a man with the help of God* (Gen 4.1), and again, *I have created sons and daughters* (Gen 5.4). David says *a clean heart create in me, O God* (Ps 51.10), asking not to be given another heart but to cleanse the one which he had. A new creature (2 Cor 5.17) is so called not because another creature arises but because the illuminated are prepared for better works. If the Father created the Son for works, then He created Him not for His own sake but for the sake of works. But what is for the sake of another and not for its own sake either comprises a part of that for which it exists or is less than it. Therefore the Saviour will be either purely a creature or less than a creature. *And so it is necessary to understand this passage to be about His humanity.*" Consequently, in such a case a new idea is obtained about primordial humanity as Wisdom in the beginning of God's ways, i.e., either about heavenly humanity, but in that case uncreated, or about creaturely humanity prior to creation. This lack of clarity thus is not eliminated and the idea not fully stated.

St Basil does not insist on his own interpretation but continues, "But another might be able to say that Solomon said this about that wisdom which the apostle mentioned, saying, 'for since in God's wisdom the world did not understand the wisdom of God' (1 Cor 1.21)." This idea remains unclear but obviously it refers to wisdom already as a property. Further on, St Basil continues, "beyond this, the one who said this was not a prophet but a moralizer. And proverbs are depictions of something other and not of the thing itself that is said in them. If it is God the Son Who says, *The Lord created me,* it would have been better to say, *the Father created me,* for nowhere did he call Him His Lord but everywhere, Father. Therefore the word 'begot' (Prov 8.25) ought to refer to God the Son, while 'created' ought to refer to the One who received on Himself the mark of a slave. Nevertheless in all these expressions we do not understand two things, not God apart and the human apart (for he was One), but only conceptually do we separate the nature of each." All the same it remains unclear how *he created me in the beginning of his ways,* before His creations, from time immemorial, could have been said about the humanity, about "the mark of a slave," i.e., about a creature. This difficulty, which as we have seen was created by a verbal misunderstanding or directly by an error in translation, led even St Basil the Great, following St Athanasius, away from examining the problem on its merits towards apologetics.

St Gregory the Theologian (Sermon 30, the fourth on theology and the second on the Son of God)[9] also occupied himself with this text for the sake of polemics: "their first and especially prepared dictum is the following, Prov 8.22. How is one to answer this? We shall not begin by accusing Solomon or repudiating his earlier words for the sake of his later fall (these words are not fully clear), nor shall we explain that here wisdom, i.e., knowledge, that artisan's understanding by which everything was created, is presented speaking. For Scripture often personifies many things, even inanimate objects, e.g., *the sea said this and that* (Is 23.4) and *the depths said he is not in me* (Job 28.14), just as the heavens are presented *as telling the glory of God* (Ps 19.1), a sword is commanded something (Zech 13.7), mountains and hills are asked about the causes of their leaping (Ps 114.6). One shall not answer in a manner similar to this, even though some among us have given this out for something firm."[10]

In this way essentially, St Gregory the Theologian does not consider the Arian interpretation of the text as the single possible one, and he only yields for the sake of polemics: "on the contrary, we suppose that these are the words of the Saviour Himself, of true Wisdom, and we will examine them somewhat more attentively. Which being does not have a cause? The Godhead. For no one will tell us the cause of God, otherwise it would be more primary than God himself. But what cause is there for the fact that God assumes humanity for our sakes? This is the cause: so that we would be saved. For what other cause could there be? And so, in so far as we find here the word *created* and another clear phrase *he who begets me* (Prov 8.25), the explanation is simple. That which is said with the addition of a cause we will ascribe to humanity, and what is said simply, without the adding of a cause, we will refer to Divinity. But was not the word *created* said with the addition of a cause? For Solomon says, *he created me the beginning of His ways in His works. The works of his hands are truth and justice* (Ps 111.7), for which He is anointed by Divinity, because this anointing concerns the humanity. But the word *begets me* is used without the addition of a cause; otherwise point out what is added to it. And so who will argue that Wisdom is called a creature according to her generation below and begotten according to her first and more incomprehensible generation?"[11]

In this manner St Gregory here accepts the distinction made by St Athanasius, but like St Basil he does not provide any explanations for it or eliminate the misunderstandings and difficulties. The chief difficulty with this exegesis that exists for all three of them equally is that in it the creature is admitted prior to creation, humanity prior to the creation of the world, for precisely the *initial* thesis says here: The Lord created wisdom before His creatures. But in the teaching of St Athanasius the Great a characteristic and fruitful distinction of eternal Wisdom and creaturely Wisdom inscribed in the world appears in connection with this, with the text of 8.22 speaking about the one and the other, in his opinion. In such a case a new question about this Wisdom arises and St Athanasius here expounds in a practical way a doctrine of Sophia as the Prototype of creation (Metropolitan Makary, in his *Dogmatic Theology* I, §38, 366, interprets this text this way, speaking with reference to the fathers of the church, particularly St John of Damascus and St Dionysius the Areopagite about prototypes *prōtotupa* and designs *paradeigmata* of things in God). In this manner the centre of gravity in the interpretation is shifted from *the hypostatic* Logos to the Wisdom of God which is disclosed through Him in the Holy Spirit. As St Gregory the Theologian says, "how was the divine thought occupied before the Almighty, reigning in the wilderness of the ages, created the universe and adorned it with forms? It was contemplating the longed-for brightness of His goodness, the equal and equally perfect radiance *of the thrice-shining* Godhead, as this is known to the one Godhead and to whom God revealed it. World-generating Mind also examined in His great mental representations the images that He had constructed of the world which was produced afterwards, but even then was real for God" (Sermon 4).[12] This pre-eternal world, the radiance of the thrice-shining Godhead, is the foundation of the created world, and about it, about this Wisdom of God Proverbs speaks. This world, in its creation out of nothing, becomes the creaturely world while remaining identical to itself according to its ontological basis. Thus it is possible to speak about the world as about the coming divine incarnation, as St Athanasius interprets this. One must observe, however, that the conception of Wisdom as the Word of God speaking about Itself, apart from straightforward impediments, is not in the least called for by necessity and as St Gregory shows, is not at all the only possible one. If one reads this and the following chapter, apart from Prov 8.21-31, it does not even tally with the conception of the Son speaking, but more naturally is understood as an instruction of wisdom, and therefore a wise instruction.

The desire to apply this explanation to Prov 9.1 as well encounters difficulties straight away, for it is necessary to interpret such that the Logos created for Himself a body or mother. Besides, this is already imprecise. Just as in the general sense the creation of humankind was clearly the work of the whole Most Holy Trinity, so in particular the preparation of the Mother of God was the work of the descent of the Holy Spirit. The result is a clear narrowing and distortion of meaning (there is no such interpretation, now sometimes advanced, among the church fathers). On the other hand, one can refer Prov 8.22f in equal measure to both the Logos and the Holy Spirit, *the spirit of Wisdom and understanding, of counsel and strength, of knowledge and piety* (Is 11.2), which in this way corresponds to the general content of chapters 8 and 9. The expression *begets* does not hinder this because it is used along side of other expressions: *I am anointed, I was an artisan, I made merry before him.* The last two expressions correspond to the Third Hypostasis in a much greater degree than to the Second. It is impossible to push this aside with the general consideration that the world was created by the Word, as St Athanasius, for whom questions about the Holy Spirit naturally are not first and foremost and remain in the shadows, primarily insists in his polemic with the Arians. The world is created by the whole Most Holy Trinity, by the Father through the Son in the Holy Spirit and precisely in the beginning the participation of the Holy Spirit is indicated: *and the Spirit hovered above the abyss* (Gen 1.2). *By the Word of the Lord the heavens are established, and by the Spirit of His mouth all their powers* (Ps 33.6). But the Arian formulation of the question about Wisdom generally speaking is in no way the sole possible one, and even the fathers of the church consider the Arian interpretation of the text about Wisdom somehow forced and unenthusiastic, without however replacing this formulation of the question with their own. The interpretation of Wisdom with respect to the hypostasis of the Holy Spirit is more preferable in 9.1 where it is a question of the foundation of the Church or of the preparation of the Mother of God. But even such an interpretation is as unsatisfactory and one-sided as the first, although it can be upheld side by side with it.

All the more natural to us seems the exegesis of this passage with respect to the Wisdom of God as a revelation of the whole Holy Trinity, of the Father in the Son through the Holy Spirit. By interpreting it this way, the meaning obtained is this: 22. "The Lord had Me" refers *either* to the whole Holy Trinity which possesses Wisdom, and in *ta paradeigmata* of the world, possesses the world *before* its creation, *or* according to another sense it can mean "the Lord (Father) had a Son — the Word in the beginning" (cf. Jn 1.1); but already 23 from the words *I was anointed* refers to the Holy Spirit resting on the Son ("anointing": The Spirit of the Lord is upon Me: He anointed Me — Is 61.1; Lk 4.18). 24, 25: *I was begotten* — again refers to the Word. 27 — "When He prepared the heavens, I was there," "the Spirit of God hovered above the waters," Gen 1.2, 30 — *I was the artisan* (the "very good" of creation Gen 1), and "with joy" (the particular domain of the Holy Spirit) are said about the Holy Spirit. In this manner the sense of this remarkable text is much more complex than was understood in the Arian epoch, at the initial time of Christian disputes when the question of the Holy Spirit had still not been placed at the centre of attention.[13]

The doctrine of the pre-eternal prototypes — *paradeigmata* — of creation is found in a whole series of holy fathers and it expresses the cosmological aspect of the doctrine of the Wisdom of God. First of all, in *St Dionysius the Areopagite* we find: "prototypes, we say, are in God as essential and wholly *heniaios* pre-existing foundations, *logous*, which theology calls predeterminations *proorismous*, the good and divine pleasures of God determinative for real and creative things, according to which the Pre-Existent has pre-determined and brought forth all reality, predetermined and produced it."[14] In his commentary on this passage *St Maximus the Confessor* (concurring here with Pachymeres) observes that "he calls the essences in God and the integrally existing foundations of the existent 'prototypes', namely, predeterminations."[15] St Gregory of Nyssa[16] says, "I suppose before an investigation of what is written it is necessary to take into consideration that word, that in the divine nature power is concomitant with desire, and desire becomes the measure of Divine power; desire is wisdom, Sophia; it is proper to wisdom to know everything, how each thing could come forth in its own species; power is inherent in knowledge." In the works of the Blessed Augustine similar ideas are also frequently encountered.[17] It is curious that similar ideas are encountered even in Tertullian (*Adv. Praxeam,* 5, 6, 7).[18]

We find the doctrine of St Dionysius the Areopagite and St Maximus the Confessor about *paradeigmata* also in St John of Damascus in his "Oration against those who reject holy icons." "In God images and plans of what will be accomplished by Him exist, i.e., His pre-eternal and always immutable counsel." "These images and plans are predeterminations, says St Dionysius . . . for in His light everything is outlined that is predetermined by Him and immutably exists before their being. In a similar manner, if anyone desires to build a house, he first outlines it in his mind and constructs its form" (1, 10). "The second semblance of an image is the idea in God about what He will create, i.e., His pre-eternal counsel, which remains always equal to itself, for Divinity is immutable and unoriginate is His counsel, in which it is decided before the ages, so that in a time predetermined by Him what is designated is also fulfilled. For, the images and examples of what will be made by Him are the ideas about each of these objects, and they are called predeterminations by St Dionysius, since in His counsel is outlined and formed that which is predetermined by Him and will be carried out without fail before its existence" (3, 19). Although these judgments are not accompanied by a reference to the texts of Proverbs 8 and the Wisdom of Solomon, they are essentially one of the possible (although not exhaustive) commentaries on these mysterious texts about the Wisdom of God.

According to its inner meaning, the doctrine of St Gregory Palamas about the divine energies concerns the doctrine of the Wisdom of God; however, the establishment of this link would require a special investigation that exceeds the bounds of the present excursus.

Endnotes

Notes to the Introduction

1. An interesting and understandable typographical error crept into the version of this encounter in L. A. Zander's study of Bulgakov, *Bog i Mir* [God and the World] (Paris, YMCA-Press, 1948). Instead of the word *zhertvennost'* here translated as sacrificial readiness, Zander writes *zhenstvennost'* or femininity/the feminine. It is an understandable variant reading because of Bulgakov's discussion of the Eternal Feminine, Sophia and the Mother of God, where the Virgin Mother does in fact represent the creaturely realization of authentic femininity.

2. As cited in Catherine Evtuhov, *The Cross & the Sickle. Sergei Bulgakov and the Fate of Russian Religious Philosophy, 1890-1920* (Ithaca and London: Cornell University Press, 1997), 44, n. 13.

3. The first happens while Bulgakov is travelling across the steppes to the Caucasus, and is an experience of the Divine in the beauty of the natural world; the second occurs in the experience of forgiveness through an elder monk. See *Svet nevechernyi. Sozertsaniia i umozreniia* [Unfading Light. Contemplations and Speculations] (Moscow: Put', 1917), 7-8, 9-10.

4. The spirit of the Silver Age and Bulgakov's involvement in it are exceptionally well told by Evtuhov, *The Cross and the Sickle.*

5. Sergei Bulgakov, *Philosophy of Economy. The World as Household,* Catherine Evtuhov, tr., ed. (New Haven and London: Yale University Press, 2000).

6. Sergei Bulgakov, "Avtobiograficheskoe [Autobiographical]," *S. N. Bulgakov: Pro et Contra. Antologiia* [Pro et Contra. Anthology], vol. 1, D. K. Burlaka, ed. (St Petersburg: Izd. Russkogo Khristianskogo gumanitarnogo instituta, 2003), 67, 68-69.

7. There is really no Orthodox Mariology comparable to the developed Mariology found in Roman Catholicism, and Bulgakov's essay may be the first such attempt to reflect on the Mother of God dogmatically. Although the present work is a separate treatise, Bulgakov clearly roots his Mariological thinking in the broader contexts of Christology and Ecclesiology.

8. Zander, *Bog i Mir,* vol. 2, 184. Italics are in the original Russian.

9. *Drug zhenikha. O pravoslavnom pochitanii Predtechi* (Paris: YMCA-Press, 1927). English translation, *The Friend of the Bridegroom. On the Orthodox Veneration of the Forerunner,* Boris Jakim, tr. (Grand Rapids, MI: William B. Eerdmans Publishing Company, 2003).

10. *Lestvitsa Iakovlia* (Paris: YMCA-Press, 1929). No English translation as yet exists.

11. A feature also commented on by Zander, *Bog i Mir,* 63.

12. See B. Marchadier, "Sergei Bulgakov i 'Rimskoe Iskushenie' [Sergei Bulgakov and the Roman Temptation]," *S. N. Bulgakov: Religiozno-filosofskii put'. Mezhdunarodnaia nauchnaia konferentsiia posviashchennaia 130 — letiiu so dnia rozdheniia* [S. N. Bulgakov: A Religious-philosophical Path. An International Scholarly Conference marking the 130th anniversary of his birth], O. B. Vasilievskaia, M. A. Vasil'eva, eds. (Moscow: Russkii Put', 2003), 278, where Bulgakov is reported to have said that it was "a blunt catching of fish in troubled waters." Marchadier and other commentators incorrectly identify the encyclical as *Ecclesiarum Dei.* In his encyclical *Ecclesiam Dei,* Pope Pius XI makes indirect reference to the calamities that have befallen Christian Slavs, their miserable plight in exile, and suggests unity with the Church of Rome as one remedy for their current sorrows. Josaphat Kuncevich (ca. 1580-1623) was the Ukrainian Catholic bishop of Polotsk, who was killed by Orthodox laymen and subsequently recognized as a martyr by the Roman Catholic Church.

13. Zander, *Bog i Mir,* 23-26. It is interesting to note that Bulgakov's main sparring partner in *The Burning Bush* is the Roman Catholic dogmatic theologian Matthias Scheeben, one of the most authoritative and respected of German theologians of the nineteenth century.

14. See "Moe rukopolozhenie [My ordination]," S. N. Bulgakov, *Tikhie dumy* [Quiet Thoughts], V. V. Sapov, ed., an. (Moscow: Izd. Respublika, 1996), 346: "Essentially, even in the state of spiritual barbarism in Marxism I was always religiously melancholic, I was never indifferent towards belief. At first I believed in an earthly paradise, but timidly, with tears. Then, beginning with that well known moment when I permitted it to myself and decided to confess, I quickly, sharply, decisively went directly to my spiritual homeland from a distant land: having returned to belief in a 'personal' God (instead of the impersonal idol of progress) I believed in Christ Whom I had loved in my childhood and carried in my heart, and then also in 'Orthodoxy'; it pulled me into my family church imperiously and irrepressibly. But years would pass in which this idea and desire to return to my Father's house remained still powerless in me, my return was paid for by hidden sufferings."

15. A. P. Kozyrev, "Androgin na 'piru bogov' [An androgyne at the feast of the gods]," *S. N. Bulgakov: Religiozno-filosofskii put',* 338, writes "The experiences and intellectual torments that he is living through in a given moment often are poured into the theological thought of Father Sergius like a mighty flood . . ."; S. S. Averintsev, "'Dve vstrechi' o. Sergiia Bulgakova v istoriko-kul'turnom kontekste ['Two Encounters' of Fr. Sergii Bulgakov in their historical cultural context]," *S. N. Bulgakov: Religiozno-filosofskii put',* 253, where he writes "As is well known, Bulgakov is generally speaking an extraordinarily emotional author; the degree of emphasis with which he speaks, shall we say, about his own tears and even sobs of grief or rapture, and about other manifested feelings, is so great that in any other author not so sincere and in a certain sense more naïve than he it would be possible to censure for affectation."

16. Marchadier, "Rimskoe Iskushenie," 279.

17. S. N. Bulgakov, "Pis'mo k P. A. Florenskomu [Letter to P. A. Florensky]" in *Pro et Contra*, 159-188. See for example page 183 where Bulgakov states that his Orthodoxy demands recognition of the Pope, and where he accepts the council of Florence, papal infallibility and universal jurisdiction.

18. The book's publication history is as dramatic as its author's life. Zander produced a typed version in 1963, but only in 1991 was the full Russian text published by A. M. Moissine in *Simvol*, no. 25. A French translation exists: *Sous les remparts de Chersonèse*, Bernard Marchadier, tr. (Geneva: Ad Solem, 1999). See his introduction, 5-19, for details.

19. Vladimir Soloviev, *Tri razgovora: o voine, progresse i kontse vsemirnoi istorii so vkliucheniem kratkoi povesti ob antikhriste i s prilozheniami* (1900), translated as *War, Progress and the End of History*, A. Bakshy, ed., Thomas R. Beyer ed., rev. tr., Czesław Miłosz, intro. (Hudson, NY: Lindisfarne Press, 1990).

20. "Iz 'dnevnika' [From his Journal]," *Tikhie dumy*, 351.

21. Tikhi "Iz 'dnevnika'," *Tikhie dumy*, 369.

22. "Iz 'dnevnika'," *Tikhie dumy*, 356; 362: "On the one hand I do not believe him, I instinctively tighten up before him as if before a snake, a type of mendacity, ulterior motive, treachery, 'Jesuitical airs,' makes its presence felt in his every habit, but at the same time in ecclesial consciousness I am with him, I am closer to him than to any of our own (with the exception of the distant and alas now mute for me Fr. Pavel), and I listen attentively to his talk, interrogate him with hidden sympathy."

23. "Iz 'dnevnika'," *Tikhie dumy*, 376-377, outlines the discomfort that Bulgakov felt in Tyzskiewicz's presence. There is also a barely disguised anti-Polish sentiment in these pages.

24. "Iz 'dnevnika'," *Tikhie dumy*, 366-367.

25. "Iz 'dnevnika'," *Tikhie dumy*, 386.

26. "Iz 'dnevnika'," *Tikhie dumy*, 357.

27. Zander, *Bog i Mir*, vol. 1, 57.

28. Marchadier, "Rimskoe iskushenie," 279.

29. "Dve vstrechi," *Tikhie dumy*, 391.

30. Marchadier, "Rimskoe Iskushenie," 277. See also Marchadier, *Sous les ramparts de Chersonèse*, 16. On the basis of Bulgakov's recently published journals, Marchadier gives a complete and telling summary of Bulgakov's dramatic rejection of Catholicism, 13-18.

31. Cited by A. P. Kozyrev, "Androgin 'na piru bogov'," 339.

32. Marchadier, "Rimskoe iskushenie," 279.

33. S. N. Bulgakov, *Sv. Petr i Ioann. Dva Pervoapostola* [Saints Peter and John: The Two Chief Apostles] (Paris: YMCA-Press, 1926).

34. See Jean-Paul Deschler, "Die Ikone Gottesmutter 'Nichtverbrennender Dornbusch'," *Die Weisheit baute ihr Haus*, Karl Christian Felmy and Eva Haustein-Bartsch, eds. (Munich: Deutscher Kunstverlag, 1999), 113-157, for a thorough discussion of this icon type, including a decipherment of the numerous written devices that decorate the icon. According to Deschler, the icon type is from the sixteenth century and represents a theological icon, i.e., the image is not narrative but dogmatic, depicting the dogma of the incarnation of the Son of God. Also useful in the same volume is the chapter by Karl

Christian Felmy, "Der mehrfach dargestellte Christus und die ikonographischen Wurzeln der Dornbusch-Ikone," 159-165.

35. *The Burning Bush* was published in 1927, but Bulgakov had finished writing it in 1924 in Prague. His author's preface is dated 1926, so he may have revised some of the book in the intervening years.

36. For an insightful and succinct discussion of Bulgakov's early Sophiology, see Bernice Glatzer Rosenthal, "The Nature and Function of Sophia in Sergei Bulgakov's Prerevolutionary Thought," *Russian Religious Thought*, Judith Deutsch Kornblatt and Richard F. Gustafson, eds. (Madison WI: The University of Wisconsin Press, 1996), 154-175.

37. Paul Valliere develops this thought in his essay "Sophiology as the Dialogue of Orthodoxy with Modern Civilization," *Russian Religious Thought*, 176-192.

38. This has been reissued as *Sophia the Wisdom of God. An Outline of Sophiology,* with a foreword by Christopher Bamford (Hudson NY: Lindisfarne Press, 1993). References are to this edition. The book was written during the intense controversy about Sophiology that saw Bulgakov condemned for heresy by the Russian Orthodox Church outside Russia, censured by the Moscow Patriarchate and gingerly protected by his own metropolitan, Evlogii.

39. *Sophia the Wisdom of God,* 36.

40. *Sophia the Wisdom of God,* 51-52.

41. *Sophia the Wisdom of God,* 74.

42. Bulgakov was one of the very first modern theologians to use the work of St Gregory Palamas constructively.

43. See Ivo Muser, *Das mariologische Prinzip "gottesbräutliche Mutterschaft" und das Verständnis der Kirche bei M. J. Scheeben* (Rome: Editrice Pontificia Università Gregoriana, 1995), 108-117.

44. See A. P. Kozyrev, "Androgin 'na piru bogov'," 333-342, for a thorough discussion. As addenda to his article, Kozyrev publishes four texts written by Bulgakov on the theme of male and female: "Muzhskoe i Zhenskoe v Bozhestve [Male and Female in the Godhead]," 343-364; "Muzhskoe i Zhenskoe [Male and Female]," 365-388; "Fragment 1," 389-390; "Fragment 2," 391-395.

45. All three are included in *Tikhie Dumy:* "Stikhotvoreniia Vladimira Solov'eva [The Poetry of Vladimir Soloviev]," "Iz rukopisei A. N. Shmidt [From the manuscripts of A. N. Schmidt]," and "K problematike [With respect to the problems]," 51-82.

46. This may simply be a generational coincidence, since Bulgakov carried forward traditional notions of what constituted male and female identity that were unproblematic for Scheeben's day. Scheeben's theological anthropology is explored in Klaus Leo Klein, *Kreatürlichkeit als Gottebenbildlichkeit. Die Lehre von der Gottebenbildlichkeit des Menschen bei Matthias Joseph Scheeben* (Bern: Herbert Lang; Frankfurt/M.: Peter Lang, 1975).

47. What appears to be a précis of Bulgakov's essay is provided by Maria Skobtsova, "Pochitanie Bogomateri," *Mat' Mariia (Skobtsova): vospominaniia, stat'i, ocherki,* ["Veneration of the Mother of God," *Mother Maria (Skobtsova): recollections, articles, sketches*], vol. 1 (Paris: YMCA Press, 1992). English translation by Fr. S. Janos, http://www.berdyaev.com/skobtsova/veneratio_Bogomateri.html, November 17, 2004.

Notes to Chapter 1

1. While acknowledging the exceptional purity of Mary and her permeation by grace at the Annunciation, Origen nonetheless ascribes to her a wavering between full faith and human doubts and in the sense of the latter interprets the phrase "a weapon in the soul" as "a sword of unbelief." Even without external foundations in the Gospel and despite the gospel's witness that knows that Mary stood unwaveringly beneath the cross, Origen claims that she together with the apostles "was tempted" on account of Jesus (*In Lucam* 17, PG 13.1845). This strange opinion, which did not receive a special condemnation at the Fifth Council of Constantinople in 543 during the general condemnation of Origenist errors, on the contrary appeared to be quite alive. It was shared even by St Basil the Great who likewise interpreted "sword" as doubt (*Epistola 260,* 9, PG 32. 968) and by St John Chrysostom (*In psalmum* 13). Chrysostom speaks about vanity at the miracle in Cana of Galilee (*In Iohannem homilia 21,* 2, PG 59.130). He calls the appearance of Jesus' mother and brothers when Jesus is preaching "useless vainglory," done in order to show her influence over Him before the people (*In Matthaeam homilia* 44,1, PG 57.464). Cf. also St Hilary, *In psalmum 118,* 12, *PL* 9.523 A; Ps-Gregory of Nyssa, *De occursu Domini,* PG 46.1176; Ps-Chrysostom, *In psalmum 13,* 4, PG 55.555; Ps-Augustine, *Quaestiones veteris et novi testamenti,* 73, *PL* 35.2270; St Cyril of Alexandria, *Comm. in Iohannem* 19.25, PG 74.661-664. On the other hand, the declaration that Mary was free of sin appears already in St Epiphanius (*Adv. haereses, lib. I, 3, haer.* 42, PG 41.778), and in St Gregory of Nazianzus, who testifies that Mary was cleansed beforehand in both body and soul by the Holy Spirit (*Oratio 38 in Theophania,* PG 36.326). But the first to begin speaking about Mary's sinlessness was St Ephrem the Syrian in 370: "You, Lord, and your Mother, You alone are completely holy in every respect, for in You, Lord, there was no stain and Your Mary has no blemish" (*Carm. Nisib.* 27, 8). In another place he calls Mary guiltless like Eve before the Fall. St Ambrose gathered together all corresponding texts and gives a generalizing picture of the sinlessness of Mary (*Expositio evangelii secundum Lucam,* 2, *PL* 15.1633-1672), "Maiden, freed by grace of every sin" (*Expositio in psalmum 118,* *PL* 15.1599), whereas "weapon" is interpreted in the light of Heb 4.12 (*PL* 15.1656). Among westerners, Jerome, Gaudentius and blessed Augustine approximate this view.

2. According to the Catholic notion, the souls of sinless but unbaptised children have their own place in the afterlife (external limbo). Orthodoxy is silent about this as indeed it is in general about the afterlife fate of all unbaptised. This whole question is linked with the doctrine about preaching in Hades.

3. St John Damascene, "An Exact Exposition of the Orthodox Faith," book 3, chapter 2, writes (what follows seems to be a paraphrase, since it is not found in the passage cited by Bulgakov) "the Holy Spirit descended upon the pure Virgin and still made her pure. Pure on account of her body and spirit's own condition, she became the purest one through the creative omnipotent operation, which was produced in her by the life-giving, purifying, renewing, transforming Spirit of God who converts his vessels. The Pure Virgin became the Most Pure, foreign to every filth both thought and sensed, she became graciously pure, *the Spirit-bearing, divine Virgin*" (Bishop Ignaty Brianchaninov, *Exposition of the Doctrine of the Orthodox Church concerning the Mother of God. Works,* 3rd ed., vol. 4 [Moscow, n.d.], 364). It is difficult to reconcile this statement with bishop Ignaty's fur-

ther statements about how "the old human came to light and operated in the Mother of God; eternal death and *sin,* implanted in human nature, could not help but become apparent" (407). However, these imprecise and unfortunate expressions in which the author by the way sees "the exact and faithful doctrine of the Orthodox Church concerning the Mother of God" are referred by him only to the presence of original sin and its consequences, but not at all to personal sins, which he too, evidently, excludes. It is possible to think the same on the basis of what he says on the same page 407: after the Annunciation "her virginity was imprinted by the spirit: in as much as she preserved herself from every passionate intention and sensation, she became inaccessible for these intentions and sensations." In another place he writes "God's Mother did not partake of or know the struggle with fleshly desires. Even before desire began to operate in her, the Holy Spirit descended upon her, imprinted her purity, and gave her spiritual delight" (423).

4. See Appendix 1, pp. 11-14 below. (Translator's note)

Notes to Chapter 2

1. I have corrected some errors in the printed Russian text, which has *hamaftēma* for *hamartēma,* and gives Rom 12 instead of Rom 5 as the source for the biblical passages. (Translator's note)

2. A collection of these can be found in any history of dogma, such as Joseph Schwane, *Dogmengeschichte der patristischen Zeit (325-787 n. Chr.),* 3 vols. (Theissug, 1869); Reinhold Seeberg, *Lehrbuch der Dogmengeschichte,* 2 vols. (Deichert, 1895-1898); Friedrich Loofs, *Leitfaden zum Studium der Dogmengeschichte* (M. Niemeyer, 1906), etc.

3. Rev 12.7-9: "And war broke out in heaven. Michael and his angels rose up against the dragon; and the dragon and his angels fought (against them), but they did not stand their ground and no place for them was found in heaven. And the great dragon was cast down, the ancient serpent who is called the devil and who seduces the whole universe, was cast down to the earth and his angels were cast down with him."

4. The ruling is contained in canon 2 of the council of Carthage of 418, Denzinger-Schönmetzer, 223. (Translator's note)

5. This very thought is expressed in the Wisdom of Solomon 7.1-3 where some people mistakenly find the trace of the doctrine of reincarnation: "and I (speaking in the person of Solomon) am a mortal human, like all descendants of the primordial, the first-born. And I was formed in my mother's womb in flesh in nine months condensed in blood from the seed of the man and delight that is linked with sleep. And having been born I began to breathe the common air and fell to this earth, my first sound I disclosed as a lament, equally with all things." The special quality of this text is that here as it were the pre-temporal eternal existence of I *is opposed to* his earthly birth.

6. The fourth prayer of exorcism in the service for catechumens directly speaks about slavery to the devil, "to the work of the enemy" of which the one to be baptised is guilty even though new-born. The priest blows three times on him with the words: "expel from him every deceitful and impure spirit that is concealed and nested in his heart."

7. "It is necessary to know that neither among the Hebrews nor in sacred scripture was it the custom to include women in a genealogy, but it was the law that no one tribe

should take women from another tribe (Num 36.7). Joseph, originating from the tribe of David and being a righteous man, would not have become engaged with the Holy Virgin against the law, if she had not originated from the same tribe. Therefore it was enough to show the origin of Joseph alone." John of Damascus, *Expositio fidei*, 4, 14, PG 95.1156.

8. The status of a human after the fall of Adam does not differ from his state in pure nature any more than a stripped man differs from a nude one, neither is human nature worse, if you remove original sin, nor does it labour more in ignorance and charity than one established in pure nature would be or would labour. Therefore the corruption of nature proceeds not from a lack of some natural gift or from the entrance of some evil quantity but from the sole loss of the supernatural gift on account of Adam's sin. Robert Bellarmine, *De gratia primi hominis*, 5.

9. In the letter to the Rom 3.23 the apostle Paul gives a short but completely comprehensive formula of the meaning of original sin for the human: all have sinned (*hēmarton* — one-time action, the aorist) and are deprived (*hysterountai* — present) *of the Glory of God (tēs doxēs tou theou)*. Here the Glory of God is Sophianicity, present in man in virtue of his creation in the image of God: the human is the creaturely Sophia. By the power of sin, the divine image becomes obscured in man and, having ceased to be sophianic by condition, he by the same means is deprived of the palpable manifestation of the Glory of God. He ceases to be himself, loses the norm of his proper being.

10. Denzinger-Schönmetzer, 1511. (Translator's note)

11. An answer to the understanding of Catholic theologians in defence of the dogma of the Immaculate Conception, which frequently is expressed, is included here: if the Virgin Mary was not preserved in her very conception from every seed of original sin, she would necessarily have proven to be under the sway of "the prince of this world" if only for a brief moment, which is obviously inadmissible. To this it must be replied that the sway of the prince of this world is realized only through personal sinfulness which has its basis in the infirmity of nature. If the Mother of God never had *personal* sin, by this very fact she remained free even from "the prince of this world." The mortality of the human being along with diseases and weaknesses of the body was determined by God himself as the consequence of sin, and the obligation of death does not signify subordination "to the prince of this world." The human who is redeemed and who makes his own the power of redemption in baptism is liberated from captivity to the prince of this world, who is expelled from "the newly branded warrior of Christ" (censuring prayer), but he remains guilty of death in keeping with the general sentence of God: "you are earth and you will depart into the earth."

12. The thought about the Mother of God participating in redemption is sometimes exaggerated in Catholic literature to the degree that she proves to be along side of and on equal footing with her Son in the work of salvation. For examples see Alexander Lebedev, *The Difference of Eastern and Western Churches in the Doctrine of the Virgin Mary. A Polemical Dogmatic Investigation* (Warsaw, 1881), a work that still has some significance. The fundamental thought of the author with respect to the personal sinlessness of the Mother of God, though in the face of her assimilation of original sin, is quite close to what we have set forth. See pages 18, 136, 137, 198, 231, 300, 302, 350, 399.

13. "Preordained in the pre-eternal and foreknown counsel of God, presented and proclaimed beforehand in various images and words of the prophets by the Holy Spirit,

she grew out of the root of David at the foreordained time." John of Damascus, *Expositio fidei*, 4, 14, PG 95.1156.

Notes to Chapter 3

1. In essence a whole series of medieval Catholic theologians stand by this point of view: Paschasius, Radbertus, Anselm, Peter Lombard, Bernard, Bonaventure, Albert the Great, Thomas Aquinas. Cf. Schwane, *Dogmengeschichte*, vol. 3, § 94; X. le Bachelet, "Immaculée Conception," *Dictionnaire de théologie catholique*, vol. 7, Alfred Vacant, ed. (Paris: Letouzey et Ané, 1899-1950), 845-1218.

2. Denzinger-Schönmetzer, *Enchiridion symbolorum definitionum et declarationum de rebus fidei et morum*, 36th ed. (Freiburg im Breisgau: Herder, 1976), 2015. (Translator's note)

3. "Unbefleckte Empfängnis," Wetzers u. Welte's *Kirchenlexikon*, vol. 4 (Herder: Freiburg im Breisgau, 1847-1860), 456.

4. Matthias Joseph Scheeben, *Handbuch der katholischen Dogmatik*, vol. 2 (Herder, 1877), 660. The passage referred to by Bulgakov comes in a section devoted to the means of the transmission of original sin and the origin of the human soul. The text in question reads ". . . or the soul, which is pure from the perspective of its origin from God, as a result of its being poured into the body which has been shaped by the generative principle and stands under its direct influence, is stained and infected by this as by a filthy and spoiled vessel and as by an attached lead weight is weighed down and bound." (Translator's note)

5. "That integrity, with which the first human was established without which all humans are born after the fall was not his natural condition but a supernatural uplifting . . . , was a supernatural gift." (Translator's note)

6. Scheeben, *Dogmatik*, vol. 2, 216. The discussion referred to by Bulgakov continues on page 217 of Scheeben. (Translator's note)

7. "The mortality of the human being both with respect to the possibility and to the necessity of its death is a consequence of the constitution of its nature, a natural attribute of the body as *corpus animale*; it has therefore its root in nature itself and not only in sin (!), as if it were substantiated through this for the first time" (Scheeben, *Dogmatik*, vol. 2, 218). "On the contrary, God only restrained it for as long as the human being refrained from sin. It is the same thing with the possibility and necessity of the disorders of this life bound up with sickness, the pangs of birth, and with the excitability and arousal of sensuality and sexual desire" (Ibid., 218-224). "Human *concupiscibilitas* which turns into *activa concupiscentia* constitutes, if not a special gift of God (Pelagians), a defect and evil of nature, mortality and death. They are not from God, who has allowed them merely to endure and arise, as He has death and sin; rather, they are at the basis 'of the constitution' of human nature" (ibid., 225-226). (Therefore they are from God after all?)

8. Die geistige Seele hat von Natur nicht nur die Kraft das animalische Leben des Körpers vollkommen zu vergeistigen und zu durchherrschen oder die *infirmitas carnis* aufzuheben und sich von der Notwendigkeit sie zu dulden, zu befreien. Auch für ihr geistiges Leben selbst ergiebt sich aus der Verbindung mit dem corruptibeln und passibeln Körper eine gewisse von Haus aus ihr anhaftende Unvollkommenheit und

Schwäche, oder eine *infirmitas mentis*. "The spiritual soul has by nature not only the power to spiritualize fully the animal life of the body and to thoroughly dominate it or to raise the *infirmitas carnis* and to free itself from the necessity of enduring it. Also for its spiritual life itself a certain imperfection and weakness inherent in it, or an *infirmitas mentis*, results from its union with the corruptible and possible body." (Ibid., 227).

9. This becomes clear from the twenty-first proposition condemned by the Catholic Church: humanae naturae sublimatio et exaltatio in consortium divinae naturae debita fuit integritati primae conditionis, et proinde naturalis dicenda est et non supernaturalis. "The raising and exaltation of human nature into a participation of divine nature was due to the integrity of the first condition, and therefore it is to be called natural and not supernatural."

10. Seventy-six (or seventy-nine) statements attributed to Baius are condemned in the bull "Ex omnibus afflictionibus," of 1 October 1567. Denzinger-Schönmetzer, 1001-1079 (old numeration); 1901-1979. (Translator's note)

11. Georg Hermes (1775-1821) was a Catholic priest and renowned theologian active in Bonn. He developed Hermesianism which used doubt as a way of establishing rational foundations for church doctrine. His system was condemned by Pope Gregory XVI in 1835. (A. Thouvenin, "Hermes," *Dictionnaire de théologie catholique,* vol. 6, 2288-2303. Translator's note.) Anton Günther (1783-1863) was a Catholic priest, theologian and philosopher who attempted to explain the central truths of Christianity on an anthropological and rational basis. His ideas had a great influence on Catholic theology in the mid-nineteenth century. (P. Godet, "Günther," *Dictionnaire de théologie catholique,* vol. 6, 1992-1993. Translator's note.)

12. A veritate catholica eos aberrasse asserimus, qui docent Dei sapientiam et bonitatem exegisse, ut homini gratiam sanctificantem a concupiscentia aut immortalitatem corporis conferret; vel qui asserant immunitatem a concupiscentia necessarie pertinere ad ipsius hominis ideam seu naturam; denique qui dona Adamo collata propterea solum supernaturalia vocanda esse dicunt, quod homini a Deo creante et non ab homine sibi ipsi collata sunt. Hubert Theophil Simar, *Lehrbuch der Dogmatik* (n.p., 1879-1880), 390-409. "We assert that they have strayed from Catholic truth who teach that the wisdom and goodness of God are to be understood so that they confer on man sanctifying grace from concupiscence or immortality of the body; or who assert that immunity from concupiscence necessarily belongs to the idea or nature of man himself; and finally, who say that the gifts conferred on Adam are therefore to be called supernatural, because they are conferred on man by God creating and not by man upon himself."

13. This is perhaps an allusion to the influential if eccentric nineteenth-century thinker Nikolai Fedorovich Fedorov (1829-1903). His major work, *The Philosophy of the Common Task,* set forth his idea that through future technological advancements, humanity could achieve its common task, the physical resurrection of all the dead in historical time. (Translator's note)

14. Cf. for example John of Damascus, *Brief Exposition of the Orthodox Faith,* book 2, chapters 26 and 27, and in the *Orthodox Confession of the Eastern Catholic Church:* "although human will was injured by original sin, for all that, it is even now in the will of each person to be good or a child of God, or to be evil and a son of the devil" (*Orthodox Confession,*

part 1, question 27). In the letter of the Eastern Patriarchs we read: "every fallen human has that nature with which he was created and a natural, free, living and active power, as a result of which according to nature he can choose and do good, flee and turn away from evil" (Archbishop Silvester, *An Attempt at Orthodox Dogmatic Theology*, volume 3, Kiev, 448-450).

15. Among church authors supporting the *generation* of souls are Tertullian, *De anima*, 27, PL 2.737-739; Rufinus, in Jerome, *Adversus libros Rufini*, 2,8, PL 23.449-450; and Ps-Macarius (Bulgakov identifies him as Macarius the Great), *Homilia spiritalis 30*, 1, PG 34.721, "the earthly parents generate children from their own nature, both their bodies and their souls." On the other hand, the majority is for the creation of the soul: St Clement of Alexandria, *Stromata* 4, 26, PG 8.1372-1381; *Stromata* 6, 16, PG 9.357-380, St Athanasius the Great, *De incarnatione contra Apollinarium* 1, 4, PG 26.1097-1100; *Contra gentes* 1,1, PG 25.4-5 (perhaps 1,2), Sts Gregory the Theologian, Ephrem the Syrian, John Chrysostom, Cyril of Alexandria, Hilary, Ambrose of Milan, and blessed Jerome. Blessed Augustine occupied a wavering position and ultimately admitted his powerlessness to give a satisfactory answer to this question. In Augustine's dispute with the Pelagians, the latter naturally tended to the hypothesis of creationism as more in accordance with their teaching about the absence of radical depravity in human nature. On the other hand, in his defence of the doctrine of original sin Augustine was compelled to incline more towards the side of traducianism. Ultimately Augustine admitted that "ego adhuc inter utrosque ambigo et moveor, aliquando sic, aliquando autem sic — even now I hesitate between the two options and am moved sometimes this way, sometimes that way" (Augustine, *De genesi ad litteram*, 1 10, s.2. The quote does not appear in the text, though the sentiment is correct. Augustine discusses the options particularly in book 10, PL 34.407-428). Following on Augustine came his pupil Fulgentius and Pope Gregory the Great, Eucharius and Isidore. With the course of time in the Western church creationism triumphed in the period of scholasticism, Thomas Aquinas and others. Pope Benedict XII condemned the doctrine of the Armenians who rejected it. (Denzinger-Schönmetzer, *Enchiridion*, 533 [old numeration]; 1007.)

16. Cf. the exposition of the question in the dogmatics of Scheeben. Also, Joseph Kleutgen, *Die Philosophie der Vorzeit*, vol. 2 (Münster, 1863); Albert Stökl, *Die speculative Lehre vom Menschen und ihre Geschichte*, 2 vols. (Würzburg, 1859); Heinrich Klee, *Katholische Dogmatik*, 3 vols. (n.p., 1835, 1861); among Orthodox theologians, the fullest outline is found in Silvester, *An Attempt at Orthodox Dogmatic Theology*, volume 3.

17. Apollinarius distinguishes three parts of the human: *nous, psychē* and *sōma,* and the Logos assumed only flesh, having replaced the human spirit with himself. Apollinarius tends also to generationism, considering that souls are born from souls, as bodies are from bodies. In the general question about dichotomy and trichotomy, the opinions of the fathers generally speaking vary, although a majority are on the side of trichotomy: Justin the Philosopher and Clement of Alexandria talk about both, Irenaeus and Tertullian about dichotomy. Athanasius the Great also wavers between both, as does St Ephrem the Syrian. Sts Basil the Great, Gregory Nyssa, Epiphanius, Ambrose, Augustine, Cyril of Alexandria, and others speak about body, soul and spirit. Supporting the dichotomous option are Chrysostom, Nemesius, John of Damascus. After Apollinarius they are sometimes inclined to number dichotomy among the dogmas of Orthodoxy.

18. This may be an allusion to the thought of the Pre-Socratic philosopher Anaxagoras of Clazomenae (500-428 BC) who spoke of everything that exists as containing everything in it, as seeds, or portions of everything else. (Translator's note)

19. Here is an analogy with the Eucharistic sacrifice, offered once and for all, but repeated over and over again in the liturgy, with the sacrificial lamb, single and yet ever anew slaughtered, always divided and not fragmented: frequency of repetition combines in a single divine act of a single execution.

20. "The soul is given by God when the body is formed and made fit to receive it, and when it enters it spreads through the whole body similar to how fire spreads in scorching hot iron." *Orthodox Confession of the Eastern Catholic Church,* question 28.

21. Here a Christological question seems essential and even decisive: *how must one understand* the incarnation of God, to what principle does the Logos correspond in the Godman? Blessed Augustine is undecided concerning the provenance of the soul of Christ: unde Adam quam de Adam (*De genesi ad litteram* 10.18,33, *PL* 34.422), and the question about whether the soul of Christ derives from Mary together with the body, or if it was created by God (in conformity with strict creationism) and consequently Mary gave only the flesh, remained open, and the rejection of Apollinarius' error, according to which the Logos replaces the soul and spirit, does not give any guidance. In keeping with the conciliatory formula of the Third Ecumenical Council in 433, following the Antiochene creed, it was likewise impossible to define confidently the doctrine of the church. Here it was stated: *Theon teleion kai anthrōpon teleion ek psychēs logikēs kai sōmatos.* In this manner the trichotomous view is adopted here, and the being of Christ consists of "perfect Deity and perfect humanity, who consists of a rational soul and a body." There are no indications as to the provenance of this rational soul. But it is conceivably conformable to the spirit of the whole Old Testament and the Gospel genealogy that the rational soul of Christ was born from the Virgin Mary, who is His Mother in the *full* meaning of the word, like every human mother who gives birth to a human in the flesh.

Notes to Chapter 4

1. To be sure, this is a neologism, but so too is Bulgakov's original *votserkovlenie.* The meaning, however, is clear. (Translator's note)

2. The Staurotheotokion, in Russian, *krestobogorodichen,* is a canticle that evokes the Virgin at the foot of the cross. It replaces the Theotokion, the hymn honouring the Virgin in the regular liturgical offices, on Wednesdays and Fridays. (Translator's note)

3. Bulgakov's identification of the author as Melito of Sardis has been emended to reflect current scholarship. For a detailed discussion of the earliest traditions concerning the Dormition of Mary, see Stephen J. Shoemaker, *Ancient Traditions of the Virgin Mary's Dormition and Assumption* (Oxford: Oxford University Press, 2002). English translations of some early homilies concerning the themes are found in Brian E. Daley, S.J., *On the Dormition of Mary. Early Patristic Homilies* (Crestwood, NY: St Vladimir's Seminary Press, 1998). (Translator's note)

4. See Appendix 2, pp. 114-16 below. (Translator's note)

5. And the Mother of God herself, in her humility, said about herself, "for the

mighty one has done great things for me" (Lk 1.49). As mother of the King of those who reign she herself already becomes a participant in royalty.

6. "Prayer to the Most Holy Theotokos," *Priest's Prayer Book,* 259.

7. The omophorion is the stole worn by Orthodox bishops. Symbolically it is the equivalent of the Latin pallium. (Translator's note)

8. The Blachernae was the most famous of all churches in Constantinople dedicated to the Mother of God. It was built sometime between 450 and 453, but suffered repeatedly from fire and reconstruction down to the conquest of the City in 1453. While praying in the Blachernae church St Andrew (±936) had a vision of the Mother of God holding her veil over people praying for her protection. (Translator's note)

9. "Service of the Dormition of the Mother of God," canon, canticle 4, troparion 1.

10. Cf. my sketch "on the veneration of sacred relics in Orthodoxy" (manuscript). According to Zander, this appeared in *Sergievskie Listki,* no. 56, 1932. (Translator's note)

11. "When the stars had been created, all of my angels extolled them with a mighty voice" (Job 38.7).

12. The third of three Old Testament lessons which is always read on feasts of the Theotokos (the first is taken from Genesis 28.10-17, concerning Jacob's vision of the ladder; the second is taken from the prophecy of Ezekiel concerning the closed gates, 44.1-3; the third comes from the Proverbs of Solomon, 9.1-18) obliquely bears witness to this. The text of Prov 9.1, "Wisdom has built herself a house and established seven pillars" is applied by the Church in this way to the Mother of God, who is just such a house or dwelling place for Wisdom; in other words, she is the incarnation of Wisdom, she is the Church established on seven pillars. The attempt has been made to interpret this text in relation to Christ-Wisdom, but without saying that it contradicts its direct application by the Church to the Theotokos, such an attempt also leads to incongruities in the interpretation of the text. Namely, if we accept that Wisdom is the Logos, Christ, then it follows that the Logos, the Second Hypostasis, created for himself a body or prepared a mother. But this constitutes a direct contradiction to the Annunciation, according to which Divine Motherhood is connected with the visitation of the Holy Spirit: "The Holy Spirit will come to you and the power of the most high will overshadow you." Therefore it is more natural in the given text to time the action of Wisdom to the manifestation in the world of the Third Hypostasis, the Holy Spirit, and this corresponds as well to the continuation of the text which has in view in a clear manner the Church and the gifts of grace of the Holy Spirit: "and she has established seven pillars, has slaughtered her sacrificial animals, and mixed in her cup the wine, and prepared her table" (Prov 9.1-2).

13. If one uses a comparison from the history of dogma for an explanation of the thought about the Mother of God as Pneumatophore, one can here apply the concept of *adoption,* a certain inner appropriation, confluence of the creaturely and divine hypostases. Adoptionism in its application to Christology was condemned by the western church in the ninth century in Spain, because it contained in itself the doctrine not about the single divine hypostasis of Christ but about two hypostases, divine and human, which then were merged into a single divine Hypostasis on the basis of adoption. It is obvious here that the church's doctrine about Christ is impaired, pronounced at the fourth and subsequent ecumenical councils. However when applied to the personality of the Mother of God and in her relation to the Holy Spirit the idea of adoption, of her full

and complete sanctification, can have its lawful application, foreign to Christological heresy. The blessing with grace or divinization of the human by the action of the Holy Spirit can be imagined generally as a type of adoption, of the more or less full penetration of human nature by divine, their living conjunction. It has different degrees, but "she who is more honourable than the cherubim" has this unity with the Holy Spirit in a degree exceeding all measure, wherefore she is also the Pneumatophore in the proper sense.

14. Bulgakov devoted considerable energy to the question of gender, especially because of his initial fascination with and then resolute rejection of the influence of Anna Schmidt on Vladimir Soloviev's conceptualization of Divine Sophia. For a thorough discussion see A. P. Kozyrev, "Androgin 'na piru bogov'," in *S. N. Bulgakov: Religiozno-filosofskii put'*, 333-342. As addenda to his article, Kozyrev publishes four texts written by Bulgakov on the theme of male and female: "Muzhskoe i Zhenskoe v Bozhestve" (Male and Female in the Godhead), 343-364; "Muzhskoe i Zhenskoe" (Male and Female), 365-388; "Fragment 1," 389-390; "Fragment 2," 391-395.

15. Bulgakov engages in an untranslatable play on words: *pol* (sex, half), *polovinchatost, nepolnota, polnota*. (Translator's note)

16. With respect to this point, the Western Church has the definition of the eleventh council of Toledo (675): "nor however ought the Holy Spirit be believed to be the Father of the Son, because it was said that Mary, overshadowed by the same Holy Spirit, conceived. Let us not seem to assert two fathers for the Son, which is certainly to be called monstrous" (Denzinger-Schönmetzer, 282/533, not 281 as in the Russian). This opinion is supported in Catholic dogmatics too, for example, Christian Pesch, *Praelectiones dogmaticae*, vol. 4 (Herder: Freiburg im Breisgau, 1900), 303: "Sp-s S. nullo modo dici debet pater Christi — the Holy Spirit ought in no way be called the father of Christ." However there are exceptions: Dubosc de Pesquidoux, *L'immaculée conception, histoire d'un dogme*, vol. 1 (Tours, 1898), 941: "Mary relates equally to the Holy Spirit as virginal spouse (!!!): *obumbravit tibi* says the Gospel." . . . There is even talk of a divine wedding announced by the angel. Similar examples of bad taste, however, are the work only of individual authors.

17. The words of the archangel to Mary, "The Holy Spirit will come upon you and the power of the most high will overshadow you" (Lk 1.35), are usually interpreted — by St John of Damascus *Expositio fidei* 3,2, PG 94.984-988 (and above all by St Athanasius the Great, St Gregory of Nyssa, St Cyprian, St Hilary) — in the sense that "the power of the most high" is the Logos, who comes to dwell in the Mother of God by the visitation of the Holy Spirit, for which reason the Annunciation is also the divine conception.

18. In the apocryphal gospel of the Hebrews these words are placed in the mouth of Jesus Christ: "My mother is the Holy Spirit." *Hē mētēr mou to hagion pneuma* (Origen, *Commentarii in Iohannem* 2, 12, PG 14.132; *Homilia in Jeremiam* 15, 4, PG 13.433; Jerome, *Commentariorum in Michaem* 7, 5-7, PL 25.1221; *In Isaiam* 40.9, PL 24.419; *In Hiezechielem* XVI, 23; Edgar Hennecke, *Neutestamentliche Apokryphen*, 2nd ed. [Tübingen: J. C. B. Mohr (Paul Siebeck), 1924], 54).

19. In his first sermon in Constantinople, Nestorius exclaimed: "you ask, can Mary be called Theotokos? But surely God does not have a mother, does He? Then one must accept paganism, which speaks about mothers of deities. No, Mary did not bear God, the

creature did not bear the Creator, but a human who is the *instrument* of Divinity; the Holy Spirit did not implant the Logos but He built a temple in which He must dwell. I honour this *clothing* for His sake, who clothed himself in it and was not separated from it. . . . He who was formed in the womb of Mary was not himself God, but God assumed *(assumpsit)* him and for the sake of his being assumed, that which is assumed is called God" (*Marii Mercatoris s. Augustino aequalis Opera omnia; ad pelagianam nestorianamque haeresim pertinentia, PL* 48, 757-765; Hefele, *Conciliengeschichte,* vol. 2. A, II, 152-153; Schwane, *Dogmengeschichte,* vol. 2, 322-323.

20. In a similar manner is imagined the generation of the human in crude creationism, appropriated in Catholicism through the dogma of the Immaculate Conception. The soul *is poured into* the embryo by God when it attains sufficient development, and in this manner inhabits the body as in a house or is clothed by it as with a garment. Therefore from the precocious dogma of the Immaculate Conception of the Mother of God Nestorianism follows with inevitability in Christology: in its own time the Logos' "soul is poured into" Christ's body, prepared by Mary, and Mary proves to be not the Theotokos but the Christotokos. Catholic dogmatics did not know how to join both ends here.

21. We encounter such an expression applied to the Divine Mother in bishop Ignaty Brianchaninov, op. cit., "she became . . . the *Pneumatophoric,* divine Virgin."

22. In sacred hymnody the Son of God is called the one who is begotten by the Father *without a mother,* and of course we do not think that it departs here from the norms of church doctrine. The begetting of the Son is accomplished by the Father; the Third Hypostasis, who already presupposes the Begotten One, does not participate in this. But in begetting, the Father proceeds towards the Begotten in the Holy Spirit, maternally embraces Him and quickens Him. Thus not only sonship is from the Father but also motherhood which, being unparticipatory in the generating, still takes part in the birthing process already accomplished, and pre-eternally contains it.

23. In one Catholic author, S. Thomas de Villeneuve, is encountered a successful definition: "if the human is created as a microcosm, then Mary is *microcosmus Ecclesiae* (J. B. Terrien, *La Mère de Dieu et la mère des hommes d'après les pères et la Théologie,* vol. 1 [Paris, 1902], 313). "The Theotokos mother is damp earth and in this is a great joy for humanity." Feodor Dostoevsky, *Demons.*

24. Works of John Chrysostom, volume XI, 1, 166; volume IV, 1, 134; volume I, 1, 308; volume IV, 2, 797. (These are Russian translations used by Bulgakov.)

25. By what manner do the angels multiply? Were they created in their full number by God or were they multiplied by their species originator? There is no answer, but equally possible is the one and the other suggestion.

26. The expression *aei parthenos* (Ever-Virgin) is encountered already in St Athanasius the Great, *Oratio II contra Arianos,* 70, *PG* 26.296; likewise Didymus the Blind, *De trinitate* 1, 27, *PG* 39.406; Epiphanius, in 2 and 6 apothematisms of the 5th ecumenical council and others. Many speak of the Ever-Virgin Mother of God; see for example the sermons of St John of Damascus, *Homilia i in nativitatem b.v. Mariae, PG* 96.966; *Homilia ii in dormitionem b.v. Mariae, PG* 96.724.

27. Hence the ascesis of voluntary virginity is so highly esteemed by the Church, as a struggle of the cross with lustful nature on behalf of uninjured human nature with

freedom from sex. In the Revelation of St John (14.3-5) we read: "they sing as it were a new song before the throne . . . and no one could learn this song except those 144,000 redeemed from the earth. These are they who have not been sullied with women, for they are virgins, they who follow after the Lamb wherever He might go. They are redeemed from the people, like the first fruits for God and the Lamb."

28. Bulgakov refers here to an idea found in the writings of Anna Schmidt, a mystic who exerted some influence on Bulgakov through Soloviev. According to her, she had received a personal new revelation, which she termed a Third Testament, in which she felt within herself the incarnated spirit of the church through which she was in communion with the heavenly Beloved, who turned out to be incarnated in Vladimir Soloviev. See S. N. Bulgakov, "Iz rukopisei A. N. Shmidt," in *Tikhie dumy* (Moscow: Izd. Respublika, 1996), 57. (Translator's note)

29. The famous Catholic dogmatician Scheeben (*Dogmatik*, vol. 3, 506-507) attempts to define the place of Mary in obscure but sometimes bold expressions: "Mary along with Christ is in such an extraordinary degree the image and likeness of God that the Church finds no difficulty in applying to her the expressions of sacred Scripture concerning the Wisdom of God. She participates in the *gloria et virtus* of the divine hypostases, has *communicatio idiomatum divinarum* in such a singular form as no other creature. Of course one cannot call her Dea, or *persona divina* or even *diva*, her divine property is always expressed otherwise: holy, glorious, heavenly Virgin. In her divine sonship lies the specific reflex of *divine daughterhood* (!!) of eternal wisdom with respect to God-Father." Further he speaks about the application of the expression Daughter of God to the Holy Spirit, *sapientia* as *filia Dei, Ruach, caritas Dei, filia Patris et sponsa et soror Filii*, with respect to humankind *Mater spiritualis* and first-formed of all creation. (All of this would require development and disclosure.)

30. St Andrew of Crete, *Homiliae iv in nativitatem*, PG 97.805-820, 820-844, 844-861, 862-88; St Tarasios of Constantinople, *In praesentationem*, PG 98.1488; Jacob the Monk (11th century), *Oratio in nativitatem ss deiparae*, PG 127.573, et al.

31. Gregory Palamas, *Homilia in dormitionem deiparae*, PG 151.468, 472.

32. See my "Chapters on Trinitarity" in manuscript form. This work is available in a new edition, S. N. Bulgakov, "Glavy o troichnosti," in *Trudy o Troichnosti*, ed. Anna Reznichenko (Moscow: O.G.I., 2001), 54-180. (Translator's note)

33. Here for example is the judgment of the latest "Mariology." "La bienheureuse Vierge est la Fille du Père, sa fille première née, sa fille unique, comme Jésus est son fils unique; *unigenita; unigenitus*" (Terrien, *La Mère de Dieu*, vol. 1, 194). "Il est le Fils de Dieu par excellence, le Fils unique, *unigenitus;* elle est la Fille perpétuelle de Dieu. Il est le premier né *primogenitus*, elle est après lui la première née, *primogenita*" (197-198). Despite all these exaggerations, imprecisions and obscurities the author nonetheless considers it "blasphémie et folie" to equate the nativity of the Son and the Mother, for "tout ce qu'elle est, elle l'est non par la nature, mais par le privilège souverainement gratuit" (168). Cf. A. Lebedev, *Differences of the Eastern and Western Churches concerning the Doctrine of the Most Holy Virgin* (Warsaw, 1881), 269.

34. In a sermon of St Ephrem the Syrian we find the following address to the Son placed on the Virgin's lips: "I am Your sister, in as much as we both have David as ancestor; I am also Your mother, in as much as I conceived You, Your spouse, according to the

gift of holiness, given to Me by You." Ephrem the Syrian, *Opera II* (Syriaco-latina) 429, *Sermo in nativitatem deiparae,* 279.

35. In his first homily on the Nativity of the Theotokos, St John of Damascus writes: "O daughter — *thugatrion. . . .* Abiding in the bridal chambers of the Holy Spirit and preserved in immaculateness as the bride of God and as the mother of God according to nature," PG 96, 672; and "rejoice, sister designated beautiful brother and beloved . . . rejoice bride whose sponsor is the Holy Spirit and bridegroom, Christ . . . rejoice, matrimonial chamber, adorned with the beauties of virginity, as it is said in the Song of Songs (5.1): *I came to my garden, my sister bride.*" *In hom. ii in nativitatem b. v. Mariae,* PG 96.693.

36. From our countrymen we will cite the sermon of Stefan Yavorsky, metropolitan of Riazan, from his book *The Rock of Faith:* "she is the daughter of God the Father, the Mother of God, the holy bride of God the Spirit." (The latter clearly is under Catholic influence. *The Mighty Deeds of the Most Holy Theotokos and Ever-Virgin Mary* [Moscow, 1845], 356.)

37. We find the most resolute likening of the Mother of God and the bride from the Song of Songs in St Ambrose of Milan, *De institutione virginis et S. Mariae virginitate perpetua,* PL 16.319-345. "Who is closer if not she who is brought near to Christ to whom the Word says: *arise, come my near one, my lovely, because the winter is past* (Song 2.10-11)?" (PL 16.319-320). Likewise in another place he adds: *your eyes are doves beneath your veils* (PL 16.320): because she is all spiritual and simple like a dove, in the image of which John saw the Holy Spirit descending, he sees the spiritual and knows the mysteries which he sees (4). See chapters 87, 88, 89 and col. 327 in St John of Damascus, *Homilia ii in nativitatem b. v. Mariae* where the text of Song of Songs 1.11, 12; 4.13,14; 7.1; 4.9,7; 1.2; 3.6; 7.5,6 is broadly applied to the Mother of God. (These verses are not used in this section of the homily. Translator's note.) Cf. the comparison of texts referring to the Mother of God in the Song of Songs in the book *Tales about the Earthly Life of the Mother of God,* Athos, 9-11.

38. One must be on one's guard against correlating the Mother of God as Bride of God not with Christ but with the Holy Spirit, who in this case is regarded as the father of the begotten son. This false inclination, proper to Catholic theology, sometimes arises in Orthodox theology as well. We find a striking example of this, in addition to the already cited extract from *The Rock of Faith* of Stefan Yavorsky, in the sermon of St Dimitry of Rostov on the memorial of the Protection of the Theotokos. He says that "in her single person I see three particular ranks of Divine work expressed; with a particular rank she served God the Father, with a particular rank God the Son, and with a particular rank God the Holy Spirit: for she is Daughter to God the Father, to her he says "listen daughter and see' (Ps 45.10). She is Mother to God the Son, and she is as a betrothed Maiden to the Holy Spirit" (*Marvels of the Most Holy Theotokos,* 246). We encounter a similar thought in the book *Tales about the Earthly Life of the Mother of God,* 7th ed. (Moscow, 1897), 9: "she is called *bride* with respect to the Holy Spirit, she is designated *not bride* with respect to people, as the one not conjoined by marriage, the unwed."

39. In conjunction with this, one remarkable feature in the church's use of the Song of Songs becomes comprehensible: *it is never* read at the Divine Liturgy, one necessarily thinks, because all of it, as indeed the whole life of the Church, is the Song of Songs in the process of being accomplished. At the same time the church's liturgy is saturated with it, its images became the most intimate and usual in ecclesiastical use.

40. Blessed Augustine.

41. This is an allusion to the major sophiological work by Bulgakov's close friend, Pavel Florensky, *The Pillar and Ground of Truth (Stolp i utverzhdenie istiny)* (Moscow, 1914). An English translation is available, Pavel Florensky, *The Pillar and Ground of the Truth: An Essay in Orthodox Theodicy in Twelve Letters,* Boris Jakim, tr. (Princeton: Princeton University Press, 1997). (Translator's note)

42. Cf. my "Unfading Light," Moscow 1917, the section on Sophia; also the sketch "Hypostasis or Hypostaseity" in the collection in honour of P. B. Struve. The latter work is normally called "Hypostasis and Hypostaseity." It is reprinted in *Trudy o Troichnosti,* ed. Anna Reznichenko (Moscow: OGI, 2001), 19-53. (Translator's note)

43. This idea about the pre-eternal and creaturely Wisdom of God forms the main theme of the theological reflection of St Athanasius the Great on this subject (cf. the special excursus about the doctrine of St Athanasius the Great).

44. Wisdom is called Holy Spirit by St Theophilus, *Ad Autolycum,* 2, 10, *PG* 6.1064, and St Irenaeus, *Adv. haeres.,* 4, 20 1, *PG* 7.1032.

45. Remarkable and in the highest degree significant is the content of this most ancient icon, housed in the most ancient Russian church of St Sophia in Kiev. It is supposed that this depiction is taken originally from a Justinianic church, but when it was painted is unknown. In any case this is the most sacred emblem handed on by elder Byzantium to young Russia as a dogmatic gift, bequest and testament. This icon has a definite Theotokos-sophianic content. It depicts the Mother of God in a chiton with a veil on her head standing beneath a canopy supported by seven columns. Her arms and hands are outstretched; her feet are fixed on a crescent-shaped moon, resting on a cloud; at her breast, as in icons of the Sign, is the Pre-eternal Child, blessing with his right hand and holding an orb in his left. On the cornice of the canopy is an inscription in Greek which reads "wisdom built herself a house and fashioned seven columns," and beneath this *hē Sophia.* On the peak of the canopy, in the middle the Holy Spirit is depicted in the form of a dove surrounded by rays; somewhat higher also in blue rays is depicted God the Father, holding an orb in his left hand and blessing with the right. Out of his mouth come the words "I have fixed her feet." This fundamental part of the composition has an obviously expressed Theotokos-sophianic meaning. The Most Pure is depicted here as the pre-eternal Mother of God, holding the Son-Emmanuel against her bosom. She is shown as the unity of divine-begetting and divine motherhood, and on her rests the Holy Spirit, overshadowing the Mother of God. Above it all rises a depiction of the Father, generating the incarnating Son and proceeding Holy Spirit, revealing himself in both hypostases. The inscriptions, which refer in a clear way to the Wisdom of God as well as to the Mother of God, leave no doubt about the Theotokos-sophianic interpretation (thus, the interpretation of these inscriptions by some theologians in an exclusively Christosophianic sense is obviously inapplicable here, namely that "Wisdom – Christ – built himself a house – the Mother of God or house of the Holy Spirit"; the house is built by the Father, as the First Principle, who generates the Son and sends forth the divine maternal principle of the Holy Spirit). All further symbolism of this icon elaborates the motif of seven, as an image of the seven gifts of the Holy Spirit, present in the Church and the Mother of God, and refers, e.g., to the Mother of God as the bearer of the Holy Spirit. On it are depicted 7 angels, 7 prophets, 7 columns, 7 steps with 7 inscriptions, 7 emblems and inscriptions on columns, from which the same number is found in

each. Seven archangels in the clouds each hold in their hands the sign of their ministry: on the right Michael holds a flaming sword, Uriel, lightning, Raphael, an alabaster jar of myrrh; on the left Gabriel holds the blossom of a lily, Selaphiel, prayer beads, Jehudiel, a crown, Barachiel, a bunch of flowers. Beneath the clouds with the crescent-shaped moon as the footstool of the Mother of God, is an ambo with 7 steps; on each is printed in ascending order from below one of the following words: faith, hope, love, purity, humility, goodness, glory (a host of Christian virtues, crowned by glory — sophianicity). On the first step is written above this: "by seven risings is her ascent." On the steps of the ambo before the Mother of God, prophets stand on both sides, Old Testament bearers of the Holy Spirit, "who spoke through the prophets." On the right of the 4th step from the top stands Moses with the tablets, on which is written: "rejoice tablets of God, on which the Word of God was written by the Father's hand," as if in intentional refutation of theologians who want to see Wisdom as Christ who built the Temple-Mother of God in the text of Proverbs 9. Behind Moses in descending order follows Aaron with the blooming rod and on the last step with Moses stands Isaiah with a charter hanging from the left shoulder on which are the words: "behold a Virgin receives in the womb" etc. Behind him in descending order on their own steps stand the prophets: Jeremiah with a scroll, Ezekiel with closed gates, and Daniel with stone in his hands. On all seven columns supporting the canopy are found emblematic depictions in circles, taken from the Apocalypse, with explanatory words from this prophetic book. On the first column to the right of the Mother of God are depicted seven eyes with the inscription "the gift of counsel," then the words "on a single stone seven eyes." On the second column is depicted a seven-branched candelabra over which is the inscription "the gift of reason," and then "I saw a golden candlestand and seven lamps on top of it." On the step at the extreme right is depicted a book with 7 seals suspended from it with the words "the gift of wisdom" above, and behind them the inscription "I saw a book sealed with seven seals." On the column closest to the left of the Mother of God are 7 trumpets, above which is the inscription "the gift of fortitude," and beneath "seven trumpets at the fall of Jericho." On the fifth column is a right hand with 7 stars with the inscription "the gift of sight," and then "in the right hand are seven stars." On the sixth column are 7 smoking thuribles over which are the words "the gift of reverence," and behind them "seven gold phials full of incense, which are the prayers of the saints." On the last column are depicted 7 flashes of lightning with the inscription "the fear of God," and then "seven thunders spoke their voices." (*The Benefits of the Mother of God to the Christian Race through her holy Icons*, 2nd ed. [St Petersburg, 1905], 672-675.) Corresponding to this symbolism here the Mother of God is depicted as the incarnation of the Church with all the gifts of the Holy Spirit, as the unity of earthly and heavenly Sophia, as the Glory of the world.

    46. "The most ancient Russian cathedrals in Kiev and Novgorod were dedicated to Sophia, the Wisdom of God; in this dedication one sees an imitation of the temples of Greece, and in the Greek East there not a few such temples of Sophia: St Sophia in Thessalonica, Constantinople, Trapezond, Tauridian Chersoneses, Nicosia on the island of Cyprus, and Sofia in Bulgaria. The esteem for this ancient tradition was transferred to us in Russia and the custom of dedicating temples to St Sophia found among us a broad dissemination: besides those in Kiev and Novgorod, temples of St Sophia are known in Vologda (1568), Tobol'sk, Moscow, Grodno, and Polotsk. One can suppose that some of

the most ancient temples dedicated to the Mother of God, e.g., in honour of her Nativity and Dormition, also have a close relationship in idea with the temples of the Holy Spirit . . . in this last circumstance, perhaps, is the reason why there were many cathedrals of the Dormition in Russia: in Rostov, Zvenigorod, Vladimir, Moscow, Yaroslavl', Riazan', Kostroma, Astrakhan, Vologda, Rybinsk, Tobol'sk, Vilnius" (A. Nikol'skii, *Sophia the Wisdom of God. Novgorod redaction of icons and services of St Sophia* [St Petersburg: St Petersburg Archeological Institute, 1905], addenda 34).

47. Published by Fr. Pavel Florensky, from a manuscript held in the Moscow temple of St Sophia on Sofiika, and reissued in Belgrade by a circle of student-theologians, lithograph. In general it represents a supplement for the service of the Dormition (correspondingly a little abbreviated) with proper stikhira and canons in honour of Sophia. In many cases Sophia is directly equated with Christ, but in others, with the Mother of God. We shall bring forth examples of the latter. Troparion: "Mighty and inexpressible is the power of Divine Wisdom, most eminent Sophia, most honourable temple, flame-coloured throne of Christ our God: in you dwells inexpressibly the Divine Word, and becoming flesh, the invisible appeared, . . . and as a child-loving and merciful queen, look upon your people." (This and other prayers, printed originally also in *Moscow Church News* 1889, No. 35, are reprinted in a collection of prayers read before holy icons at molebens, all-night vigils, gathered from akathists and church services approved by the spiritual censor of the Most Holy Synod, by archpriest A. Stavrovskii, St Petersburg, Sinodal'naia tipografiia, 1909.)

> ***Kontakion:*** Let us hasten, Orthodox people, and see the miraculous icon of the Wisdom of God, His Most Pure Mother: for it brilliantly shines in the most honourable temple of God and gladdens the hearts of those who approach with faith and gaze on this most pure icon with fear and reverence; pondering in our hearts how in truth the Mother of God is for the hope of the faithful, let us look at her flame-coloured image, and let us bend the knee to her true and immaculate virginity in birth and after birth. . . .

> ***Ikos:*** Establish my mind and meditation in goodness, God and Father Almighty: for I dare to sing the defender of the world, the most immaculate bride virgin. You have named her virginal soul your divine church and on account of the incarnation of your word you have called her Wisdom of God, and in that name you commanded emperor Justinian to build a church, and in an appearance you gave the most divine Cyril the chosen virgin, Sophia by name, that is Wisdom of God; you portrayed the visage of her face flaming, from her proceeded from Your divinity, that is, Your only-begotten Son, consuming our bodily passions . . . for this reason let us all sing for she is in truth the Wisdom of God, the refuge and heavenly canopy, bestower of all good things. . . . Canon ode 8, troparion 3: The rational vineyard is the temple of Sophia, the Wisdom of God, that is, the womb of the most holy Mother of God, from which came forth the divine one, burning the corrupt passions of our soul. . . .

Cf. also, A. Nikol'skii, *Sophia the Wisdom of God.* On the basis of his analysis of a service for St Sophia the author reaches the conclusion that its composer "understands under

Wisdom of God at one time the incarnate Word, and at another time the Mother of God," and in the troparion "Mighty and inexpressible is the power of the Wisdom of God" understands both Jesus Christ and the Mother of God under the term "wisdom of God" (10). The author comments: "the compiler did not form for himself a clear and precise concept of Holy Wisdom" (ibid.).

The doubling in interpretation of Wisdom, which in one case is taken as Divine revelation in creation in general and in another case is directly equated with the Second Hypostasis, becomes apparent in the canon of Great Thursday. Here are some examples: Ode 1, troparion 1: *"cause of all and bestower of life, the measureless wisdom of God built a temple for itself* from a Mother who had no experience of men: wrapped in the bodily temple Christ our God is greatly glorified." Here the thought is doubled: the cause of all and the bestower of life — this is the power of both the Word and the Holy Spirit, operating in creation, to which is ascribed (in agreement with Prov 9.1) also the building of a temple in the Mother in which Christ was clothed. So too from Proverbs 9 are taken images of the third irmos, where it is again said of Wisdom in a general sense "let us, all the faithful, listen to the uncreated and natural wisdom of God summoned by a exalted preaching, for it sings: taste and see that I am good (the Slavonic translation reads "Christ" but this is an incorrect translation of the word *Chrestos* which is clearly confused with *Christos*), shout out: Christ our God is greatly glorified!" Ode 9, Troparion 2 has the same thought (likewise on the theme of Prov 8.22f.): "Before the ages the father begets me the co-worker and wisdom, he established the beginning of his paths in works now secretly done. For being by nature the uncreated word, I have made his voice my own, and now I shine him forth" (clear vagueness in the translation). On the contrary, in other cases a clearly Christosophianic meaning is given to Wisdom. Here are some examples: Ode 1, troparion 2, "Instructing her friends in the mysteries, the true Wisdom of God prepares a soul-saving table and mixes a cup of immortality for the faithful: let us approach reverently and cry out: Christ our God is greatly glorified!" Ode 5, troparion 1: "containing the uncontainable water of the firmament in the air, and restraining the abyss and holding back the seas, the Wisdom of God pours water into the wash basin and the master washes the feet of his slaves." Similar examples of a doubling of meaning are found in other church hymns.

48. In St Dimitry of Rostov we find such a passage (cited on page 251): "run to her, O priests, because she was the divine Priestess or sacrificer when she offered to the Lord in sacrifice her Son, the spotless Lamb, on the altar of the cross for the sake of all the world."

49. In his painting of the Last Judgment, Michelangelo wanted to paint this countenance of the King and Judge which is so different from that of the Teacher meek and humble of heart.

50. The antinomy of justice and mercy in the fate of humankind is expressed by the divinely inspired teacher of antinomic theology, the apostle Paul in conjunction with the question about the fate of the Jews: "for God has locked everyone in opposition so that he may have mercy on everyone" (Rom 11.32). (The printed version reads Rom 11.12. Translator's note)

Notes to Excursus 1

1. These prefigurements and prophecies are often enumerated in the appropriate collections. See for example the excellent comparison in the book *The Mighty Deeds of the Most Holy Theotokos* (Moscow, 1845), 8-68.

2. A reference to Dan 2.34, a text used in stichera on the Sunday of the Ancestors (the Sunday between December 11 and 17, before Christmas), and on December 22 and 26; also from the Octoechos, tone 5, Theotokion on Saturday at Small Vespers. The mountain not hewn, or the stone that was cut out, not by human hands, is understand as a prototype of the Theotokos in Orthodox theology. See Karl Christian Felmy, "Der mehrfach dargestellte Christus und die ikonographischen Wurzeln der Dornbusch-Ikone," *Die Weisheit baute ihr Haus,* Karl Christian Felmy and Eva Haustein-Bartsch, eds. (Munich: Deutscher Kunstverlag, 1999), 164. (Translator's note)

3. The epithet refers to Hab 3.3 and is part of the Irmos of the first canon of Canticle Four for Orthros on Christmas Day. It is also sung on December 27 and 29, and on the Sunday of the Holy Ancestors, and is found in the Octoechos, tone 5, ode 4, Theotokion, for the Sunday Midnight Office. (Translator's note)

4. "Rejoice, pillar of fire, leading humankind to a higher life," (Akathist of the Mother of God, Canon, ode 9). "Brilliant cloud . . . in truth, Graced One, you have been shown" (Octoechos, tone 5, ode 5, Sunday Orthros; canon 1, prokimen, ode 9, Theotokion).

5. *The Mighty Deeds of the Most Holy Theotokos,* 31.

6. This is corroborated in church hymnody: "miraculously the bush and fire show a miracle to the hierophant Moses: seeking an end in the passing of time, he said I shall gaze on the pure Girl" (Canon for the Annunciation, ode 9, troparion 4); "Moses perceived in the bush the great mystery of your nativity, Holy Virgin" (Akathist of the Mother of God, ode 8, troparion 2). Note that this verse comes from the Akathist Canon used on Friday vespers during the fifth week of Great Lent. (Translator's note)

7. From the abundant liturgical material pertinent to this point we will introduce only the well-known "dogmatic" in the 2nd tone: "The canopy of the law passes, when grace appears: for as the bush was burning without being consumed, so the Virgin gave birth and remained a Virgin; instead of the pillar of fire the sun of justice shines, instead of Moses, Christ the salvation of our souls." (The text comes from the Octoechos for Sundays. Translator's note.)

8. Bulgakov's text reads Gen 18-69, which makes no sense; however, the whole of chapter 18 suits the point he makes here. (Translator's note)

9. It deserves attention that in a few texts (1 Sam 4.4, Lev 16.2) it is said that above the lid of the Ark of the Covenant in the midst of the depictions of the cherubim God himself is revealed, but in 2 Sam 6.2 we read "the ark of God on which is written the Name of the Lord Sabaoth, seated on cherubim." The inscription of the name is equivalent to the presence of God — this idea is generally characteristic for the Old Testament where the temple of God usually is called "temple of the Name of the Lord" (see for example 1 Kg 8).

10. Cf. 1 Kg 19.11-12. (Translator's note)

11. Octoechos, tone 7, Canon of Nicholas the Wonderworker, ode 3, Theotokion, tone 2, Canon of the Theotokos, ode, irmos, Canon of the Meeting of Our Lord (February 2), ode 5, Troparion 3, 2.

12. "We glorify you the Throne of the Word of God, O Theotokos, on which as a man God appeared seated, and you are higher than the Cherubim." Octoechos, tone 2, Canon of the Theotokos, ode 5. Cf. Octoechos, tone 6, Canon to John the Forerunner, ode 3, Theotokion; tone 2, Canon of St Nicholas, ode 6, Theotokion.

13. The text reads 12.22, but this does not correspond to Bulgakov's point. (Translator's note)

14. "Wonderous Ezekiel, you have been revealed as the Prophet of God, you foretold to all the incarnation of the Lord, this Lamb and Creator Son of God who appeared in the ages." Kontakion of the prophet Ezekiel.

15. In St Andrew of Crete we come across a general indication that among the fathers the appearance of Glory to the prophet Ezekiel signified the Theotokos. *Selected Discourses of the Holy Fathers in Honour and Praise of the Most Holy Theotokos,* 4th ed. (Moscow, 1896), 53-54.

16. Tertullian, *De resurrectione carnis,* 6, PL 2, 848-849.

17. Octoechos, tone 7, Wednesday morning, canon 2, ode 8, troparion 3.

Notes to Excursus 2

1. Bulgakov uses two words that have the same meaning: *Premudrost'* and *mudrost'* which I have translated as wisdom and understanding respectively. (Translator's note)

2. In the English translation this text reads as follows: "Jahweh formed me as the beginning of his creation, the first of his works, in days of yore." Crawford Howell Toy, *A Critical and Exegetical Commentary on the Book of Proverbs* (New York: Scribner, 1899), 172.

3. The English text reads, "in the primeval time was *I fashioned*/In the beginning, at the origin of the earth."

4. 8.24, "when there were no depths was *I brought into being*/No fountains full of water."

5. Coming near to this conception is the depiction of Wisdom in the book of Job 28, only in less defined features: "when he placed on the wind everything and distributed the water according to measure, when he indicated the path for rain and the path for thunderous lightning, then He saw her and revealed her; he prepared her and tested her still." Job 28.25-27.

6. Theophilus, *Ad Autolycum* 2, 10, PG 6.1064: "houtos oun on Pneuma theou kai archē kai Sophia kai dunamis Hupsistou, katercheto eis tous prophetas — this one, being the Spirit of God, comes down in the prophets as principle and wisdom and power of the Most High."

7. Irenaeus, *Adversus haereses* 4, 20, 1, PG 7.1032: "Adest enim ei semper Verbum et Sapientia, Filius et Spiritus. To Him (the Father) is always present the Word and Wisdom, Son and Spirit."

8. The distinction between the authority of canonical and uncanonical books is generally hard to define and in certain cases in fact even directly dismissed by the Church which for the Divine Liturgy and scriptural readings makes use of excerpts from these books and others (in particular from the *Wisdom of Solomon*). This distinction was generally very exaggerated by the Protestants who at one time practically removed them from

the Bible. In Orthodoxy there is no doctrinal levelling in the authoritativeness of these and other books, as is the case in Catholicism particularly after the Council of Trent, but practically speaking almost no such distinction is made except for some dubious cases.

9. In the Russian translation for some reason an imprecision was allowed: *she is the spirit.*

10. To see in this text an indication of the Holy Trinity in its three hypostases seems to us strained, first of all on the basis of the very structure of the phrase in Greek: *boulēn* and *sophian* are used without an article, which would scarcely be possible if the divine hypostases were understood here. Secondly, there is no basis to see in *will* the hypostasis of the Father, without falling into anthropomorphism. Our interpretation comes to this, that "Your will" refers to God's will for us, to the right path of salvation, to walk along which people are taught by Wisdom, through the inspiration of the Holy Spirit (the relationship of Wisdom and the Holy Spirit observed in the book of Wisdom is elucidated in the text). In favour of such a conception the further continuation of the text states "and thus the ways of those living on earth were set aright and people learned what was pleasing to You, and they were saved by Wisdom" (9.18). The verse is erroneously identified as 7.18-29 (Translator's note).

11. Notice that in this verse the Word and Wisdom are in no way identified with each other but are distinguished though not opposed.

12. Precisely in this way does the Church speak about Wisdom "in the prayer service for youth at the beginning of study," in the petitions of the Great Litany: "that he might grant to them *wisdom who is seated near His throne* and place her in their hearts so that she may teach them what is pleasing in His sight, we pray to the Lord." It is obvious here that the words do not deal with the Second Hypostasis, even if they are about wisdom in an ontological sense. On the contrary, in further petitions for wisdom it speaks already as about property: "that he may prosper them with wisdom and growth into God's glory . . . that they may have wisdom and a virtuous life . . . joy and consolation" . . . etc. The exclamation "Wisdom" frequently repeated in church has a similar meaning, calling to wisdom those praying (before dismissal) or drawing attention to the particular significance of what follows (before the reading of the lessons, the apostle or gospel, even sometimes only a prokimenon).

13. It is by the way instructive to compare chapters 11-12 of the *Wisdom of Solomon* with chapters 44-50 of the *Wisdom of Jesus ben Sirach* (the so-called *humnos tōn paterōn* — praise of the fathers). Here are extolled the deeds of Moses and others. In the first book is said that they are inspired by Wisdom and in the second, directly by God.

14. 1.5 which in the Russian translation reads "the source of wisdom is the word of the Almighty and her going is the eternal commandments" is absent in some editions of the Septuagint, e.g. in H. B. Swete, ed., *The Old Testament in Greek according to the Septuagint*, 3 vols. (Cambridge: Cambridge University Press, 1887-1894).

15. Cf. in particular the texts "I came out of the mouth of the Most High," and the psalm "By the word of the Lord the heavens were established and by the Spirit of his mouth all their power" (Ps 33.6), though under "by the Spirit of his mouth" is usually understood the Holy Spirit.

16. Here in the following excursus, called forth only by the needs of a special exposition, we consider ourselves in the right to be limited only by these negative results not

about what Sophia is but rather about what she is not. We consider a positive doctrine about this question an as yet unresolved problem of Orthodox theology. It is called upon here to develop an Orthodox doctrine concerning the Divine energies in their distinction from the hypostatic essence of God, connected with the name of St Gregory Palamas. The author attempted within his power to express this theological theorem in his essay "Hypostasis and Hypostaseity" (in a collection in honour of P. B. Struve — there is a German translation), to which interested parties are referred. We consider it appropriate, however, to add that no really new doctrine is given in it but only an attempt to give meaning to the fact of veneration for Divine Sophia already existing in church tradition, as well as a certain interpretation of this fact. As a result a new dogma is not established, only some theologizing about a dogmatic fact which already is present in the Church. And the one who denies the very question takes the liberty of denying this fact as well and therefore in the first instance the *onus probandi* of such a denial of church tradition rests on him.

17. "Actually after the Holy Virgin expressed her consent, in keeping with the Lord's word, announced by the Angel, the Holy Spirit descended on her, purified her and gave her the power to receive in herself the Divinity of the Word as well as to give birth. Then the Son of God overshadowed her, as if a Divine seed, the hypostatic Wisdom and Power of the Most High God, one in essence with the Father, and from her spotless and most pure blood formed for Himself the first beginning of our composition — flesh animated with a thinking and rational soul, — not through impregnation by a seed, but creatively through the Holy Spirit" (St John of Damascus, *Expositio fidei*, 3, 2, PG 94.986). Most sanctified Feofan the Recluse agrees with him.

"Look, how was the Son of God incarnated of the Most Holy Virgin? The Holy Spirit came and incarnated Him. Is the Son of God not God? Was not everything through Him? Does He not carry everything by the word of His power? And besides when it was fitting for Him to be incarnated, the Holy Spirit wove flesh for Him from the most pure blood of the Most Holy Theotokos. Surely He could have done this Himself! He could have, but this is what the trihypostatic God preferred, and as a result, when his Son was being incarnated a body was made for Him by the Holy Spirit," etc. (Bishop Feofan the Recluse, *Letters to diverse persons about various subjects of faith and life*, 2nd ed. [Moscow, 1892], 153.)

18. The iconographic interpretation of the text of Proverbs 9.1, given in one of the most ancient icons "Wisdom has built her house," is instructive (Likhachev, *Russian iconography*, No. 266). In this icon in conventional iconographic style there is a landscape with seven separate rocks (four from the right above and three from the left below) which correspond to the seven pillars on which is the depiction of a throne; above it to the left in a medallion is Christ and beneath the rock-pillars in a medallion is the Mother of God with Infant; on the top are seven small medallions with symbolic depictions of the seven gifts of the Holy Spirit (and their corresponding inscriptions: spirit of wisdom, spirit of understanding, etc.). The general meaning of this sophianic-iconographic theological theorem is clear: Wisdom is in her appearance both Christ and Mother of God — both Logos and Holy Spirit with His gifts, the Church as the Body of Christ, blessed by the Holy Spirit. In any case the content of this icon is not confined within the frame of a simple theological schema: Wisdom = Logos.

19. An exegesis of this text will be given in a special work on the Forerunner, the

Friend of the Bridegroom. This is available as *The Friend of the Bridegroom. On the Orthodox Veneration of the Forerunner,* Boris Jakim, tr. (Grand Rapids, MI: Wm. B. Eerdmans Publishing Company, 2003).

Notes to Excursus 3

1. "God, who willed to fashion creaturely nature, saw that it could not receive into itself by any means the untempered hand of the Father and the Father's creative power, which is why He produces and makes first and alone the One only and names Him Son and Word, so that with His mediation, through Him all the rest could come into existence (Arius, Eusebius, Asterius)" (*Oratio II contra Arianos,* 24, PG 26.200). St Athanasius correctly points out here that "if it is possible for the Word, so too does all nature necessarily have this same possibility, or, if it is impossible for nature not to have this possibility, it is likewise impossible for the Word . . . and by all necessity, there was need of a mediation at His creation . . . otherwise it will be impossible for the creature to subsist" (26 *PG* 26.201). However it is scarcely right to object to this ontological argument with a reference that "by confirming something similar, the weakness of the one who prepared is shown all the more, namely that alone He does not have the powers to create the universe but produces for himself an instrument like a wood-worker or ship-builder who does not have the possibility of working anything without an axe or saw" (26 — Bulgakov's version seems to be a variant; it may refer to *PG* 26.204-205, Translator's note). "For what reason will God, in willing to make us, look for an intermediary as if His will were insufficient for the production of what is pleasing to Him? If His one will is sufficient for the creation of everything, then again the necessity for an intermediary is superfluous according to your doctrine" (29, *PG* 26.208). But with such arguments the opposite side could object to Athanasius' own doctrine of the creation of the world by the Word. It concerns of course not the limitation of the divine omnipotence but the ontological incompatibility of God and the world without an intermediary; otherwise it would be possible with similar arguments to deny the omnipotence of God, in that all the features connected with creatureliness and limitation are improper to Him.

2. "The Father, as with a hand, made everything with the Word and He creates nothing without It" (*Oratio II contra Arianos,* 31, PG 26.212). "The Word of God builds and creates, and is the Father's will" (31, *PG* 26.213). "What is pleasing to God and thought by Him is quickly brought into existence and completed by the Word" (31, *PG* 26.213).

3. Correcting the Russian "for his sake" (Translator's note).

4. Eusebius, *De ecclesiastica theologia,* PG 24.978, is the first to turn his attention to the variant readings of this text, noting that in the Hebrew text there is no direct indication of creaturehood and that several Greek manuscripts contain *ektēsato.* Blessed Jerome says the same thing in Ep. 139, *Comm. in Isaiam* 26,13, PL 24.308. Thus he inserted into the Vulgate *possedit me* instead of *creavit.* The Russian translation of the synodal edition reads "The Lord possessed me as the beginning of his ways." See the foregoing excursus.

5. This is not exactly what 1 Jn 2.23 says (Translator's note).

6. Hilary of Poitiers, *De trinitate,* PL 10.452-453, 455-456, 459, though the reference given by Bulgakov is not exact. (Translator's note)

7. Ps-Basil, *Contra Eunomium IV-V, PG* 29.704. Bulgakov knew the text as an authentic work of Basil of Caesarea, which is now not accepted by most scholars. See Franz Xaver Risch, *Pseudo-Basilius. Adversus Eunomium IV-V. Einleitung, Übersetzung, Kommentar* (Leiden, New York, Cologne: E. J. Brill, 1992).

8. This statement, overstated in essence, represents an extraordinary concession to Arian exegesis, especially if one reads the whole eighth chapter first; the introductory words of Wisdom cannot be considered the words of the Son.

9. Gregory of Nazianzus, *Oratio* 30, *PG* 36.104-133.

10. Gregory of Nazianzus, *Oratio* 30, *PG* 36.105. (Translator's note)

11. Ibid.

12. I have been unable to locate this passage. (Translator's note)

13. The thought of Blessed Augustine also has to do with the Athanasian distinction of hypostatic and incarnated Wisdom. *De trinitate* 1.12, 24, *PL* 42.837: In the form of God it is said that *Before all the hills he begot me* (Prov 8.25), i.e., before all the immensities of creatures; and *Before the daystar I begot you* (Ps 109.3), i.e., before all times and all things of time; however in the image of a servant it is said *the Lord created me in the beginning of his ways* (Prov 8.22). Augustine considers the question, is the Son alone Wisdom, and arrives at a negative conclusion: "Therefore the Father himself is wisdom: and thus the Son is called wisdom of the Father, just as he is called light of the Father; i.e., that just as light is from light and both are one light, so may wisdom from wisdom, and both are one wisdom, be understood; and therefore also one essence, because there to be is the same as to be wise. For what it is for wisdom to be wise and for power to be powerful and for eternity to be eternal, for justice to be just, for greatness to be great, this it is for essence simply to be. And because in that simplicity to be wise is no different than to be, there wisdom is the same thing as essence" (*De trinitate* 7.1, 2, *PL* 42.936). "And therefore one essence because one wisdom. Since indeed wisdom is also Word, but not Word in the same way as wisdom, for Word is understood relatively, wisdom essentially." [Bulgakov omits a significant section here.] "Let us accept it to be said Son and image. . . . *Whence Father and Son are together one wisdom because they are one essence, and one by one they are wisdom from wisdom and essence from essence. . . .* But both together are one wisdom and one essence, where to be is the same as to be wise" (*De trinitate* 7.2, 3, *PL* 42.936).

Why is the Son primarily called Wisdom? "Therefore wisdom the Son is from wisdom the Father as light from light and God from God so that the Father alone is light and the Son alone is light, and the Father alone is God and the Son alone is God; thus also the Father alone is wisdom and the Son alone is wisdom. And as both together are one light and one God, so are both one wisdom. But the Son *was made for us by God wisdom and justification* (1 Cor 1.30), because temporally we turn to him, i.e. at a certain moment in time, in order to abide with him for ever. The Word too at a certain time *was made flesh and dwelled among us*" (7.3, 4, *PL* 42.937-938). (In this manner the naming of the Son as Wisdom is connected with the fact of incarnation.) "This therefore is the reason that whenever something about wisdom is being declared or narrated in Scripture, either by her own speaking or when she is spoken about, it is primarily the Son who is introduced to us" (7.3, 5, *PL* 42.938).

But as Wisdom is the Father and the Son, so too is she the Holy Spirit as true God: "Therefore the Father is light, the Son is light and the Holy Spirit is light; [Bulgakov omits a significant section here] and together they are not three wisdoms but one wisdom, and because in their case to be is the same as to be wise, the Father and the Son and the Holy Spirit are one essence" (7.3, 6, *PL* 42.939).

As follows from the cited texts, the doctrine of Blessed Augustine cannot be reduced to a direct equation of wisdom with the Second Hypostasis; on the contrary, he considers her in relation to the whole Holy Trinity, not only to the Son but also to the Father and the Holy Spirit.

14. Ps-Dionysius the Areopagite, *De divinis nominibus,* 5, 8, *PG* 3.824. Cf. the notes of Corderios, 829-830, and the paraphrase of Pachymeres (844-848). A modern English translation is available in Pseudo-Dionysius, *The Complete Works,* trans. Colm Luibhed (Mahwah, NJ: Paulist Press, 1987), 104 (Translator's note).

15. Bulgakov identifies this as *PG* 4.442; however, it is not a work of Maximus the Confessor but a paraphrase of Ps-Dionysios by George Pachymeres (Translator's note). Cf. F. A. Staudenmaier, *Die Lehre von der Idee (Die Philosophie des Christentums oder Metaphysik der heiligen Schrift, 1-er Band)* (Giessen, 1840), 321-324.

16. Gregory of Nyssa, *Apologia in hexaemeron, PG* 44.68-69.

17. Augustine, *Tractatus in euangelium Ioannis, PL* 35.1387; *De diversis quaestionibus LXXXIII,* qu. 46, *PL* 40.30.

18. "Now as soon as God willed to put forth in their own substances and forms those things which he had ordered within himself with Wisdom's reason and word, he first put forth the Word Himself having within Him His own inseparable Reason and Wisdom so that through him all things might be made through whom they had been thought and ordered, indeed already made, as much as they were in the understanding of God. For this was lacking them, that they should also be known and kept in their forms and substances. Then therefore does even the word himself assume his own form and garb, sound and voice, when God says, let there be light," etc. Tertullian, *Adv. Praxeam,* 6-7, *PL* 2.184.

Index

Adam (first): choice/self-determination (freedom), 21-23, 24-25, 29, 31; creation of, 22, 59-60; dichotomy/duality of being, 59-60; and Divine image in humankind, 80-81, 102-3; individuality, 21-23; mode of procreation, 93-94, 96; original sin of, 19-27, 29, 31

Adoptionism, 168n.13

Akathist of the Dormition of the Theotokos, 114-16

Alexander VII, Pope, 49

Ambrose of Milan, St, 161n.1, 166n.15, 166n.17, 172n.37

Anaxagoras of Clazomenae, 167n.18

Andrew of Crete, St, 178n.15

Andrew the Fool, St, 76, 77, 168n.8

Angels: difference between angelic world and Mother of God, 78-80; and humanity, 25, 79-80; and original sin, 25-26, 162n.3; and procreation, 170n.25

Annunciation, 66-69, 87-90, 91-99, 169n.17; compatibility of the grace of the Annunciation/grace of Pentecost, 67-68; and Divine Motherhood, 68-69, 89-90, 98-99; and Elizabeth, 68-69, 89, 98; and the indwelling/overshadowing by the Holy Spirit, 66-67, 87-90, 91-92, 97-98, 99-100, 169n.17, 180n.17; Mother of God and the suf-

fering of the Son, 69; and Pentecost, 67-68, 91-92, 100-101; and the preservation of Ever-Virginity/the virgin birth, 92-99, 170nn.26-27; and temptations of Mother of God, 69

Anselman–Duns Scotus doctrine, 50

Antiochene creed, 167n.21

Apollinarius, 57, 166n.17

Arianism: anti-trinitarianism, 143-44; and Church Fathers' interpretations of Wisdom of God, 140, 143-56; doctrine of God and the world, 144-47; and Old Testament doctrine of the Wisdom of God, 133, 140

Athanasius the Great, St: and creationism, 166n.15; on dichotomy/trichotomy of the soul, 166n.17; and Ever-Virginity of Mother of God, 170n.26; interpretations of the doctrine of the Wisdom of God, xxiv, 140, 143-56, 173n.43

Augustine, Blessed: and Athanasian distinction of hypostatic and incarnated Wisdom, 182n.13; and baptism of infants for remission of sins, 27; and creationism, 62, 166n.15; on dichotomy/trichotomy of the soul, 166n.17; and humankind's freedom, 24; and personal sinlessness of Mother of God, 161n.1; on prove-

184